Claretta

Claretta : an Impression.

Roberto Gervaso

Claretta

the Woman Who Died for Mussolini

Edited and Translated by

Tony C. Loring

Summerstown Books
Cornwall, Ontario

This book is printed on acid-free paper.

Summerstown Books
P.O. Box 93
Cornwall, Ontario
Canada K6H 5R9

All photographs are taken from the original Italian edition published by Rizzoli Editore, Milano (Italy), in 1982, and used with the permission of that publisher.

National Library of Canada Cataloguing in Publication Data

Gervaso, Roberto.
Claretta : the woman who died for Mussolini.
Translation of: Claretta.
Includes bibliographical references and index.
ISBN 0-9687793-0-1
1. Petacci, Clara, 1912-1945. 2. Mussolini, Benito, 1883-1945.
3. Mistresses—Italy—Biography. I. Loring, Tony C.
II. Title.
DG575.P455G4613 2001   945.091'092   C2001-902554-8

Designed by **Thomas & Brière Inc.**

Printed and bound in Canada by Transcontinental Printing.

First printing – March 2002.

Contents

	Editor's Preface	7
	Author's Preface	11
One	An Adventure in Ostia	13
Two	Love Blooms	17
Three	The Man from Ostia	22
Four	A Sleepless Night	26
Five	A Declaration of Love	30
Six	Believe! Obey! Fight!	36
Seven	The Man's the Man ...	51
Eight	The Fun and Games Begin	59
Nine	Italians! To Arms!	75
Ten	A Sad Love in Rome	83
Eleven	Dying for Love	97
Twelve	No Peace at Home	106
Thirteen	Ready for Anything	114
Fourteen	Duce, Don't Go!	128
Fifteen	A Revolver, Please	139
Sixteen	The Little Slave	144
Seventeen	The Unwilling Mayor	155
Eighteen	Miss, or What?	165
Nineteen	Following the Master	175
Twenty	Go, Duce, Go!	185
Twenty-One	The End Is Near	193
Twenty-Two	A Lame Horse for a ...	209
Twenty-Three	The End Is Here: Part 1	218
Twenty-Four	The End Is Here: Variation: Part 2	233
	End Notes	239
	Bibliography	243
	Index	248

Editor's Preface

(Lies, Damned Lies, and History *or* Comparative Demonology, Anyone?)

I deally, the writing of history presupposes the usage both of science and of art, i.e., includes "warts and all." The scientific part of the task requires the gathering of factual materials, the weighing of hypotheses, the discarding of unworkable ones, and the marshalling of explanations for questions or problems being reviewed. In this way, the facts are led to the "analytical couch." As well, the sources and previous work on the topic are considered. The artistic aspect sees the putting together of the "findings" from the several scientific steps. This means differentiating the layers of events; giving a coherence to the sum-total; putting in "shading" and "colour" along with attention to style; and using the language felicitously so that the finished product will not afford the readers too many roadblocks in their efforts to find something of value in the work done for them.

After the "word painting," the research is ready to be given to the "audience." While the work may not necessarily be free of bias, or of an "unusual" interpretation, it may be ready now to make its contribution to an understanding of the past. And, if the writer has the skills, his scholarly qualities will shine implicitly throughout the work. The reception accorded to the author's labour then will depend mainly on whether the reader agrees or disagrees with the writer and the "truth" he has established.

But, as Pontius Pilate asked wisely, "What is truth?" Truth is a very elusive concept which must be redefined by the author, and depends much on where that person "comes from," especially so in specialized studies. However, too many writers follow specific agendas at their desks, drowning their theses in virulent polemics. These can include economic, ethnic, national, political, religious, scientific or social notions, amongst others. Unfortunately, since 1919, and accelerating at an ever-faster pace, has been the author using the criteria listed above not to explain, but merely to sow consternation amongst the reading public.

The case of Napoleon Bonaparte may be cited as an example. During his years of ascendancy, the British and other reactionary forces opposed and derided "Boney," although many Europeans praised him. After he was finally destroyed at Waterloo, and safely out of the way, new imperialistic adventures forced his former foes to reassess his reputation in order to obtain the support of their earlier French enemies. Now Napoleon was praised grudgingly in the salons of his opponents even though he remained the same man, with the same deeds on his ledger. Time and realpolitik had healed most wounds. The "he must be wrong because our own leaders were so right" delusion that brought about the original condemnation of the French Emperor, therefore, is the bane that all writers face when they abandon balanced evaluations of historical events in order to "force the result" due to partiality. It is necessary to reject this "evangelical" approach and concentrate on logical presentation and interpretation, something very difficult for many biased, skeptical, demonizing general or academic writers to do well. Once writers and their readers understand that the main differences between heroes and villains may be merely in the cut and colour of their clothes, progress will have been achieved in understanding the past and in learning the valuable lessons that history provides.

All this presupposes that the writer of history is an expert in the field, treats his materials with the respect of a specialist, or is a generalist in the social sciences or in some other scholarly endeavour, rather than a dabbler merely seeking the desirable, illusive several minutes in the limelight.

Curiously, a certain cynicism has arisen in the field of historical studies in recent years. Some writers claim today that history cannot be known and imply that it is almost futile to record evaluations of the past. When we look a little more closely at some of the persons making such preposterous claims, we become aware quickly that they aren't trained historians, social scientists, or other scholars to begin with, but are mere daubers attempting to "practice history" as a sideline to their chosen vocation in some other field; or they are chroniclers "gone wrong." Having rejected the methods used by Otto von Ranke, Arnold Toynbee, Renzo de Felice, or other illustrious historians, the "facts" die in their hands. The results of their harvesting of factual material remain stillborn, and the readers are given work that is so much closer to agitprop and makes little contribution to a proper reassessment of the period under discussion. Thus the writing becomes more or less an exercise in verbiage, littered with gaps and assumptions.

Some authors prefer to use the very fallible faculty of memory to fill in the gaps. This use of recollection, then, gives to the work a romantic, fabulous quality very close to that of fiction. While it is possible to get the "flavour" of a particular period through drama, film, or fictional reconstruction, it is fundamental to remember the great differences between a concoction and a re-evaluation of a particular period. Only a skilled scholar, or someone who prepares text using historical or social science tools and nuances can help make sense of the materials he has gathered. The unskilled dabbler merely manipulates the "facts" a bit, and voilà, history is born! The would-be historian is now ready to throw out the historical baby with the unhistorical bathwater!

Hollywood has been particularly flagrant in its cult of distortion where history is concerned. Probably we have all heard of the director or producer tearing his hair out trying to find a piquant episode to include in one of his "epics" that will fill his pockets but which will misrepresent the period depicted. This "nudge, nudge, wink, wink" approach then, with variations, can also be found in the history writing trade, and does much to discredit a field that has reaped much honour in the past.

And, of course, all historical writing is revisionist since historical studies are not static. New factual material, previously unavailable, becomes known thus engendering a re-interpretation. Anything other than a revised view degenerates into myth for the faithful. Myth is fine for temples. It very definitely is objectionable in the world of thinking human beings, especially when it masquerades as something else.

Roberto Gervaso's illuminating biography of Claretta Petacci, and of her stormy, obsessive, and lengthy relationship with Benito Mussolini, the Italian dictator, presents a view of the couple from a perspective that does not seem to have had much currency in the English-speaking world. In any case, Mussolini and Italian Fascism remain thorny issues both within and outside Italy. As such, this book is presented now with the hope that some of the legends that have accrued to the subject matter of Italy and World War Two since the 1940's may be dispelled, and a much closer reading of the events leading up to, and including that conflict, may find resolution in the consciousness of the discerning reader of the English-language edition of the book. While "Dead men tell no tales," it is essential that the tales told about dead men —and women—be plausible ones.

Tony C. Loring

Author's Preface

No love story has moved and divided contemporary Italians as has that of Claretta Petacci and Benito Mussolini.

It is a story that began long ago, and yet as recently as April 1932, on the Via del Mare, between Rome and Ostia, and ended on the banks of Lake Como, at Giulino di Mezzegra, on the 28th of the same month, in 1945.

Claretta doesn't merely love Il Duce, she worships him to the point of obsession, to the heights of the most lofty and tragic of self-sacrifice. At least at the beginning, he feels for her a mixture of physical attraction, and a paternal, or childlike tenderness.

They die together: he condemned by history, she by passion. To re-evoke this love story—the ecstasy and the disappointments, the disillusion and the pain—is not to apologize for a political system that died and was buried on 25 July 1943. It is to experience again an extraordinary human adventure that involved a highly praised, and much hated middle-aged dictator, and a very romantic, a very devoted, too happy, but too unfortunate young woman.

Roberto Gervaso

One

An Adventure in Ostia

Claretta Petacci and Benito Mussolini meet for the first time on the 24th of April of 1932, on the Via del Mare, between Rome and Ostia.

It is a leaden and windy Sunday. The clouds chase each other across the sky, bunching up from the southwest, propelled by a strong libeccio. On the road, despite the holiday, just right for a trip to the country, traffic is light since the threat of bad weather has kept most Romans in town.

In the Lancia Asturia limousine bearing Vatican license plates and driven by Saverio Coppola, the former Neapolitan cabby but now house chauffeur to the Petacci family, are riding Signora Giuseppina Petacci, daughters Miriam and Claretta, and the latter's husband-to-be, Riccardo Federici, second-lieutenant in the Royal Italian Air Force.

After passing the Roman Forum, Coppola heads for what, even at that time was already the City's beach, although the residents then did not quite descend upon the area as do today's boisterous and unruly hordes.

In mid journey, rain begins to fall. Sig.ra Giuseppina is all for going home, but her daughters and Federici insist on proceeding, going against the wishes of the chauffeur who is not keen on driving in the rain, and who shows his displeasure by further reducing the already slow pace.

At a certain point, the persistent honking of a horn shakes the lethargic Coppola who, without realizing it, has strayed to the center of the road thus blocking whoever is tailgating him and wishes to pass ahead. With a sharp swerve, he moves to the right, throwing the passengers off-balance: Sig.ra Giuseppina nearly strikes the windshield, while Miriam finds herself on Riccardo's knees. This only takes a moment, but it is enough time for Claretta to recognize the motorist at the wheel of the first car, a speedy red Alfa Romeo, similar to the one driven by Tazio

Nuvolari, the current racecar sensation.[1] "The Duce, it's the Duce!" she screams, grasping Federici and wrecking havoc on the sleeve of his blue uniform bearing the decorations. "He's the one, really him!" echoes Miriam who has provided the emotional recollection of this historic event of long ago. "Faster, Saverio, faster," urges Claretta, "we've got to catch up to him!" But the Alfa in which, besides Mussolini, clad in a white suit, sporting a blue beret, and dark glasses, is seated a blond officer, speeds by, followed by a black sedan with five men on board, agents of the security service, the very watchful protectors of the Duce, who miss nothing of the little scene.

Coppola speeds up for a few hundred metres, then, seeing that everything is in vain, reduces the pace; at this, rebelling in her seat, and ever more excited, Claretta spurs him on to the chase. The driver bursts out in his Neapolitan dialect, "Signurì, chillo è 'o Duce!" ["Miss, that's the Duce!"]. But very stubborn, and gesticulating wildly, she repeats, "Faster, faster, we've still got time!"

Suddenly, at a sign from Mussolini, the red and the black cars ahead slow down, allowing the pursuing vehicle to catch up. Thus Claretta is able to see the dictator again, who smiles at her, only to take off once more.

The young woman is completely overwhelmed. Her fine Florentine straw hat is pushed back onto the nape of her neck; her previously freshly pressed white organza dress is now a formless shape. She no longer shouts "Duce, Duce," since her spirited cry has shrunk to become a plaintive whisper.

Her heart resumes its normal rhythm, but her feelings are in an uproar. That sighting stuns her, and she almost doesn't believe what she's seen. And yet, that hadn't been an illusion. That was really Mussolini!

"Catch up to him, catch up to him!" she presses the driver again, while her fiancé tries to calm her down, but without the desired results. The dictator moderates his speed a second time, only to step on the gas again, after winking with an amused air at the girl. The remarkable, unexpected game continues until the Head of Government shifts into fourth gear and disappears.

At this point, Claretta sinks back exhausted into her seat, staring with astonishment at the wet road flanked by a double row of shade trees that appear to fly by. She seems to be in a trance, and neither Riccardo, nor Miriam, nor Sig.ra Giuseppina dare to address her, or even speak amongst themselves.

Only after reaching the terrace at Ostia, a few metres from the water's edge, and the Duce re-appears leaning against a railing bristling with barbed wire, looking at the sea, does she come out of that strange, or perhaps, very natural torpor. Another opportunity like this one would not happen to her again.

"I'm going to introduce myself," she announces to her traveling companions. "I want to know him, I want to talk to him!" Sig.ra Giuseppina doesn't make a sound, but Miriam coaxes her on. Federici would have preferred to remain in the car, but Claretta won't listen to reason, and dragging him with her, impatient and very resolute, she gets out.

At this point, the security agents, standing in a fan formation around the Head of Government, try to block the progress of the couple, but with a gesture, the dictator stops this from happening. "Excuse me, Duce," Claretta breaks the ice with a weak voice, "but it gives me such joy to see you that we took the liberty to disturb you. I am Claretta Petacci, and this is my fiancé."

"You are related to the Vatican physician?" asks a pleased Mussolini.

"He is my father."

"And you, lieutenant?"

"I am stationed at Orbetello to prepare for the trans-Atlantic flight." [2]

The Duce questions Riccardo briefly about his activities and his line of action, then turns to Claretta. "And you, what do you do?" The dazed young woman stammers, "I write, I play the violin…" Then, after a moment's hesitation, with the audacity of the timid when they are emboldened with enthusiasm, seizing courage, she cries out: "Duce, sometime ago I sent you some poems. They were in a green folder, tied with a ribbon the colors of the flag. I sent them to Palazzo Venezia, but perhaps you didn't even receive them."

Mussolini who is ready for anything except for that childlike declaration, biting his lip and stroking his chin with his hand, stammers: "Poems? I seem to remember. I must have them." Then, after a brief pause: "When are you getting married? Do you like the sea? How is your father?"

While leaving, Claretta's dress gets caught in the barbed wire of the fence. Mussolini gallantly helps her to free herself, after which, seeing that she's trembling, asks her if she's cold. "No, it's the emotion," answers the young woman, who takes her leave with a loud "Long live the Duce!" while Federici salutes him.

Returning to the city, no one talks of anything else, and later, with both Doctor Francesco Saverio, her father, and Marcello, her older brother present, the extraordinary meeting is discussed with passion and in detail. As Miriam will later write: "My sister's euphoria extends to everybody, somehow. Claretta continues to repeat: 'What a man! What eyes! Do you know that he asked about you, papa? Did you see how unaffected he is, mama? Can it really be true that he remembers receiving my poetry?' "

True or not, she'd never quite felt so happy. She had finally met the Duce, her Duce, and talked to him, and he had actually kept her back for a few moments.

If that is the nicest day of her life, the ensuing evening is the most romantically restless. She does not close her eyes (and how could she have done that?) going over the transitory sequence of events of the fateful meeting, touching it up in her imagination, and projecting it into the thrilling realm of otherworldly love.

Two

Love Blooms

C laretta had just turned twenty in April 1932 when she met Il Duce, her birth having occurred on 28 February 1912, a leap year. Her mother had chosen her name in honour of St. Clare of Assisi, associate of St. Francis, and founder of the Poor Clares. Ever since childhood, however, she was called Claretta, or Etta, a pet name to correspond to her small stature.

Although she was of medium height, she had Lilliputian feet (she wore a thirty-three size shoe of the era[3] with special orthopedic heels), which required that she move in quick, small, almost mincing steps; straight and beautifully shaped legs; a slim body, in contrast to opulent breasts, the anatomical feature that most struck Mussolini as a good native of the Romagna, appreciative of female cleavage.

Her face was very sweet: a determined chin; a regularly shaped mouth rendered very lovely by magnificent teeth; a softly-angled nose; eyes of a radiant Andalusian melancholy; tiny ears, crowned by a head of curly brown hair, wispy like cirrus clouds; a smooth, light, translucent skin thanks to the liberal use of face powder; small hands; slim fingers with carefully lacquered nails.

She took several hours to get ready: from ten when she rose after having had breakfast in bed, to noon. Her favourite article of clothing was a chiffon robe that she wore over blue pyjamas. She'd go into the bathroom, turn on the radio—a small Marelli model[4]—remove the curlers, and with a hot curling iron primp up her hair, cover her face with crème, and her eyelashes with mascara, choose between her three favourite perfumes—Arpège, Fleur de Rocaille, and Tabac Blond—the one most suited to the dress she would wear that day.

She had dozens of ensembles, some made by the elderly family seamstress, others from two well-known boutiques downtown: Gabriellasport in Piazza di Spagna, and the Montorsi Sisters in Via Condotti. She preferred suits in dark colours, especially brown, which were her choice for winter wear; and flowery dresses decorated with frills, lace, or embroidery kept for spring and summer.

She adored small hats, fur muffs, and one-piece silk underwear, in pastel colors and split on the side.

She didn't enjoy very good health and she feared illness almost as much as Il Duce who was absolutely terrified of the same thing. She'd had all the childhood ailments, but her weakest point was her throat: the least variation in temperature, a draft that was barely noticeable, a mere few degrees in humidity, brought on throat difficulties (when her already suggestive voice became deep and guttural with the passage of time). She was often stricken with influenza, colds and headaches of a nervous origin, just as nerves caused the nausea that she experienced in the morning after waking. She also had stomach problems, sudden swellings, and reddening of the skin that no one could explain.

She got tired very easily, but this didn't prevent her from participating in sports: she took her first horse ride at twelve, at thirteen she discovered canoeing, skiing, and tennis. However, she began swimming at six, learning so well that at fourteen years of age she saved a young girl who was drowning in the water at Ostia.

She ate little though she devoured sweets, especially chocolate, and artichokes in oil. Her usual meal consisted of a thin soup, some meat, greens and fruit. No wine, or a few drops thinned with water. At night, she normally skipped supper, not because of dieting, since, actually she would have preferred to put on a few pounds in an age when women were considered, and appreciated, for an abundance of curves, especially in the gluteus.

Although the member of a family of rank and wealth, she did not go too far in school. After having completed elementary studies with the Sisters of Nevers,[5] where her father was physician, she had studied at the secondary level. But she'd not continued beyond that.

As was the case with Mussolini, she was, in fact, self-taught. She loved Beethoven, and Chopin even more, especially his *Nocturnes*. The verses of Leopardi, Gozzano, and Petrarch moved her to tears;[6] she played the harp, the violin and the piano, and she wrote sonnets, ballads, and madrigals. She even composed songs and romances—words and music—that she would have consigned happily to the voice of a Gigli, or a Tagliavini.[7]

Another passion of hers was painting, having been introduced to that hobby by a cousin (in 1936 she'd have an exhibition). To the want of technique she made up with a streak of natural inspiration, even though her choice of themes was somewhat commonplace: friars in prayer, swallows on branches, dolls, country scenes, or the sea. As well, she designed her own clothes that the house seamstress then made up.

Her amateur artistic streak was of an emotionally romantic nature, as was her changeable disposition: easy to give in to irrational enthusiasm, or to depression, always wavering between the most thoughtless optimism, and the blackest pessimism. Her physiology and her psychology coalesced and drove her forward, nourishing the myth of the Superman of which she would be the amorous victim.

If she'd had her first admirer at the age of nine, and her first suitor at sixteen (someone of almost the same age, son of a rich industrialist from Cipriano, where Claretta spent her holidays with her family), the fire for Mussolini came even earlier, having burst into flame in the summer of 1920 when she was eight years old.

From then on, she begins to snip pictures of the future Duce from the newspapers, to devour his articles in *Il Popolo d'Italia*, to memorize his speeches, to carve his name in school desks, to hide his picture under her pillow, or between the pages of her textbooks, up to the point of pelting with stones a bricklayer from Grottaferrata who had commented rather sarcastically after he heard the braying of a donkey: "Mussolini is speaking!"

This was idolatry, pure and simple, aided and abetted by governmental propaganda, which the passage of time did not weaken, but rendered more and more intense.

In October 1922, Claretta is in the Piazza del Quirinale with her grandmother, attending a military review held by the *squadristi*, veterans of the March on Rome. When the new Head of Government, in a black coat, chin jutting out, arms akimbo, appears on the balcony with the King, she throws him a kiss. "Kisses are aimed only at the pope," scolds her grandmother, but she continues to clap her hands frantically, bewitched by the authoritarian expression.

A nun at school declares to her that Mussolini is ugly. The girl rebels at this, and she no longer looks at the bold defamer in the face.

At twelve years old, after hearing the rumour that her idol has rented a villa at Grottaferrata, a stone's thrown from that of the Petaccis, she climbs up to the roof of her family's abode, carrying her violin, in the illusory hope that the dictator will peer out of a house nearby. She also walks ten kilometres to participate in a Fascist rally, and she begs a friend to go with her to the Senate where Il Duce is to deliver a speech (to be noticed, she wears a showy, crimson dress).

Her Fascist cult reaches its highest point when she climbs onto a large cornice and she begins to parade back and forth, or when she tries to convince a young friend to pretend that she is drowning in the sea off Ostia so that Claretta can "save" her, and be received at Palazzo Venezia as an "heroic child." But the ruse doesn't have the desired result.

She doesn't give up, however, and during an aerial display, she mounts upon an unused drum that lies before the official stand of the Head of the Government. At the most strategic moment, the membrane of the percussive instrument breaks, and she falls through it. Mussolini, who has been following the shenanigans, laughs, though there is no subsequent follow through.

Her letters, cards, postal notes, and telegrams which she obstinately dispatches, signing her own name, congratulating him for his latest speech, for a new slogan, a new law, a new measure, or railing against this or that political adversary, do not have a better effect.

She writes him after the attempted assassination by Violet Gibson [an Irish woman living in Italy]:

Duce. For the second time there has been a villainous attempt on your person. And by a woman! What infamy! What vileness! How disgraceful! But she is a foreigner, and that's that! Beloved Duce, why has someone tried for a second time to take you from our strong and assured love?[8] Duce, my very great Duce, our life, our hope, our glory; how can such a pitiless person try to deprive our beautiful Italy of her dazzling destiny? O Duce, why wasn't I present? Why wasn't I able to strangle that murderous woman who wounded you, divine being? Why wasn't I able to get rid of her from Italian soil forever, the soil that was sprayed by your blood, by your great, good, fine blood of the Romagna? Duce, I want to tell you again, as in the previous very sad incident that I would wish fervently to put my head on your breast to allow me to hear the beats of your great heart which is still alive.[9] These painful and memorable dates will remain forever etched on my heart: 4 November 1925, 7 April 1926.
O, Duce, you who are the man of our future, you who are the man who is loved with a growing fervour and feeling by the

Italian people, and by whoever doesn't desire your downfall, must never be away from us. When I heard the sad news, I thought I'd die because I loved you deeply as a young Fascist from the very first moment. Duce, how your good and sensitive heart must have suffered knowing that a foreign hand had tried to break your holy, regenerative and important work. Beloved Duce, eternal loyalty has been pledged to you anew by your Black Shirts, and I, youthful but ardent Fascist, with my favourite slogan, understand all the love that my young heart feels for you: Duce, my life is for you! The Duce is safe! Long live the Duce! – Clara Petacci (fourteen years old), Lungo Tevere Cenci, no. 10.

Mussolini doesn't answer, just as he hadn't replied a couple of months previously when she had invited him to supper on her birthday (hopeful of his arrival until the very end, the young hostess forces her guests to delay sitting at table for an hour). She would console herself by kissing his photograph over and over in bed that night, the picture kept as a treasure under her pillow, and focusing ecstatically on the walls of her room where the dictator seemed to be towering in the most martial of uniforms.

Her parents let her be: even they were Fascists, as were almost all other Italians. Besides, what could they do, even if they wanted to do something? Claretta was not the only one to worship Mussolini, to magnify his undertakings so zealously. Some people existed who, at the moment of death, would request to be buried in the Predappio cemetery, in a black shirt and swathed in the Italian flag.

The big lictorial drum was programmed to achieve such fanaticism. The radio and newspapers, tied to "directives from above," choreographed resonantly by Starace,[10] acted powerfully on the fantasies of a fickle and impressionable population who, after so much chaos, had found once again—or was it an illusion? —peace and order. In the blacksmith's son, they saw not only a firm hand, but also a sleepless demi-god, a saviour of the nation, and a restore of ancient virtues.

Three

The Man from Ostia

The archives in Trieste, which trace lineage back to the fourteenth century, prove that blue blood ran in the veins of the Petacci family. In 1384, a certain Anselmo Petazzi, or Pettazzi, leads a mission to Leopold of Austria; about fifty years later, in 1427, Benvenuto, a part-time pirate and local nobleman, owner of a small castle called "di San Servolo," above Trieste, writes a will in favour of unknown heirs.

The descendants of the dynasty whose coat of arms—a dozen gold disks on a red background—adorned, and adorns still, with twelve additional disks, the Castle of San Giusto, get lost in time, re-emerging about 1763, when a branch of the family moves to Milan, and then on to Rome. Here the name Petazzi, or Pettazzi, is modified to Petacci. At the end of the eighteenth century, these members are entered into the Capitoline lists of nobility with the title of marquis.

From the beginning, relations are established with the Vatican, when entry is obtained into the old Roman bourgeoisie, the influential cadres on the payroll of the Pontifical administration, the source of its strength. The social status of the members of this family was very obvious: besides occupying quasi-hereditary posts in the church government, "they lived in comfort, possessed an estate, and had a coach."

The first Petacci to work within Vatican walls was Giuseppe, the uncle of Claretta's father, a medical doctor of good repute who, on the death of Doctor Lapponi, the main Papal physician, assumed the post and, in 1915, had his nephew taken on as health officer.

Francesco Saverio was born in Constantinople in 1882, where his father Edoardo was a high civil servant in the Turkish state (he was the one who was to organize the first postal service and to introduce the first postage stamps in that country).

In 1902, Francesco Saverio leaves his parents, his three brothers and four sisters, and comes to Italy to pursue his university studies. Having completed these, he marries Giuseppina

Persichetti, his first cousin, the daughter and niece of noted medical people and rich proprietors of lands, who is a distant descen-
dant of a pope.

Francesco Saverio was a quiet and reserved man, a good
Catholic, a serious professional who liked to live in his particular
shell, pursuing simple and upright goals. He went to the theatre,
especially to the opera, but very rarely was he found in the drawing rooms or at official receptions, and then always accompanied
by his wife. He did not spend too much time at home and, because
of this, he was not always noticed very much.

Within the family compound, the vigorous and effusive Sig.ra
Giuseppina laid down the law. She was always ready for anything
or anyone, on whom everything depended, regulating by the
minute and in detail the very lives of her husband, her children,
and her hired help: a sleepless and energetic woman who even
found time to recite the Rosary.

If her influence over her husband was total, her authority
over her children was absolute. They were accountable to her for
even the most insignificant action, not even turning a leaf without
her consent: after evaluating the pros and cons, she'd give her
thumbs up or thumbs down categorically. She expected to have the
last word, whatever that might be.

Above all, Sig.ra Giuseppina watched over her daughters,
especially Claretta. This was not because she didn't trust her, but
because at twenty years of age, it was necessary for her to begin
thinking of marriage.

The second born had many suitors, but how many were worthy of her? The Petaccis enjoyed a good standing and reputation,
and Sig.ra Giuseppina would never have given her daughter's
hand to anyone. A mistaken choice would have prejudiced the honour of the family.

Except for some platonic and short-lived crushes, Claretta
had never been in love until, in 1932, she meets a twenty-seven
year old Air Force second lieutenant on the streetcar. After a quick
exchange of glances, the courteous young man approaches her.
They trade a few pleasantries, plus the usual hope that they will
see each other again.

In his blue uniform, with the eagle and collar badge of a pilot,
Riccardo Federici appears to Claretta to be "a praetorian flier":
vigorous, lean, very masculine features with a sulky expression
that women love so much, and many of whom were hoping to nab.
At dances—and he never missed one—the eyes of everyone were

always on him. Also, the fact that he was in the Air Force made him still more irresistible. He had had many flirtations, but none of these had been serious. And this for Claretta and Sig.ra Giuseppina was important.

Offspring of a good middle class family, in July 1930 he had received his official pilot's license from the Air Force Academy of Caserta.

Claretta was quickly conquered, at least in respect to him, but, perhaps nothing would have come of it if, a few weeks later, during a military ceremony, they hadn't met again at Viareggio. If the accidental meeting was a bolt of lightning, this one was the coup de grace. They danced until dawn under the eagle eyes of Sig.ra Giuseppina who, from her table, watched every move of her daughter and her escort.

Unfortunately, he was neither a nobleman, nor a millionaire, but his perfect manners, his good looks, and his spirited self-assurance seemed to compensate for his lack of wealth and family tree.

The next day, mother and daughter return to Rome where Federici shows his interest by phoning often. Then, obtaining a short leave, he comes to see the Petacci parents and announces that he wanted to become engaged to Claretta, who also seemed to want exactly the same thing. Marriage was brought up quickly, however without setting a date.

When Claretta meets Mussolini at Ostia, her bond with Riccardo was thus official. Perhaps Federici was not yet aware of what the Duce meant to the young woman whose Fascist obsession disconcerted him at the beginning, though not so much as to wound his self-respect, but causing an understandable jealousy. Not only did she talk to the young man about "Him" from morning to night, but also she forced him to read, and listen to, his speeches, to attend the ceremonies of the Government, and to involve himself in the rituals of the Regime.

From the beginning, Riccardo takes a faint interest in these rites, but then, even though he may have been submissive, he shows his disappointment. A few quarrels also break out, but these do not threaten the intended marriage.

The Ostia episode could, essentially, itself appear as homage to the Chief by one of the many victims of the messianic rhetoric of Fascism. And such is the call that Mussolini makes a few days later to Claretta, that Miriam remembers this way. "One afternoon, rather late, the telephone rang and I went to answer it. I heard a deep voice which asked: 'Is the young lady in?' I was nine years old and I had a great wish to be considered an adult. Therefore, full of haughtiness, I reply, 'Which young lady?' The voice at the other end hesitates for a moment. 'The young lady ... Clara.' 'Who wants her?' Another pause. Then, 'Tell her that it's the man from Ostia.' I call Claretta. 'It's for you. He says he's the man from O ...' 'Great heavens! He's calling!' Claretta takes the receiver and begins to stammer. She doesn't know whether she should say 'Duce,' 'Excellency,' or 'Prime Minister,' she just didn't know how to reply. All in all I'd say she made a rather poor showing.

" 'I've telephoned you to let you know that I've found your poems,' Mussolini was saying. 'They are here on my desk. Ask permission of your mother and of your fiancé and, if you wish, come to see me at seven o'clock. I'll be waiting for you.' And he hangs up."

Four

A Sleepless Night

Claretta is stunned. Her heart beats in her throat; her legs become soft and wobbly, and she is speechless. No less moved, her mother and her sister can't believe their ears. And yet, the one that had called was really he, Il Duce.

If he'd decided on that course of action, it meant that he'd really been favourably impressed by the young Petacci girl.

Recovered from the shock, mother and daughters rush to Claretta's bedroom to choose an outfit.

While on other occasions the preparations would have taken a long time, now they are extremely rapid. Helped by Miriam and by Sig.ra Giuseppina, Claretta puts on a tan and brown suit, with matching shoes, handbag, and small hat. When she is ready, she calls the chauffeur, and with her mother who'd also changed her dress, leaves for Palazzo Venezia. She is overwhelmed, and this shows, as is also the case with her mother.

Arriving at the piazza in front of the main entrance, the one reserved for guests (Mussolini usually entered through the nearby door on Piazetta San Marco, to the left when the palace is seen frontally), the car stops. Claretta gets out, but not before having received last minute instructions from her mother. This included that of not lingering for more then twenty minutes, almost as if the length of the interview depended on her.

She crosses the threshold with trepidation, troubled by a multitude of thoughts, remembrances, sensations, almost as if under the influence of drugs. She climbs the long stone staircase, her heart almost wanting to burst. She is early, and she takes this opportunity to catch her breath while she leans against the balustrade.

At the second level, she meets a doorman to whom she shows the pass obtained at the entrance. Having reached the waiting-room, she is handed over to Quinto Navarra, Il Duce's long-time clerk, the holder of so many secrets. "Please follow me," he tells her, leading her towards the Sala del Mappamondo where the dictator had his office.

"I enter the room," Claretta will recount later (which Miriam will subsequently relate) "and I see, faraway in the distance, his solemn form, upright behind a huge desk. I sense that I don't have the strength to reach him. He, as if instinctively, gets up and comes towards me."

"Were you expecting my phone call?" he asks.

"I didn't dare hope for such a thing, Duce."

"I've located your poems. They haven't been brought here to me yet, but one day we will read them together. How old were you when you wrote them?"

"I was between eleven and fourteen; I sent them to you in 1926."

"So now you are twenty. Is it possible? I'd give you sixteen, or seventeen, at most."

With an inquisitorial, paternal air, he asks her then what studies she'd done, what books she'd read, what music she liked, what sports she played. Then, changing tone, with tenderness and care, he inquires: "Will you remember the day of the libeccio at Ostia?"

"I'll never forget it."

"But is it true that you were not trembling because of the cold?"

"It's true."

Looking at her fixedly in the eyes, he confides: "Do you know that you gave me a strange sensation? I couldn't sleep because I was thinking of you." Then, almost authoritarian: "But it is already late. You must go. I'll call you again to read the poems. If you have others, bring them along. You'd be pleased to come again?" Claretta doesn't reply but limits herself to nodding assent.

He takes his leave of her—as Miriam again recalls—with a "Goodbye, Chiara" (not Clara), to which she replies with a weak, "Good night, Duce." Then, he summons Navarra who accompanies the guest to the stairs that an overawed Claretta descends, in her eyes, in her head, in her heart, holding the image of her god.

In her mind spin over and over the words that "He" had uttered, the confession that he had made to her: "I couldn't sleep because I was thinking of you." Il Duce was not sleeping because he was thinking of her, and he was asking her to see him again: this really did seem to be a dream!

She gets back into the car and, even before the vehicle begins to move, she launches into an excited summary of what had taken place.

About twenty days later, Il Duce telephones her again for another get-together which lasts longer than the first one, and which more than the first visit is more intimate and almost romantic. "Were you expecting my second call?" begins the dictator. "Really yes? May I use the familiar 'tu?' " Then, without pausing for an answer, going with her towards the window: "Do you feel the spring? I feel it very much in this city where, despite everything, I live alone, without a friend. I am isolated. But you can't understand."

At which she reassures him weakly: "I think I do, really." He then surmises that he'd made an error: "Perhaps you are right," he says. At this point, he gently takes her arm and, tracing with his hand the flight of swallows, he pulls her to him.

They turn to the topic of music. He confides to her that he loves Chopin, she replying that she adores that composer, knowing his *Waltzes* and his *Nocturnes*. They also agree on Petrarch and on Leopardi, from which they recite a few verses. When it is necessary to say goodbye—how those twenty minutes had flown!—and without her asking him to do this, he promises to call her again.

"Why does Mussolini continue to see her?" her sister Miriam asks herself at this point, and we with her. "The answer is not difficult to understand: because he'd fallen in love without realizing it, or, at least, without wanting to admit to himself the possibility of such a feeling, given his age and his position. He was captivated because Claretta represented for him the ideals of youthfulness.

"Benito Mussolini was a man of the nineteenth century, and he carried with him all the romantic and sentimental hues of his century. Having been raised when madrigals and perfumed notes were in vogue, when poetry was the essential ingredient of love, and softness the synonym of femininity, he felt a stranger to 'the new way of doing things' that the Great War had brought in. The relations between men and women had changed, and young girls had, in general, an approach that left him cold because he didn't understand the transition. With her nineteenth century upbringing, Claretta broke the barrier and she gave him the almost magical sensation of having gone back to former times.

"But there is more. In his youth, Mussolini had never happened upon the love ideals of his generation. The many women with whom he'd had liaisons had been from various social strata, and varying ages, but they all had one thing in common: an energetic and independent disposition, almost masculine for those times ...

"And now he finds himself confronted by a young woman who, age-wise, could have been his daughter, but who in spirit, belonged to his century, to his youthful years. It was as if, suddenly, one of those damsels whom he'd seen twenty years before, travelling in carriages with coachmen in livery, had come back to life. And to that woman, he did not appear to be the poor country schoolteacher, but was a prince charming, actually something much more than a prince charming. What was really lovely was the touch of fate, possibly needed. But that she admire him sincerely, without reserve and without established goals, was necessary.

"I don't know how long it took Mussolini to realize all of this. Perhaps he discovered his true emotions from the early encounters when Claretta had the feeling of being studied and scrutinized. But when he finally understood, everything was, in fact, over. That man who was powerful and feared, that man who was preparing to conquer an empire, was in love like a young boy."

And Claretta?

"She wasn't aware of all this because she didn't want to analyze her own emotions. For her, it was enough to be received by her mythical man, spend some time with him, and to listen to him. Here was a splendid dream that it was convenient to prolong while holding her eyes very tightly shut."

Miriam is right. Mussolini had had many women, and he would have plenty more. But no one, with the exception of his wife Rachele and, perhaps, Margherita Sarfatti, the journalist, had convulsed him in such a way.[11] Up until then, his dalliances had been transient, adulterous ones of the senses. He seized them and discarded them, without fraud or illusions, without promising or demanding anything.

With Claretta things were different because, young and persistent Vestal virgin of his cult, he fell in love at first sight, not only because she was young, not only because she was lovely, and not only because she was a fanatical devotee. He fell in love because he fell in love. A flame broke out in him, actually seared his insides, all of a sudden, because of the incomprehensible cosmic mystery that bewitches, that carries one away, and that captivates.

Five

A Declaration of Love

I n the next twenty months after these meetings, the Petacci girl
and Mussolini see each other at least another dozen times,
each meeting not longer than a quarter hour since the dictator
had little time to spare, and the minutes were already apportioned
to other work. For Claretta, all that matters is to be admitted to
his presence, even if for only a moment. If the Duce, then, has her
sit down beside him on the soft cushions on the stone step beneath
one of the two mullioned windows, next to the famous Balcony,
this is ecstasy for her, the tip of happiness so much more inexpressible than just merely unexpected.

With the temporary shedding of his lictorial trappings, with
the self-confident frown discarded, he would affectionately take
her hand in his, and he'd return to the memories of his past, to
that of his bitter childhood. He'd talk to her of his atheist, revolutionary, extremist father; of his mother Rosa, a devoted, young,
patient schoolteacher; of his studies; of brawls with his friends; of
punishments; of the first Socialist militia; or his early dreams of
becoming the secretary of the local trade union. And she'd listen to
him enraptured, as if in a trance. Then, he'd ask her what she'd
done that morning, when she was getting married, if she truly
loved Federici.

Before too long, she'd be Riccardo's wife, but her heart beat
for the one who lingered in the shadowy solitude of that austere
sixteenth century chamber, remembering years long gone, and
previous struggles – my how this was obvious and perceptible!

With the dictator's deep and soothing voice—so different
from the bombastic and rhythmical one, now threatening, now
humouring, that he used in his speeches when haranguing the
vast delirious crowds—there was something of childlike rapture.
The difference in their ages—almost thirty years—seemed to render their rapport so much more harmonious, soon making their
relationship an indivisible coalescence.

She appeared to be totally submissive to him and he was
awkwardly allured. A silent undercurrent, but pregnant with
meaning, seemed to suffuse their minds and to knit their very

30

souls. The spark had burst into fire, but it was necessary to shield this fact from impertinent eyes and ears. Who was it who said that in the purgatory of marking time, love's embers cool and die out? If that love is real, it grows, becomes more noble, becomes more perfect.

Even if Riccardo did not understand, or did not wish to examine the feelings of his chosen mate for Mussolini, he could not but be aware that those meetings would, sooner or later, disturb and eventually compromise his own relations with Claretta.

He could leave her, saying goodbye, but he loved her; and even she deceived herself, or tried to do so, that she reciprocated the feeling. An equivocation that could have been resolved had all three dropped their masks. But who had the will to do this? Claretta let Mussolini understand that she loved him, but she didn't tell him directly. Even if Mussolini didn't show his hand, he behaved as does a lover. Riccardo found it more convenient to believe that he was dealing with a passing fancy.

In any case, Riccardo doesn't hide his vexation for the too frequent visits to Palazzo Venezia, which render him neither pleased, nor "very happy," as, in fact, maintains Miriam. He endures all this in silence, not foreseeing the inevitable consequences.

But, he does make a few jealous scenes which nearly cause the forthcoming engagement to be called off. Many quarrels erupt, and one more violent than the others keeps them apart for a number of months.

During the summer of 1933, Federici is assigned to service at the Giorgio Filastri seaplane base on the east side of the La Spezia Gulf, near Muggiano, about fifty kilometres from Viareggio, where Claretta was spending the season with her mother and sister.

The idea of being dumped at the church door, after the wedding had been arranged, upset her. She'd spend her time locked in her room, crying, and writing imploring letters which elicited no replies. Sig.ra Giuseppina was in despair: to see her daughter suffer like that made her also extremely uncomfortable.

One day, she talks to a guest in the hotel, a certain Luigi de Vincentis, author after the war of a mean libel against the Petacci family, whose advice was to confront Federici directly. Next day, mother and daughters, accompanied by de Vincentis, drive out to the base.

While the women wait in the car, the enterprising go-between heads towards the gate. He asks the gatekeeper if he might see the young officer, who quickly comes along. He explains to the latter his reasons for being there, telling him that Claretta was not eating, couldn't sleep, and that she was depressed, and that her family feared for her well-being. If there had been any misunderstandings, if the daughter or the mother had wronged him in some way, they were ready to repair the injury.

Riccardo listens impassively to his visitor's pleadings, then replies in a courteous but firm voice: "In marrying her, I'd be marrying her mother as well." De Vincentis presses him to see Claretta at least, but Federici refuses dryly. After which, using the excuse, feigned or otherwise, that he had another meeting that he couldn't miss, he says goodbye to the mediator. The latter immediately rushes back to the three women to report the results of the talk. Claretta begins to weep again, which causes her mother and sister, already disappointed and angry, to try to console her fruitlessly. Two days later, they return to Rome.

The next day, Sig.ra Giuseppina goes to see Maria Ausili, Federici's mother, who succeeds in convincing her son to resume his relationship with his fiancée. Following this, a few other disagreements in fact do occur, but nothing as serious as the previous one.

On 27 June 1934, Cardinal Gasparri, one of the authors of the Concordat, officiates at the wedding in the San Marco Basilica, just next to Palazzo Venezia, chosen not because it was a few steps from where Mussolini was quartered, but because this had been the site of Sig.ra Giuseppina's baptism. Witnesses for the bride were Gino Gasperini, president of the Audit Office, and Duke Cesare Rivera, commander of the Knights of Malta; for the bridegroom, Air Force Colonel Briganti, aide-de-camp to the King, and gold medal holder Cupini.

Claretta wore an Empire-style dress, adorned with a silver lamé cloak, and an ermine flounce (the same as her mother had worn when she married Dr. Saverio), while Riccardo had on a full dress uniform. The Cardinal bestowed upon the couple the special benediction of the Holy Father who had recently received the about-to-be-married Petacci girl in audience.

A very large banquet was held on the eve of the wedding, lasting until late, with two hundred guests in attendance, chosen by Sig.ra Giuseppina from amongst her husband's friends and acquaintances, especially from the Vatican. Her daughter wore a stunning gold lamé dress, with huge bird of paradise plumes, which symbolized, ironically, the fragile future. Just promoted lieutenant, Riccardo wore a magnificent blue uniform. They seemed happy.

But when the lights go out, and the noises of the festivities cease, Claretta is overcome by a restless melancholy. She recalls what Mussolini, her Duce, told her rather awkwardly and fearfully in their last meeting: "Believe me, long engagements are the death of love." She sees his hand on her shoulder again, almost an urging to break the delay, and speed up the calendar. She'd agreed, she'd even smiled at him, but without being convinced, fearing not to be able to see him again (the same silent fear that he had). They hadn't uttered this out loud to each other, but my, what eloquence could be read in their looks! Were there really to be no other meetings after that one? What if they never saw each other again?

With Claretta's marriage, perhaps, Mussolini hoped to free himself from a sensation whose range and effects he'd underestimated. What he felt for her was much more than a mere frivolous physical attraction. Thinking of her one night, he hadn't slept a wink. What else could this be but love?

As for Claretta, her thoughts were only of him. She'd only just married, and she had wifely duties to carry out, but how could she forget the long, languorous, platonic meetings in the Sala del Mappamondo?

The honeymoon turns into a disaster. At Venice, the first violent altercation breaks out, apparently due to a preventive action by Federici, rejected by his wife.[12] The next day the couple makes up, and for the rest of the trip—a lengthy meandering that included stops at Istanbul, Athens, Palestine and Egypt—no other quarrels occurred.

Upon returning home, towards the middle of July, after a brief stop in Rome, they move to Orbetello where Riccardo had been assigned a post as pilot to the special group commanded by Italo Balbo.

Not yet having a house, they stay at the Hotel Nazionale, occupying first apartment Number six, then twelve. They rent, subsequently, lodgings on the upper floor of a small villa still under construction, the property of Luigi and Giuseppina Bini: three large rooms that they furnish simply with furniture picked up here and there (the dining-room set was on loan from the Air Force Officers' club, while for the bedroom, they had to content themselves with a matrimonial bed and a large armchair provided by Sig.ra Giuseppina who also sends her daughter one of her domestic servants).

Even at Orbetello, actually here less then elsewhere, was there peace between them. He went out at dawn to return, when he did return (the training often took him away from the main establishment), late at night, weary and stressed. If she hadn't slept well, she'd greet him gloomily, as one greets an undesirable stranger. They quarrelled over trifles, and kept lengthy grudges.

Whether for right or wrong reasons, Claretta hated Orbetello because she felt herself neglected, and also because the weather caused her terrible migraines and worrisome autonomic nervous system distress. She had no friends, and neither was she seeking any. Rather than wasting time with the wives of other pilots, she preferred to remain indoors to read Petrarch, Leopardi, and Gozzano, to listen to the radio, and to write endless letters to her mother, who telephoned her everyday.

Late in the morning, or in the afternoon at dusk, she'd wander tediously along the deserted banks of the lagoon, sometimes wearing a light blue cloak, lined in white silk, deep in thought, accompanied by her lovely memories. Then, when she was sadder than usual, she'd reach out for Miriam and her mother, her sole confidantes.

Sig.ra Giuseppina who had so wanted that marriage, tries to keep the union afloat against impossible odds. But every effort is useless. "The scenes," recalls Miriam "follow one after the other, and sometimes even erupt in our house, where Claretta and her husband came to spend Sundays. Matters were always more heated, more and more insufferable. One day, our brother Marcello, having come home on leave (he served aboard [Italy's] SS *Colleoni* as medical officer), notices a strange mark on Claretta's cheek. Right away he guesses what is going on and, asks incredulously: 'My, oh my, are beatings the order of the day in these parts?' Trying to maintain her sense of decorum, Claretta denies that anything is happening, and the incident would probably have been closed if I, who was still living in a 'realm of honesty,' hadn't blurted out 'If only that were the first one.' Worse happenings were avoided only because Federici made himself scarce very quickly, staying away from our house."

But one Sunday in September 1935, "Claretta and her husband came to see us in Rome, though they returned home earlier than expected. We were all out, even the servants had a day off," continues Miriam. "Federici was very impatient because he said he had an appointment. Not being able to get into the apartment, he goes to a public telephone in a bar; Claretta pushes open the door of the booth to inquire if he would like her to order something for him from the establishment, but he yells that he had not given her permission to listen in on his conversations. Accompanying the shout is a slap that causes Claretta to fall on the floor. Bad luck had her collapse against a sharp corner, striking her head behind her left ear, at a spot where, a few years earlier she'd had an operation for a mastoid problem. The result of this blow was a concussion."

That was enough to cause a split-up, helped along by Riccardo's leaving for Eritrea (he went as a volunteer), from where he mails long conciliatory letters to his wife, which she answers in the same tone. But these were mere words, trite and sterile intentions, which had little to do with his true feelings, or with hers, divided as they were by a chasm that could not be bridged because of bitter distrust.

When Federici returns, his wife goes to Naples to pick him up, but the arguments soon begin anew. After another spat in their endless series of such confrontations, Claretta returns to her family, not wanting to live alone in a large apartment on Viale Angelico that she had received as a gift from her parents. A short time later, Riccardo leaves for Tokyo, where he will remain as air attaché for the entire war period. First, however, in agreement with his wife, he seeks a legal separation, granted at the beginning of autumn. He disappears soon afterwards.

After a few months, Claretta meets the Duce again who, being aware of her marital woes, once more invites her to Palazzo Venezia.

How often they see each other, we do not know. But we are assured—at least as Miriam tells us—that Mussolini, not less bewildered than his ecstatic visitor, keeps from making any suggestive advances. He behaves as usual, respectfully and gallantly: seated beside her on the stone step beneath the window, hand in hand, searching the sky, caressed by westerly breezes, and crossed by flocks of swallows.

The dice was cast, however, and the arrow was aimed. All that was needed now was the maternal consent.

One day, Sig.ra Giuseppina is summoned to the Sala del Mappomondo where the stilted Duce, in the formal uniform of an honourary corporal of the Militia, omitting the pleasantries, brusquely asks her: "Signora, will you permit me to be Clara's lover?"

It was a warm night of October 1936, the year of the African conquest, and of Empire.

Six

Believe! Obey! Fight!

When Benito and Claretta's romance changes from platonic to sexual (there are some who maintain that the two had already become lovers), the dictator is at the height of his renown. He has just founded an empire, and, on his pedestal, praised by the entire population, his star had risen like that of an Olympic god.

Never had he enjoyed such approval, never, even outside of Italy, was his name making so much news, and his spectacular feats roused either admiration, or condemnation. "The only European giant," the Archbishop of Canterbury said about him; "the greatest genius of the modern era," had extolled Thomas Edison; "a superior human being," had exalted Gandhi.[13] Almost another Hannibal, a new Caesar, a twentieth century Napoleon.

By now, he'd been in power for fourteen years, and nothing seemed to shake him. He'd been needed to bring order to the country, but once having achieved mastery, he exercised it, through thick and thin, amongst peers and inferiors, with a fist of iron, trusting to his own infallibility, his indispensability, and his invulnerability.

After the Ethiopian triumph, his wife Rachele, with the wisdom of a housewife, advises him to step down, to pass the mantle of leadership to one of his designated successors.

But how could he possibly give up to others the scepter that he'd desired for so long, and for which he'd fought so hard?

His had been an inspired rise, worthy of the pages of Plutarch, beginning on 27 July 1883 at Varano dei Costa, in the village of Dovìa, a corner of Predappio, province of Forlì, where he was born under the affected sign of the lion.

His father Alessandro, son of failed land owners, was working as a blacksmith, but the small shop brought little food to the table, forcing his wife Rosa to hold school classes in a small room off the kitchen, in the very house.

Here Benito shared a bed with his brother Arnaldo, a mat which was really a straw pallet stuffed with corn husks, while his sister Edwige slept in one of the other two small rooms.

His name was not of local derivation: Benito was the name of Juarez, the Mexican revolutionary, executioner of Emperor Maximilian; neither was his brother's name of the immediate area, but echoed that of the unlucky Brescian reformer.* Having thus named his two sons, Alessandro clinched his position as international Socialist, enemy of bourgeois order, and champion of the disinherited and of the oppressed.

Alessandro's extremism, as later also that of Benito, his fighting barricade spirit and his own anticlerical stance, show all the frustrations and humiliations of the impoverished and marginalized class. Because of this, he preached revolution.

Towards the end of the century, he joins the Socialist International, earning his stripes as deputy mayor. He also writes polemical articles for the newspapers, promoting the most worn out ideas of the era, denouncing the "tired and bastard society," praising Socialism, "the precise ideas and upward movement that lights up the world," and dumping God as a "bourgeois expedient." In his head are jumbled a holy yearning for justice, with a strange messianism, and a utopian humanitarianism.

That these notions should fire up fantasies in Benito was inevitable, counter-balanced only by the good sense of the gentle Rosa.

The future Duce begins to give his parents anxiety from infancy. He'd not yet begun to talk in his third year, and his mother takes him to the doctor who tells her reassuringly: "He'll talk, he will talk, and talk even too much!"

But he presents the first serious problem to his parents after having completed his elementary schooling at Predappio, when he is enrolled in the Salesian boarding school in nearby Faenza, something that Rosa desires, but that Alessandro, the extremely rabid priest-hater, does not.

The boy quickly finds himself in difficulties, not only because he has such a father, but also because the pupils are grouped on the basis of wealth and, in the dining hall, the poorest children are to make do with the leftovers. He is not offended, essentially, by the inedible food, but rather by the privileges of the others.

He has no friends, not even from amongst his classmates, who are afraid of him, although they defer to him. He reads a great deal, but in a disorganized fashion: revolutionary and anarchist writers, and the French social novels of Hugo and Zola, which fulminate against capitalism and the bourgeoisie.

---

* Arnaldo da Brescia (d. 1155), opponent of the temporal power of the popes.

He does not remain long at the Faenza school because he wounds a schoolmate on the leg with a knife, and he is expelled.

He moves next to the Royal teacher-training institute in Forlimpopoli directed by Valfredo Carducci, the brother of the famous Giosuè.[14] But even here he is put out, to be re-admitted as day student, thanks to the good will of Carducci, who appears to have had an interest in him.

His relations with the other students are not any better than at Faenza. The few times that he draws close to them, or that they seek to be friendly with him, is to protest against the abuse of the power of the supervisors in the punishment of a fellow pupil. He feels himself already to be a leader, albeit a misunderstood one.

At sixteen years old he has his first contact with the local Socialist chapter, but because of his youthfulness, he is refused entry into the party. At eighteen, in 1901, he receives his teaching diploma, and soon afterwards sits for the competitive exams for the position of public clerk, without success, however.

At this point, he accepts a post as a substitute teacher in the Socialist town of Gualtieri, a farm centre in Reggio Emelia.

He falls in with a crowd that have similar views, arguing politics till dawn, then going home drunk. In any case, neither his drinking, nor argumentative nature cause him to lose his job, but rather an intrigue with the wife of a Socialist man who had moved in with him; this unleashes an uproar amongst his friends, proponents of free love, just as long as this wasn't practiced with their own women.

The only thing left for him to do is to move on to Switzerland where for two years, from 1902 to 1904, he becomes a jack-of-all-trades—from manual labourer to warehouseman to mason—sleeping under bridges in a wooden box, skipping meals, or eating apples and cooked potatoes.

The experience, nevertheless, is a useful one, since in the Swiss Confederation he comes into contact with Italian Socialist émigrés.

He quickly embraces their cause, becoming their champion and, after a mere four months, is elected secretary of the Italian Union of Masons and Manual Labourers.

His most pleasing quality is his roaring Manicheism. He divides humanity into the good and the evil, the exploited and the exploiters, the revolutionaries and the bourgeois. He is against popes and priests, against kings and aristocrats, he doesn't want war, and he attacks the constitution. He becomes excited over a trifle, peppering his indictments with curses and fulminations and, in a public debate, often reaches the point of challenging God! "If you exist," he'd yell, taking his watch from his pocket and indicating the dial, "I give you two minutes to strike me dead!" The two minutes pass, God doesn't smite him, and his prestige soars.

He has many mishaps, is arrested for seditious assemblies and expelled from the country (but he manages to get back in through another canton). One time he has to leave to rush to his mother's sick bed, but he returns to Switzerland quickly since he is drafted into the Italian Army with the rest of his age group. For this, he is sentenced to one year in default.

At Lausanne, he attends the lectures of Vilfredo Pareto, the great economist, whose theories dealing with the limits of democracy, on violence, and on the leading role of minorities, fill him with enthusiasm. The concept of the masses as the instrument to use in the pursuit of power dates, perhaps, from that period (if Marx teaches him to love the idea, Nietzsche the Superman, raises in him a feeling of contempt for the notion).

Another decisive meeting is with Angelica Balabanoff, the Russian *pasionaria*, an Amazonian woman of thirty-three, of bourgeois origin, who repudiates her social class for that of the proletariat. With her fiery temperament, she takes hold of Benito, who is a dozen years her junior, placing him under her wing, and in her bed. She trains him in ideology, introduces him to other exiles, and is the first to understand that the young man with the wild eyes, with the thread-bare clothes, with the worn-out shoes, is much too full of himself to think of others, and much too cocksure to even consider following the advice of others: in his world, there is room only for his personal self. More than a revolutionary, then, he is an anarchist: rather than a follower of Lenin, he seems to be a disciple of Kropotkin and Sorel.

Towards the end of 1904, thanks to an amnesty, he leaves Switzerland, and returns to Dovìa. But he only stays for a short time there as he goes soon afterwards into the Army, heading for Verona. With the end of that military stint, he heads home for two months, then on to Tolmezzo where a teaching post is available. Here, according to some biographers, he seduces a woman, comes to blows with her husband and, perhaps, contracts the pox (although no one ever succeeds in establishing the proof of this). From Friulì, he continues on to Oneglia, in Liguria, and finally to Trento, no longer as a school teacher but as the editor of *L'Avvenire del Lavoratore,* a Socialist periodical.

La Balabanoff and other friends obtain that post for him, and never was a better choice made. Within a short space of time, the circulation of the journal increases due to his extraordinary bite, bringing down upon him a sea of troubles. In a few months, he is fined six times, eleven issues are seized and, finally, he is fired, which perhaps doesn't displease him: amongst his many talents, he also ranks that of martyr.

Thus, he returns to the Romagna, heading this time, not to Dovìa, but to Forlì. His widowed father has closed the blacksmith shop, and has established a trattoria that he manages with the aid of Anna Guidi, a former lover of his, and helped at the counter by her nineteen year old daughter, Rachele.

Mussolini had met the girl when she was seven years old, then, they had lost contact. Seeing her again, he is struck not only by her fresh loveliness, her generous shape, and her golden hair, but also by her vigour and her determined, strong will. He understands quickly that she can't be tamed easily, but this really spurs him on. Here is a challenge not to be missed and, in actual fact, he makes the conquest.

His father does everything to try to dissuade him until, one day, Benito takes out a pistol, and threatens: "If Rachele doesn't want me, this weapon holds six shots, one for her, the others for me." Rachele is actually not opposed to the liaison, but since she involves herself so dramatically, the ultimatum becomes better still and even more effective. All this has the desired results. The next day, they move into two bare rooms in Via Merenda (they would marry in a civil ceremony five years later).

Benito is without work and they might have had a hand-to-mouth existence if Cesare Battisti, an acquaintance from Trento, hadn't requested him to prepare a novel to be published serially in his newspaper. Mussolini throws together a pathetic banality whose title indicates its very contents: *Claudia Particella, the Cardinal's Mistress*, a publication that had an astonishing success.

Rachele would have preferred to see him return to teaching, but all he could think of was the written word, and politics.

Meanwhile, the Forlì Socialists entrust him with the editorship of their new journal for which he himself suggests the title: *La Lotta di Classe* [*Class Struggle*].

The issues of the paper sell out quickly because of its extreme leftist polemics, its crude but effective personal attacks, and the fierce demagoguery against proprietors and their accomplices.

Benito shoots from the hip at anyone who doesn't agree with him, whether bourgeois leeches, conformist moderates, Republicans, or even the reforming Socialists. As a result, he is chosen to be the Party secretary of the local chapter.

The Party congress of July 1912 makes his name even more widely known. Once he is at the podium and begins to speak, it is as if he is brandishing a spear against the reformers, all eyes being glued to him.

This is his great day, even if the applause, more than his own ideas, let loose the rhythmic sentences, that erudite use of pause and pursuit, the clever variance of tone, from attenuated to high-falutin', from conciliatory to imperious. More than a victory, this is a triumph, and resounds mightily throughout the country. The newspapers hail him as the "New Man" of Socialism, as the "Rising Star" of the proletariat. This was only the beginning, but what a beginning!

Five months later, he is called to the editor's chair of *Avanti!* which forces him to move to Milan, leaving behind in Forlì Rachele and Edda, his first-born. No one doubts that he is the right man, for the right job, at the right time.

One of his first actions is to reduce his salary from seven hundred to five hundred lire, perhaps to underline his disinterest in money, and his absolute devotion to "the Cause."

The paper's circulation quadruples—from twenty-eight thousand to one hundred thousand—but, above all, he creates his ascendancy over public opinion and over the political world.

The results are seen at the next elections when the Socialists increase their portion of the vote by three points, from eight to eleven, despite the Bissolati bloodletting.[15]

On 18 October 1914, like a lightning bolt out of a clear blue sky, an editorial appears in *Avanti!* whose headline says it all: "From absolute neutrality to an active and working neutrality," in contrast to an earlier piece the previous July with the hardly less eloquent opening: "Down with war!" How could the author, within the space of three months, first be hostile to, then support intervention, against the official party line, thus causing the Party to yank the editor's pen from his hand?

He is not out of a job for long as, in mid November, he is once again at the head of a newspaper, *Il Popolo d'Italia,* founded according to some, to provide an alternative voice to the interventionists, according to others, to divide Socialism.

The Party reacts by expelling Mussolini, who defends himself by proclaiming his personal, revolutionary faith: "You hate me because you still love me!"

During the war, he is sent to the front where, gravely wounded, he undergoes twenty-seven surgical procedures, some without anesthesia. He remains in service for seventeen months and, on 23 February 1917, he is promoted to corporal, and then discharged. He returns to Milan at the helm of his *Popolo d'Italia*.

With the war over, it soon becomes apparent that the conflict has been a traumatic affair for Italy. Not only has the country reaped 600 000 casualties, and the treasury has a debt of twelve billion lire but, what is worse, the nation having suffered a psychological blow, must now live through one of the blackest periods in its history: to the disbanding of the Armed Forces is joined an economic and social crisis fostering brawls between the parties, and quarrels amongst the ruling classes.

With his uncanny intuition, Mussolini senses that his time has arrived, but he also recognizes that he needs a political party.

To supply him with such an organization are the paramilitary groups, the *Fasci di Combattimenti*, organized on 23 March 1919, in the headquarters of the Industrial and Commercial Alliance of Milan, in Piazza San Sepolcro: a fateful meeting, with few in attendance—trade-unionists, anarchists, soldiers, who are volunteers from the beginning, and Futurists—a jumble of men without work or money, with few ideas, and even fewer ideals. They are ready for anything, but also the opposite: possessing a great will to beat up others and impose order (their own, naturally).

The situation is becoming red hot, the government isn't governing, strikes occur without end, d'Annunzio occupies Fiume, chaos is everywhere.

Mussolini presents a slate of his *Fasci* for the elections that are called for November. Without having an active party, he overcomes the hurdle by presenting "personalities" such as Marinetti, Podrecca, and Toscanini, but even with such names, the result is a bitter one.[16] He receives only 4657 votes as opposed to 170 000 for the Socialists. To console himself, he takes fencing and driving lessons.

He can always rely on his newspaper which he uses with devilish skill, keeping his distance from d'Annunzio, but having his followers adopt the odd clothes and bizarre rites of the legionnaires: from the black shirt, to the skull-cap type fez with tassel; from the grey-green pants to the shorts with puttee; from the Roman salute, to the martial "A Noi," to the nonsensical cry "Eia,

eia, alalà," to the motto "Me ne frego," ["I don't give a damn"]—
which really sum up the feelings of the new-born action squads.

The peninsula becomes a battle zone between the groups of
Black Shirts, and the Reds, while the government looks on, and
public opinion, tired of the whole thing, demands a restoration of
law and order.

The editor of *Il Popolo d'Italia* fans the flames cleverly, now
urging his "braves" on, then restraining them, now attacking the
government, then seeking dialogue.

Great tactician that he is, Mussolini understands that
democracy is out of breath, the patient is on his death bed, and
only by speeding up his demise with a knife can the country find
a little peace. In short, a surgeon is needed, and he himself is the
ideal candidate as the elections of May 1921 are about to show.

This time, he receives more than 172 000 votes, obtaining
thirty-five seats in parliament: a determined and close-knit
minority, against a divided and skidding majority.

In this political climate, the bewildered and frightened Facta,
when not allowed to declare a state of emergency by King Victor
Emanuele III, throws in the sponge. It thus becomes obvious that
his successor can only be the son of the blacksmith.

The Fascist squads, meanwhile, are mobilized and, on 28
October 1922, begin to move. First they take over the prefectures,
then the police headquarters, followed by the railway stations,
other local public offices, and finally, Rome.

Once summoned here by the King, Mussolini proceeds to the
Capital by night sleeper, arriving late in the morning. After leaving his few bags at the Hotel Savoia, in black shirt, overcoat and
gaiters, he presents himself to the sovereign who, without delay,
appoints him Head of Government. He is not yet forty years old.

The Italians, besides Claretta, breathe a sigh of relief, while
the newspapers, with very few exceptions, vie with each other to
see who could heap the most praise on the new Prime Minister.

The newspapers showed him to be husky, of medium stature
(he was one metre, sixty-seven centimetres tall, two centimetres
taller than Napoleon),[*] with powerful shoulders, the chest of a
tenor, a head more rough-hewn than sculpted, a bull neck, muscu-
lar nape, a high forehead, accentuated by a receding hairline and
a wart, with an energetic forehead, thick and ever-moving lips, a
strong chin, the lower jaw heavy and determined. However, his big
black eyes are his most striking feature: avid and dazzling, hun-
gry and searching, rolling like the blades of a windmill, fixing

---

* About 5 feet, 6 inches.

them intently on whoever is before him, after which he'd move them on to some other interviewer, or to the crowd with the same speed.

His voice varied in tone depending whether he was speaking publicly or privately. The official one was shrewdly modulated, now cutting, now thundering; the private one, soft and devoid of melodrama.

He moved quickly, back erect, chin out, a stance he often exaggerated while at the lectern or podium, haranguing the crowds, thick legs astride, with his heavy hands on his hips, in a manner both provocative and dominating.

Physically he was somewhat clumsy, and his body gestures revealed him as having a melodramatic and imperious character, a man born to rule, ambitious and intransigent, the saviour of the Nation, and a future tyrant.

He was said to be stubborn and pedantic, hated wasting time, was maniacally punctual, didn't confide in anyone, didn't want to be the confidante of anyone else, and that he had no friends.

He was also said to anger easily, though he did not hold grudges, didn't smoke and didn't drink.

Having become Head of Government, and then Duce, many of his habits change, but his little, private quirks remain. He continues to rise at six in the morning, to be shaved by his wife Rachele, later supplanted by Sciarretta, the security service agent, to take at least a couple of baths a week, to wash himself using Viset, an almond-scented soap, to brush his teeth with Eutimol, or with Chlorodont.

As to clothes, although never too particular here, except for uniforms, an essential feature of the Fascist iconography, he preferred white suits for summer; grey, blue or brown for winter. He wore a vest, suspenders, a belt, garters, and gaiters for many years, the delight of caricaturists, and long johns, later replaced by cotton shorts. He preferred shirts with stiff, downward pointing collars (only the black shirt had a soft one), and classical, conservative ties. For a while, he slept in a night shirt, then changed to pyjamas. He used Arab-style sandals instead of slippers, and he didn't wear a wristwatch.

He was moderate, in fact, very frugal, even at table, where he remained just long enough to swallow a light broth, or a vegetable soup, consumed many vegetables and fruit, and drank a glass of milk or of effervescent mineral water.

The speed with which he downed his food was, perhaps, one

of the causes of his gastritis, something which caused him much suffering, but which was not his only ailment. He was also prone to constipation which he relieved with San Pellegrino Milk of Magnesia; worrisome mouth sores, and annoying colds, perhaps due to his disdain for umbrellas, insultingly referred to as "bourgeois relics," or the "weapons of papal soldiers."

He abhorred, no less, armchairs and cushions, symbols of a sedentary, soft life, in contrast to the spartan ideals of the Regime. For other reasons, he hated flies, and every time that he would hear one buzzing about, he would summon Navarra to come with the insecticide. As well, he couldn't stand noise as all solitary persons (he was even bothered by the sounds of the Faraglia band in Piazza Venezia, and this despite his love of music, especially opera, and his weakness for waltzes, mazurkas, and polkas).

Traditional holidays, in particular Christmas, New Year, and Easter, put him in a black mood, and he'd spend this time working in his office, or pretending to do so (one afternoon, worried about his long silence, Navarra opened the door to the Sala del Mappamondo, and saw him with folded arms, staring into space).

But what alarmed him the most was sickness, his and that of his family; death and funerals which caused him to touch iron when he happened upon them, to make the sign against the evil eye, or to put his hand in his pants (extremely susperstitious, he was wont to say: "I fear the bearer of spells and bad luck more than that of an anti-Fascist"). As well, he dreaded sudden changes in weather and humidity (exactly like Claretta).

But he loved cats, though not black ones, and animals in general, horses above all, (at Villa Torlonia, he had thirteen, amongst which was Frou-Frou, the arab). Every morning he took a brief ride on a horse and, time permitting, played a game of tennis, or of soccer with his sons. He was known to ride a bicycle, to fence, and to swim, he had an absolute passion for cars, and he was a good airplane pilot.

Some of his other hobbies included the game of solitaire, the playing of the violin, accompanying himself on a player-piano before proceeding to his office (his favourite piece was *Ramona*). As for the cinema—every night was film night at Villa Torlonia—he relaxed, and was diverted by the performances of Larry Semon, Laurel and Hardy, Wallace Beery, and Greta Garbo.

He even found time to read. To one of his *gerarchi** he boasted of leafing through the pages of 350 newspapers and magazines every day, and of underlining with a red or blue Faber pencil the

---

* *gerarca* (s.); *gerarchi* (pl.) - a Fascist leader.

important parts which he'd annotate rather pedantically—nothing, he said, escaped him.

He also read many books, especially in history and, above all, biography, and he was the author of a large number of them.

The Mussolini described here is only part of the one that assumed power in 1922. His myths didn't spring, full blown, overnight and, to construct them, the Predappio teacher spends sixteen years preparing his legend, the most active ones of his happy and tragic career.

He begins by showing up at his office in Palazzo Chigi at eight in the morning (he'll move to Palazzo Venezia later) before his associates, whom he quickly puts in line, thundering: "I want forty or fifty thousand men who work as well as the mechanism of a clock." No one dares protest, especially since he, implacably diligent, sets the example.

He wanted to know everything, to see, to control, even traffic: if, having moved aside the curtains, he spied from the Balcony, or a window, a driver committing a road infraction, he'd note the license plate number, then he'd inform the requisite official who was to see to it that the ignorant transgressor be punished. He even tried to regulate the direction of the coming and going on the sidewalk, though the experiment fails, but his campaign forbidding the needless sounding of the horn is more successful. In a puritanical frame of mind, he orders the closure of dozens of brothels in greater Rome, despite his having been an avid frequenter of these establishments in the past. He abolishes, or perhaps deludes himself into thinking that he has done so, illegal gaming houses, and revokes the permits of thousands of bars, mindful possibly of legendary youthful drinking sprees.

In the early years, he is not without opponents and problems. The Fascist squads itch for action and, with some difficulties, he manages to bring them to heel, to redirect their energies and to organize them into a voluntary, faithful Militia.

His *gerarchi* also need to be attended to, especially those in Farinacci's circle, and he manages to meld them into the Grand Council of Fascism which becomes the supreme consultative body of the Party.

Much graver is the crisis following the kidnapping and murder of Giacomo Matteotti, the Socialist legislator, enemy of the new Regime and denouncer of its arbitrary actions. The Socialist's vigourous parliamentary attacks against the results of the last election seal his doom. In parliament, a row breaks out and the speaker barely succeeds in quelling the denunciation.

Seemingly impassive, Mussolini listens to the accuser, then he rushes soon afterwards to Palazzo Chigi and Marinelli's office, the Party's administrative secretary, who also has links to the Cheka, a type of low-level secret police, assailing him with these words: "If you weren't all such cowards, no one would have dared make such a speech."

At this, the much too zealous secretary orders Dumini, one of the leaders of the Cheka, to settle the matter. Matteotti is abducted by five men, including Dumini, a short time later from the Lungotevere where he lived, forcing him into a car which then speeds off towards the Milvian Bridge.

The disappearance of the Socialist parliamentarian creates consternation and anger in the entire country—the press is still unfettered at the time. The anti-Fascist parties walk out of the chamber, and Mussolini's government is on the verge of falling. This does not happen because of the Duce's sang-froid, and of the support of the King, aware of the grave dangers that might result to the country were the Head of Government dismissed (and to substitute him with whom?).

The Prime Minister seeks to distance himself from the abduction, denying any direct responsibility in the murder for which—he says—he would be the first to pay the price. Some believe him, others not and, finally, taking advantage of the absence of the opposition, away in protest "on the Aventine," he returns more determined to the fray.

Although what he decides to do had many risks, quite suddenly he institutes a dictatorship.

The excuse for this action is offered him in the sitting of 3 January 1925. He utters a few sentences, but very effective ones: "I declare here and now, in the presence of this Assembly, and before the Italian People, that I alone assume the political, moral and historical responsibility for all that has happened ... If Fascism has been a criminal organization, I am the head of this association." Obviously, from that moment on, he would be the boss, with full and absolute power.

The result of all this is a series of attempts on his life (that of the Honourable Zaniboni, of the fanatical Irishwoman Violet Gibson, of Anteo Zamboni, the fourteen year old Bolognese boy), which merely causes the Regime to become ever harsher by bringing in a special tribunal for the defense of the State.

The approbation for the Government increases in the interim, orchestrated by a propaganda in which the dictator leads the way, supplying the slogans: "Believe, obey, fight," "Many enemies, much honour," "The plough digs the furrow, the sword defends it."

The son of the blacksmith has ever grander visions and, for him more and more, his Italy becomes "a people of saints, poets, heroes, and discoverers." In 1927, he revalues the lire to ninety to the pound sterling, with a subsequent decrease in the level of salaries. As a proponent of national self-sufficiency, he declares that the country could, and should, supply its own needs. Thus he launches the "battle of the granary," threshing wheat himself, and promotes a campaign in favour of rice, even to the point of show-ing how to cook it. Convinced that the strength of a nation lay in its fecundity, he encourages couples to have children, fining bach-elors, and ordering officers of the Militia to greet pregnant women with the Roman salute.

The Pontine Marshes are drained, he sends Mori, "the Iron Prefect," to Sicily to combat the Mafia, forbids strikes and lock-outs, laying the foundations for the Corporate State, one of the most solid achievements of the Regime.

But his master stroke is the Concordat with the Holy See, after decades of misunderstandings and quarrels. No one expects this agreement, least of all the reinsertion of religious instruction in the schools. And in 1925, the dictator and Rachele marry in a religious ceremony.

The sensitive negotiations are carried out in the greatest secrecy, without any leaks. When the question is finally closed, Pope Pius XI, in a rush of gratitude, hails Mussolini as "the man that Providence has brought forth to bring us together."

All that is left for Il Duce is to give himself a similar boost. Now that he enjoys the support of both Throne and Altar, Palazzo Chigi is no longer worthy of his new rank. Thus he decides to relo-cate to the ancient, battlemented Palazzo Venezia.

He moves there on 16 September 1929, to the magnificent Sala del Mappamondo, twenty metres long, and with a width and height of thirteen metres, lighted by two windows and a Balcony which would become his legendary pulpit.

The only furniture in the room is an armchair and a desk, on which he places an inkwell flanked by two toy lions, a round clock-barometer, a small flowered porcelain vase for pencils, a silver paper-cutter, a blotting sheet, a lamp with a yellow silk shade, and a miniature of his mother Rosa, (later he'll add a toy in the shape of a cabin and a heart, a gift from Claretta).

Of the three telephones, one is a direct line to the protective service's main switchboard, another is for long distance calls, the third for local calls (since he uses this line only when he leaves his office, he usually doesn't remember it's number). As well, he has a keyboard linked to the immense chandelier, used to soften the light, according to the rank of his visitor: the more important the latter, the brighter the light. Distances absolutely had to be maintained.

Even at Palazzo Venezia he is the first one in and the last one out. Until eleven in the morning, he'd receive the Party Secretary, the Police Chief, the head of OVRA, an overseer of the police, the chief of the gendarmerie, and various ministers. Then the interviews began: heads of foreign states, diplomats, industrialists, cultural leaders, besides the usual delegations. In the afternoons, the rounds began anew, lightened—if Navarra's memoirs don't lie—by brief erotic meetings with former lovers and young pursuers.

His day never ended before nine-thirty, after having settled all the daily business, and meticulously clearing off his desk, leaving on the light: the Italians needed to know that he was always working, even at night ("Il Duce is working; let's let him work," counseled one of the many lictorial refrains).

He no longer lives in Via Rasella, but in the baroque Villa Torlonia, offered to him by Prince Giovanni for one lira a month. If Palazzo Venezia is his Palazzo Quirinale, and his body guard his Praetorian Guard, this is his Villa Ada [where the King lived].

Amidst military bands, plumes, and praises, is celebrated the March on Rome in 1932, the highest point of the Fascist Regime. In the same year Ludwig, the German biographer, interviews him for a famous book. In 1933, Balbo sets off for a second crossing of the Atlantic, Chicago naming a street after the group leader, while in Germany, Hitler, the Duce's admirer, comes to power, the same Hitler to whom Mussolini refused an autographed photograph in 1926.

At this point, all he needs is an empire, but where is one to be found? The English, and to a lesser extent the French, have grabbed Asia and Africa: very few open territories were available for the taking. But, there was Ethiopia, bastion of slavery, which would justify a civilizing and liberating mission. In this way, Italy could also have her "place in the sun."

This, then, is the magic moment for Fascism, and the apotheosis of its Superman who, at 22:30 on the night of 9 May 1936, announces to the New Romans from the Balcony of Palazzo Venezia, the birth of the Empire, founded once again on its "fateful hills."

Also in the piazza, with throngs of other people, is Claretta, more radiant than ever, more than ever in love, and more than ever elated over the miracles of her Duce. It seemed to be a dream, or a fairy tale, but it really wasn't. That night she doesn't sleep either, as is also the case with her Benito. And they hadn"t even exchanged a kiss yet!

Seven

The Man's the Man ...

B esides the young Claretta, at least one hundred thousand women of all ages and rank show up in Piazza Venezia that night to praise the Founder of the Empire. These women had been electrified by the events in East Africa, spurred on by the radio, newspapers, and billboards that they had read enthusiastically, and in which events they themselves seemed to feel that they'd had a hand.

In the Caesar from Predappio, they saw embodied their ideal man, their eternal male. The son of the blacksmith knew this and, with his poses, his tone of voice, and his looks, encouraged a consensus, even if suffused with hysteria.

To millions of women, not only those cheering that night as if in the magic circle of an enchanted theatre stall, Mussolini was something more than just the "Man of Providence," of the Redeemer, of the Father of the Nation: he was their man. They dreamt of him at night and, in the arms of lovers, fiancés, or husbands, had him in mind (a young Piemontese schoolteacher, on the eve of her wedding, sought in vain, for him to enjoy the ancient *droits du seigneur*).

And how many wrote to him, offering themselves to him! As, for example, the Roman noblewoman who, once admitted to his presence, slips off her fur coat, revealing her naked body beneath.

All this was not merely about the worship of the Powerful One. If so many Italian women, infatuated because of their physical nature, felt themselves down deep to be the bride of the Head of Government, fantasizing about marvelous embraces, always to the tune of the typical masochistic refrain, "Torture me, but with your kisses nurture me!" others, more clear-headed, though no less inflamed, seduced by the lictorial ideology, were ready to sacrifice themselves with him, and for him.

Still others, less eager but more practical, were really grateful to him for having furthered their social advancement. Children of the proletariat, or of the lower middle classes, had been able to rise to a higher order without being considered parvenues, in fact, making of their backgrounds a social symbol (and this with the blessing of the Regime which, in part because of demagoguery, and a little because of the common plebeian spirit, found the snobbish affectations of class laughable).

Finally, there were the women of the middle or upper middle bourgeoisie who identified Fascism with order, security, social peace, the respect for religion, and the growth of comfort allowing their husbands to take a larger, more generous share of the national wealth. They, and others, had never been so well-off in Italy, and the motto "Today better than yesterday, tomorrow better than today," summarized a satisfaction for a state of things that nothing, and no one, seemed to be able to threaten at the moment, and on whose long existence everyone, or almost everyone, would have sworn.

Even amongst the women, of course, there were opponents such as the wives of militant and persecuted anti-Fascists, but this was merely a Fronde, an internal conflict, at least between 1936 and June 1940, a thin and defenseless one, that the Regime's police kept easily at bay.

The problems begin when the nation will enter the war. Defeat and bombing will hammer it into the ground, the fronts, especially the Russian one, will gobble up millions of young men, and brass bands will give way to funeral dirges, pushing the Invincible Colossus into the abyss.

The same followers—excepting the uncompromising recruits under the flag of the Italian Social Republic—will then turn their backs on him, dismayed not only because of the defeat of the Leader, but also because of the weakness of the man, overwhelmed by a woman recklessly determined to monopolize him. Mussolini, the man who flitted about everywhere, belonged to everyone; the Mussolini who settled down in bourgeois fashion with a "coquette" and was committing collective adultery, belonged to no one.

Better not get too far ahead. In the fall of 1936, when Benito and Claretta become lovers, the Duce is as he had never been, and as he was never to be again. He was the idol of millions upon millions of women, and not only Italian ones.

Every day, on the tables of his personal secretarial staff were placed large piles of letters which a special section of the Ministry of Internal Affairs examined and catalogued. If the persons writing had done so previously, the letters were delivered to the dictator who would open them personally; but if this was a first message, the experts examined the contents, noting the information on the sender, after which a part of the letter was sent to the repository, another part went to Mussolini's attention, the latter deciding which should receive a reply, and which not.

Some letters included pictures that could be misleading at times, but the receiver was satisfied easily, and somewhat uninterested in physical beauty. What aroused him most, what really set off his heat meter (the somewhat conceited Claretta will confide this to the very gossipy Navarra) were breasts. He also had a weakness for hips which he adored round and nubile. As for legs, he preferred them firm and opulent (hairless or not made little difference). Even hair colour was of slight importance: he loved the blond Rachele, the red-haired Sarfatti, the brunette Claretta, and an unknown number of chestnut-haired women.

He loathed aristocrats, who loved him, however, no less than did the working women, and the farm workers, from whom he made sure to keep his distance. He liked lower, and middle, class bourgeois females; better if they were journalists or young schoolmistresses. Unlike others before him such as Pope Formoso and Casanova, the fresh breath of young girls held no fascination for him, something common to many mere mortals who prefer the bitter young flowers to that of mature fruit.[17] If he had to choose between a young woman and an older one—Claretta being the exception—his favour always fell on the latter, perhaps because such women were always more tractable and accommodating.

A lover of a more mature age would save him the hypocritical preliminaries, the clumsy affectations, the debilitating skirmishes which, far from making him more ardent for the daring lunge, merely humiliated him because of the delaying tactics.

He mounted his women on the carpet beneath his desk, if he'd already enjoyed their favours; on the stone steps in the embrasure of one of the windows, if that was their first such encounter. He didn't remove his boots—a very labourious procedure, in any case—neither did he insist that his partner take off her clothes. He was satisfied if she simply pushed aside only that singular garment that blocked access to the Portals of Venus, so as not to complicate his virile conquest.

Some assert that he did all this with unbridled profligacy and frightful cursing; then there are others who assert that he never went too far, that he was actually always tender and respectful. According to Monelli, "He was brusque and vulgar at the beginning, while at the end he was all sugar and spice. He was not a silent and delicate lover; for the entire period that he held the woman in his arms, he shouted and made noises ... He'd get up quickly and probably took his violin and played a light tune for the woman." We'll never know for sure, of course, since the statements are contradictory, and they bear a terrible stench of revenge.

What is certain is that he scorned coaxing and ceremony; he didn't offer any because his time was always counted (Cécile Sorel, the famous French actress, exited from the Sala del Mappamondo "red-faced, preoccupied and radiant" after a mere fifteen minutes); he promised nothing and he asked for nothing. He displayed no jealousy because, for him, these adventures were absolutely, and only, erotic. Should any woman attempt to change him, he cut her off quickly.

Every so often—according to Rachele—he was even able to refuse a liaison, as in the case of the young widow of an aviator fallen in war. While he was using soothing words to try to comfort her, she began to eye him "full of desire and without any sorrow." At this point, he brusquely sent her away. "Another time,"—as his wife has stated—"he showed me a letter from a princess who had written him bitter things because Benito had never paid her any attention. That time I had my doubts. So, rolling up one of his sleeves, Benito said to me, 'Look, Rachele, just thinking about this incident gives me goose pimples. If I'd find myself in the woods with that woman and a monkey, I'd choose the monkey.' "

It really was a blot on his character that, where women were concerned, he was never very subtle: in his very crowded and ever-changing harem, he refused almost no one, even preferring the ugly, always adhering to the self-made motto: "Beauty must be distrusted; even the shrewdest men lose their heads over it."

People of his era and their descendants have asked themselves if he was ever in love. This is a question that cannot be answered easily because, for him above all else, career and power were of the utmost importance.

The first to make him seriously lose his head was Rachele, the eighth woman to fall into his bed after a plump and mature practitioner of the trade "in an unmentionable establishment" had initiated him into the pleasures and mysteries of sex. Armed with so much instruction, he had seduced a girl his own age on the stairs of his house, followed by another girl to whom, in order to avoid misunderstanding and responsibility, he'd addressed with precocious cynicism these frightful lines: "Don't look at me, girl; perhaps you love me in a serious way, but the heart that you hanker after is full of poison."

He never tired of repeating—he would even say this to Claretta—that he loved women in the natural state, and that before marrying one, he'd have to try her out (crafty hesitation of many libertines). Arrogant and aggressive (perhaps to overcome his inherent timidity), but also shy and retiring, and with so many other inconsistencies, nevertheless even he was not able to escape the insidious ties that bind.

Except for the relationship with Rachele, the others did have some effect on his tempestuous nature. But, even if they shook him, they never succeeded in turning him up side down.

The love affair with Leda Rafanelli, the anarchist from Pistoia, was a strange one culminating—it seems—with a single, furtive kiss.

Benito meets her on 18 March 1913, after a memorial ceremony on the Paris Commune. His words, his fiery and demagogic oratory inflame even her, who then sings his praises in the weekly *La Libertà*. Mussolini, who read everything (he bragged about having swallowed the entire *Treccani Encyclopedia*, except for the scientific entries), eats up her words, loves them, and thanks the author with a note. Then, he requests to see her alone. Even if involved with someone else, the woman invites him to her house.

Benito arrives in his Sunday best, sporting a bowler, and light-colored gloves, as he'd decided to take advantage right away of the situation with the eccentric and capricious anarchist who, it seems, had eastern blood flowing in her veins.

And her appearance was really oriental as she was wearing a tight-fitting, white "gelabiat" held together by a striped sash, a dark frock, a silver-embroidered veil, and dangling from her neck, a necklace of bright stones. The furniture was no less unusual: an ottoman, a sofa, cushions, mats, a water pipe, and a brazier from which rose aromatic whiffs of incense, of benjamin and sandalwood.

Accustomed to the rough smells and heavy odours of the luxuriant Romagna, and reacting as a good provincial to that display of the exotic, the editor of *Avanti!* initiates his plan quickly, and when she asks him if he is free, he lies, answering, "Like the air." Afterwards, strutting about like a peacock, he admits that two other women, besides his wife, love him: one, Angelica Balabanoff, "ugly, good-natured, and true;" the other, Margherita Sarfatti, "lovely, stingy, and self-assured." Then, to be even more forceful, he adds: "I must become a unique man ... I think I'll become a great politician ... but different from the others ... I want to become great fighting the wars of the people."

At this point in his life, he is violently pacifist, like Leda, who could never imagine that the devilish forecaster would change tunes. She saw her guest, perhaps, with the same disenchanted stupor that her guest viewed—and was viewing—his hostess. Outward appearances notwithstanding, they had very little in common, and when Benito shifts from pacifism to interventionism the following year, she bids him goodbye.

After La Rafanelli—or perhaps at the same time as that with Sarfatti (the dates don't always correspond exactly)—Mussolini begins a turbulent relationship with Ida Dalser, from Trento, a woman of a middle class Austro-Hungarian family. The two meet in Trento, and in the fall of 1913, they see each other again in Milan. Older than he by three years, beautiful, imperious, and very well-dressed, she owned a beauty-salon in Lombardy's largest city.

She charms Benito immediately, just as he quickly captivates her. They begin to see a great deal of each other until, in April 1915, the "Austrian," as Rachele insultingly refers to her, becomes pregnant. On 11 November of the same year, she bears a son, Benito Albino, that her lover acknowledges.

Problems begin when Ida claims to be his wife (according to some, she really was, but there are no proofs of this). Since Benito seemed to be hesitant, raising all sorts of excuses, she begins to hound him.

One of their most violent encounters takes place in the hospital in Treviglio, near Bergamo, where Mussolini the soldier has been taken because of a severe form of jaundice.

She accuses him of not only having deserted her, but that he has ruined her financially (she'd made him a loan for *Il Popolo d'Italia*). Being caught without money, he doesn't know what to say. To save the day, along comes Rachele who claims quickly to be his spouse (married in a civil ceremony, naturally).

All this embitters La Dalser. As soon as she hears that Mussolini has been transferred to a Milan hospital because of a forehead wound caused by a mortar blast, she reappears noisily. This time Rachele grabs her by the throat and doesn't strangle her only because of the intervention of the doctors and the nurses.

This is followed by a legal suit by the "Austrian," to whom Mussolini will contribute a two hundred lire monthly allowance for their son, increased in 1926 to an annuity of one hundred thousand lire.

But the story doesn't end there. Benito refuses to see Ida again, though she continues to keep after him until, becoming Head of Government, he has her restrained in various asylums, the last one in Venice. In December 1937, she will die there, preceding her son by five years.

Less tragic is the long affair that Mussolini carries on with the refined intellectual, Margherita Sarfatti. They meet in 1913, he the editor of *Avanti!*, she an art critic for the same paper. They take an immediate liking to each other, but the spark will only ignite in 1918.

Both had a great love of culture, and the printed word, besides, naturally, political ideas. All that divided them was their upbringing: she was sophisticated and a bit of a snob; he was plebeian and somewhat rough.

Whether the affair was brought to life more due to the congeniality of spirit, or to the enticements of the flesh, is difficult to say. Certainly no other woman, besides Claretta, succeeds in keeping him very interested for so long. Of course, he was not faithful to her, but to whom was he ever so?

As with all his love affairs, this one was not free of protests and reprisals by Rachele since certain pills—and this one was definitely a large one—she could never swallow. She even reaches the point of having La Sarfatti dismissed from her husband's newspaper, forcing him to burn the letters that the woman had written to him. "But when," as we read in Rachele's already cited memoirs, "perhaps in 1931, opening the pages of *Il Popolo d'Italia*, I found again Margherita Sarfatti's signature at the end of an article on an entire page, the blood rushed to my head. 'My, look who's returned!' I said to myself."

She hurries to the post office (at that time it was in Merano), and sends a furious telegram to Benito who telephones her angrily that same night from Rome saying, "I don't know what article you're talking about. All that I know is that I've let her go, and I don't want to hear further talk about her." "Okay," replies Rachele, "I believe you, but listen carefully once and for all, and also tell Arnaldo. If I see Sarfatti's name in the paper again, I will go to Milan and I will blow up *Il Popolo d'Italia*. You know that I am capable of doing this. Even more, since I'd make a lot of people very happy because very few of them like *Il Popolo d'Italia* anymore. It's become an indigestible lead weight."

The two will continue to see each other until one day—in 1936—although she very rarely went to Palazzo Venezia, Margherita comes to Navarra requesting to see the Duce. The usher leads her to a small salon and, after a wait of two hours, he returns to tell her that Mussolini cannot receive her. She rises and leaves. Not only from her former lover's palace, but also from his life.

She will die suddenly on 30 October 1961, at seventy-eight years of age, in her Villa Cavallasca near Como.

The Founder of the Empire had an infinite number of women – about four hundred according to unverifiable estimates – but only those fleetingly remembered here count for much, though none like Claretta. She was the one he loved the most, and who most loved him.

Eight

The Fun and Games Begin

To Mussolini's question, "Signora, will you permit me to be Clara's lover?" the flattered and confused Sig.ra Giuseppina answers, "My daughter is no longer a minor, and she is separated from her husband. I cannot stop her from loving you. The idea of knowing that she is by the side of a man like you would comfort me greatly."

That was exactly what "He" was hoping to hear as he was suffering the pangs that result from Cupid's arrows. The platonic idyll, if, in fact, it was still platonic at that time, was transforming itself into a passionate affair.

How the next meeting with Claretta unfolds we do not know since direct evidence is lacking (perhaps only her diary could fill us in). Therefore, we must be happy with secondary sources: from Pasquale Donadio, a friend of the young Petacci girl, and from Paolo Monelli, who, in due course, gathers the intimate details from one of Claretta's friends.

According to Donadio, she "is summoned to Palazzo Venezia by telephone, by Mussolini's personal secretary. She goes there alone, in the afternoon, driving her own car, and she is received in the Sala del Mappamondo. After a few greetings, Mussolini who was in any case in his fifty-fourth year, broaches the subject without beating around the bush. He tells her, amongst other things, since she was now separated from Federici she was the mistress of her own fate. Clara nods in agreement; he becomes tender, pressing, and grips her tightly. She gives way joyously to the game of love because he was really the man she'd dreamt of, adored, and wanted. This way, and in no other way, Clara becomes Il Duce's mistress."

For Monelli, or more exactly his female informant, the beginning went differently. The Founder of the Empire "receives the girl with a furious scowl and upbraids her bitterly about an affair that she'd supposedly had during the summer with a man from Genoa, according to some information he'd received. 'While I respected you, while I esteemed you first because of the girl you were, and then because of you as a bride, you were betraying your husband with the first man you found, flitting about here and there,' amongst other strong language. Claretta begins to cry, and she maintains and swears that all this is a slander. Finally, Mussolini calms down, becomes tender, pressing and devil-may-care. Claretta doesn't know how to defend herself, or she doesn't want to …

"Perhaps she was overcome by her own infatuation without being floored and shocked by the crudeness of the man. She wasn't like other women invited by Mussolini, or having sought to meet him due to curiosity, coquetry, or because of greed, find themselves face to face with a sudden unprecedented attack in the game of love, rather than be prepared by the slow, patient minuet of seduction. He'd been her idol since her tenth year; she'd had lots of dreams and fantasies about him; and there had been those meetings, hand in hand, eyes glued to each other, with the sky turning to dusk, like a long engagement. This was something different even for Mussolini. Perhaps due to her young years, her lively personality of that period, her ready laugh, her ever-present wit, and her ability to give way easily, with a willing and soft gratitude; perhaps because he was completing his fifty-fourth year, and he was feeling the coldness of being alone, of a life without friends, without confidantes. The fact is that he latches on to the young woman with a degree of impatience, a tenderness, a jealous and violent fire that was new for him."

Which version is to be believed?

We incline towards Donadio's. Having left her husband, Claretta could have all the friends she wanted and get together with them, but—and this is certain—she becomes nobody else's lover; her heart had only room for her Duce. From others she could only accept a kindness, an invitation, or a bunch of flowers. Of course, being separated from Federici, she didn't have to account to anybody for her love choices, but it is also true that, after having met Mussolini, she no longer felt free, neither did she want to feel so.

Although she married Riccardo, and she'd interrupted her visits to Palazzo Venezia, rather than causing her to forget the dictator, she'd actually become more dependent on him.

As for Mussolini, he could never ignore her relations with others, including a certain Luciano Antonetti who, according to Ferruccio Lanfranchi, having enjoyed the favours of La Petacci, was "denounced as an anti-Fascist, arrested, and subjected to a far from gentle treatment" (after which, "stricken with consumption," had ended up in Santo Spirito Hospital where a seizure carried him off. On learning this news when the funeral was over, an overcome Claretta is supposed to have let drop from her lips the following terrible words: "They've killed him and they didn't even allow me to see him for a last time"). A slander, without doubt, since if La Petacci really knew Antonetti, she did not have a love intrigue with him. Her heart beat only for Il Duce, even if they saw each other so little, and always for such short periods.

Actually, they never spent more than a half hour at a time together. But how intense those moments were, how many things they said to each other, and with such ardour! "Blessed be the day, the month, the hour, the year when my eyes first fixed upon you..." he'd reiterate to her, seated beside each other on the step beneath the window, or standing behind the Balcony windows, at early dusk, with the flocks of swallows and pigeons fluttering about.

Absolutely radiant, she'd reconfirm her absolute, total devotion to him. Her mind would return to the past, to the meeting at Ostia, fantasizing about the future, and she'd dream, dream, and dream some more. This was ecstasy for both, that state of grace that though inexpressible, seals love in a cocoon for two.

To have her closer to him, Mussolini puts at her disposal her own apartment in a wing of Palazzo Venezia that overlooked Via del Plebiscito.

True love requires intimacy and a place where its own rites can be celebrated, used up and renewed, far from prying, profane eyes and official hype. The Sala del Mappamondo had been, and was, for everyone. The Cybo apartment would be for her alone.

The rooms were called that after their namesake, the cardinal who had continued the work left incomplete by Pietro Barbo, its builder, elected later to the Holy See as Paolo II. Included were an antechamber, a study with an oval table, a desk, a sofa, and the so-called Room of the Zodiac with a vaulted ceiling painted the color of the sky, decorated with golden symbols of the twelve constellations: a large room, but dark, with only one window looking out onto the courtyard, the walls covered in light green silk and with a great mixture of furniture styles, some from the Venetian era, some modern, inclining towards confusion and without taste. From October 1936 until 25 July 1943, Claretta came here every afternoon, except, naturally, when her Lord was traveling, on holidays, or sick. In the morning, she actually stayed home.

As we've seen, she would never wake up before ten, she'd breakfast in bed, telephone her friends, the dressmaker to re-confirm a fitting, the hair-dresser for an appointment, and to her brother Marcello to whom she was very close. Then she'd get up, put on her face, get dressed, and at 1:30 go to lunch with her family. She'd eat little and spoke hardly at all, being preoccupied with her own thoughts, always waiting for "Him" to call. She'd run to her room as soon as she heard the ring of the telephone with the very long wire.

Then she'd drink some coffee, smoke a cigarette, say goodbye to her parents and, in the limo driven by Saverio Coppola, leave for the centre of town (in 1939, when she moves from Via Spallanzani to Via della Camilluccia, because of security, Coppola's place is taken by Silvio Gasperini, an officer of the road police).

At mid point, the car would stop at a florist shop where Claretta would buy a bunch of violets and a rose, to which she'd add a small envelope addressed to Ben as she'd renamed Mussolini, emulating d'Annunzio (on 18 December 1934, the Omniscient Sage had written to Il Duce: "My dearest Ben, I've already said to you at Schifamondo that amongst the many arts of divination that I practice is also that of prediction based on the interpretation of names, and that 'Ben' is a god of the sea, a type of northern Neptune, and that in 'ito,' I read the imperative verb from our Latin '*itur*,' 'you go, you go, you go' ").

In about ten minutes—there was little traffic at that hour—the car would arrive near Piazza Venezia, where a red motorcycle with sidecar, made by Guzzi and driven by an agent of the protective service, was waiting.

La Petacci would alight from the car and, protecting her long curly hair, climb into the sidecar which would then proceed to the nearby Via degli Astalli, to the back, the secondary entrance of Palazzo Venezia. Crossing the large entranceway after getting out of the sidecar, Claretta would make her way towards the elevator and ride up to the second floor where Navarra would be waiting for her.

"What's his mood like today?" she'd ask Navarra with a smile while the latter would lead her to the Zodiac Room. Here she'd place the violets in a small vase, handing the rose and the note to the usher instead. Navarra would return at five with a tea tray.

Left alone, she'd light up a cigarette, not before having opened a window, however (Mussolini could not stand smoke, and he would certainly not have made an exception for her, as he did for nobody else). Then, she'd put a record of Chopin's *Nocturnes* on the turntable, alternating these with currently popular songs. She would happily have listened also to Rabagliati, but the dictator hated that singer, guilty of having spent four years in the abhorrent United States.

To better enjoy the music, she'd recline in an armchair, or she'd stretch out on a daybed, holding in her hands a collection of verses by her favourite poets.

Navarra would reappear at five on the dot. "Did he see any woman yesterday?" she'd ask him, ill-concealing her actual jealousy (she saw cheaters and rivals everywhere). "Nobody, I assure you," would answer the diplomatic usher, sometimes lying. But she would persist cheekily. "But if he himself admitted to me last night that he met with Signora So-and-So." Then, after a brief pause, accusingly, "I can never find out anything from you ... Is it possible that you are all such cowards?"

Navarra would try to re-assure her. "Don't pay attention to everything he tells you ... He does that to tease you." At this, she'd shrug her shoulders, emphasizing with that gesture of resignation her actual disbelief.

She knew that Ben was not sexually faithful to her, and she'd complain about this in vain since the Neptune from Romagna considered his adultery as a primitive, harmless sensual escape. In fact had he not admitted to Luciana Frassati one time: "My flesh does not permit me to be a saint"? And how many times, in the illusory hope of being forgiven, would he urge Claretta "not to be jealous of this part of my animal self. It is as if I free myself from a coarse rind to be purer and more worthy of you."

She did not seek such moral nobility from him; neither did she demand his purity. Since she'd never betrayed him, since she'd never allowed the thought of another man to graze her spirit, why shouldn't he be only, and exclusively, hers? Why was he deluding her, violating that marvelous union that Destiny had reserved for them that rainy Sunday in April?

Navarra would seek to comfort her, to restore her lost, happy mood, but he'd succeed only with difficulty. The green-eyed monster was the most painful and hurtful one for Claretta to deal with as she was wounded and offended by the least suspicion.

To relax, she'd spend long periods alone, listening again to favourite recordings, summon Navarra once again to find out how much longer she'd have to wait, when the audiences would end, how the ones that were completed had progressed.

The time never seemed to go by, making her impatient, vexing her, and humiliating her. Why did her Lord delay so? Was he really in conference with Ambassador Tom, with Minister Dick, or

Industrialist Harry, with the Party secretary from Lucca or the Mayor of Avellino? Or rather was he losing himself in the arms of some dissatisfied, ambitious, parvenu strumpet? The attendant would try once again to reassure her: that day was a particularly busy one for the Duce, with work lasting until late night, but no woman had been to see him, unless for official reasons.

With the much anticipated meeting hour at hand, Claretta would go into the little bathroom—washbasin, bidet, toilet, hand towel, and soap—to freshen her make-up, spoiled by her tears. She'd remove her dress, and pull out from the mirrored wardrobe situated in the small dressing room between the Zodiac Room and the bathroom, a light blue swan decorated robe that she'd slowly pull on.

"He" had given this robe to her, and the garment brought back to mind one of their recent late-night conversations.

"The dressing gowns have been delivered to you?"

"Yes, Ben, darling. You are really such a sweetheart, and, above all, you have an absolutely exquisite and delicate taste."

"So they please you? I feared I'd choose wrongly ..."

"You're never wrong, though I must admit to you that I was not expecting so much since we women are very difficult where clothes are concerned."

"What you tell me flatters me as even I wasn't aware of this quality and I feared that..."

"Instead you have guessed my taste and my desire precisely. Dressing gowns have always been my mania ... though don't you think that there are just too many of them?"

"What can I say... They were so lovely that..."

"Then you bought all of them?"

"That's right."

"Bad Benny! I'll wear a different one every time we see each other."

"I'd be happy."

"I'll give you a kiss for every dressing gown."

"The compensation may far outweigh the value of the gift, so let's not exaggerate now."

"Then I'll give you a little discount, just to be even."

"Agreed. Goodbye, love."

"Thanks... I'm happy."

The ardour was at its highest point, even if her jealousy seemed, at times, to want to stifle the momentum.

Moved by the memories, Claretta would return to lie down on

the couch, her thoughts beyond the room, in her heart the verses of Elizabeth Barrett Browning, the English poet, that she'd discovered during those years, and whom she felt to be so close to her:

I love thee to the depth and breadth and height
My soul can reach, when feeling out of sight
For the ends of Being and ideal Grace ...
I love thee with the passion put to use
In my old griefs, and with my childhood's faith ...
_____ I love thee with the breath,
Smiles, tears, of all my life! _____ and, if God choose,
I shall but love thee better after death.[18]

The nearby clock tower of San Marco Basilica was sounding eight o'clock, but Ben hadn't shown up yet.

Finally, here he'd come, in uniform, gloomy or festive, depending on how the day had developed. She'd run up to him happily, throw her arms around his neck, kissing him with all the fire of a schoolgirl and the devotion of a long-time lover. He would pull her tightly against him, placing his head affectionately on her shoulder, and he'd thank her for the rose: "I've placed it at its usual spot, by my mother's picture."

They'd sit on the daybed, hand in hand, and she'd ask him apprehensively: "Whom did you see, what decisions did you make, did you think of me, do you love me?"

If they did not give way to their physical passion, they'd talk, or joke. He'd tell her many small secrets; she'd reveal what she'd done that morning and how she'd spent the afternoon. Sometimes they'd recite a poem together or listen to a song by Verdi, Mascagni, or Puccini; sometimes, they'd play the violin, he on his precious Stradivarius, she on the more modest instrument she'd received from her parents.

Then she'd slip away to the dressing room, get into her street clothes and, preceded by Navarra, they'd make their way together to the elevator. At the ground floor, he'd wish her a courteous and formal "Goodbye, signora," she replying with a meek, "Good night, Excellency." He would then head for the Piazzetta San Marco side exit, while she'd go out into the courtyard where the security service man, standing beside his red sidecar, waited for her to take her back to the automobile.

She'd re-enter home at about ten, when her family was already at table. Having greeted her parents and her sister, she'd go into her room where she'd write her daily letter to her lover on pink handmade paper with the motto *Nec tecum nec sine te vivere possum* (I can live neither with you nor without you) and a white dove next to a black eagle.

She kept a copy of each letter in a small wooden strong box, whose keys she always carried with her or, after the move to Via della Camilluccia, in a small safety deposit box placed in a dugout in her bedroom wall. First, however, she'd read the letter to her mother who would go up to her daughter's room after supper to have news about the meeting, to console her if she were sad, give her advice, or just to wish her a good night. As she'll write in the future, "My daughter had no secrets from me. I was mother, friend, and sister, and our hearts were as one. I could read her soul as if it were an open book, and I knew and understood all her feelings."

As soon as Sig.ra Giuseppina would leave the room, her daughter would pull out from her desk, or the safe, a diary that she kept continuously from 1933 to 1943, entering in detail all that had occurred in the afternoon visit to Palazzo Venezia.

After putting down her pen, she'd don her usual blue silk pyjamas, remove her make-up, imprison her hair in a nest of curlers and she'd get into bed to await Ben's call which usually came between eleven and midnight, only occasionally later.

A conversation of a few minutes, sometimes full of protests and declarations of love, sometimes full of nasty reproaches due to his not-always-justifiable oversights.

"What are you up to?"

"I was reading. Why this long silence?"

"I am extremely busy these days."

"My poor Ben, you are absolutely right."

"There's a continuous coming and going..."

"I can well imagine it..."

"It is necessary to keep my eyes open and note everything, especially since some people use whatever means, without noticing where the blows land. The French are especially perverse, but they'll be the first to pay."

"What's happened that's so serious?"

"Earth-shaking, nothing, but disagreeable, yes. Just consider that *Europe Nouvelle*, other than attacking Fascist policy in international affairs, and me personally who is responsible for it (which is perfectly normal), descends into vulgarity and publicizes facts and incidents about my strictly private life."

"And?... So?...

"Yes, but, the important thing is not what you think, but the damage that can be done to me."

"Try to be patient about all this."

"But even patience has its limits." [19]

Claretta never went out at night, or if she did, always accompanied by her mother or her sister, to attend a public function, or theatrical performances, where Mussolini would also be present, and not being able to show her off publicly, wanted her nearby. Seeing each other in the crowd, they'd greet each other with conventional and imperceptible nods or furtive smiles. Only once, at the Baths of Caracalla—*Carmen* was being performed—passing in front of his mistress seated in the first row—he stared at her, receiving in exchange an embarrassing bow.

But the pleasure of meeting, even in such a fleeting manner, was quickly ruined by Claretta's jealousy: she saw a potential rival in every other woman. One night at Hadrian's Theatre, becoming suspicious at the way a particular woman was looking at her Ben's theatre box, she follows the latter to the foyer during intermission where the Duce, surrounded by his bodyguards, was speaking with two strangers. Coming closer to her lover, she gives him a defiant look. At this, with an unassuming air, he asks her, "Lovely concert, isn't it?" Claretta replies sarcastically, "Also lovely the woman who's been staring at you." He then turns around, sees the woman, and angrily returns to his box.

Other spots where they met were on the Via Appia where, with Miriam, the couple went horseback riding, and at the Royal estates at Castelporziano, King Vittorio Emanuele having put two cottages at the disposition of the dictator: one, with a terrace, for him, the other for his companion.

Ben would go there at one in the afternoon during the summer, when he was not at Riccione, of course. Later, Claretta and her sister would join him with lunch (salad, vegetable broth, various puddings), the work of Pia the cook, and of Sig.ra Giuseppina. "They were short, but peaceful periods," recalls Miriam. "I swam while they went to pick seashells, which Claretta then saved. Sometimes she'd help him to pore through the newspapers; sometimes the three of us would amuse ourselves playing with a large ball on the beach. His behaviour was always very correct: it took him a long while before he began to use the informal "tu" with Claretta when I was with them, and he never came to the point where he'd forget himself and display even a hint of their relationship. He'd talk to her with an infinite sweetness, and often he seemed to be eating her up with his eyes. But the protective agents who were nearby never saw anything that would have brought on a scandal, or gossip."

The mistress was often present at the hunting events held under the auspices of the King, which the Head of Government joined only with reluctance, so as not to offend his royal host. He was an expert shot but he hated venison, and to shoot a hare, a pheasant, or a quail caused him to suffer greatly.

During one of these hunts, he pointed his rifle at Claretta as a joke, the latter pushing aside the barrel of the weapon just in time to avoid the shot that went off. "Mussolini was extremely upset," continues Miriam. "He wanted to withdraw from the hunt right then and there, but my sister had to talk to him extensively to convince him to continue. For many days afterwards he'd touch Claretta's shoulder every time he'd see her as if to convince himself that she was still alive. And for many days he'd repeat to her on the telephone, 'I could have killed you, little one, I could have killed you.'

"Claretta always responded with a joke: 'I have a tough hide,' or 'Obviously fate hadn't ordained me to leave that way.' One day, always with a smile, she said to him. 'After all, you know that I'd be ready to die for you.'"

Where they met most often, however, was at Terminillo, the winter resort of the Romans, for which Mussolini was for years the diligent and unwitting advertiser. From the beginning of December to March, his responsibilities of state permitting, and until snow remained on the ground, he'd go there every Sunday and holiday (even Saturdays if he could manage it).

Actually, he was not a great skier, but he remained standing, performing the left ski turn well, but the right one badly. He'd stay on the trails six to seven hours, from eight in the morning to three in the afternoon, wearing a heavy white sweater that he'd remove in the warm sunshine; blue pants and a Norwegian-style peaked cap. He had a trail all to himself from which even the special agents, hidden behind trees, stayed away. For a while he used the Albergo Savoia, later he switched to the Roma, the property of Signor Giocondo and of his wife Florinda, who'd built the establishment with his help. He'd occupy a small apartment (bedroom, small salon, bathroom), while Claretta used a large double room that she'd share with her sister, her usual companion.

"The excursions to Terminillo," writes Miriam, "were part of the 'appointments in public places' to which, as usual, I also had to be present. Above all, they were a very tiring thing for me. I'd begin to grumble from the morning, bothered by having to rise close to the crack of dawn that, with his mania for getting up extremely early, Mussolini required even of me who would have preferred to remain in bed until eleven. Then, arriving on the ski hills, he'd initiate the "sprint stage." Mussolini had an incredible, almost inhuman, amount of energy. He'd ski without stopping, and, since a ski lift didn't exist, this meant a continuous climb up steep hills, with laboured breathing and skis that sank into the snow. We'd have to remain behind him, and woe to us if we stopped for an instant. He'd turn around to peer at us, with an amazed look on his face. 'Now, ladies, don't tell me that you're tired. Come on, come along, hurry up.'

"Fortunately, we were both fairly good skiers. Nevertheless, it often happened that we'd check our watches, awaiting anxiously the arrival of Signor Giocondo bringing our lunches. But even when he'd come, the time for rest was short. Mussolini would have the small baskets opened, would glance indifferently at the good food inside, and he would choose a small portion that he'd eat unwillingly and with great speed. Generally, he'd be happy with a fruit and some broth from the thermos. Then, he'd return to ski...

"One day, since I had gulped down the food just too quickly and it weighed heavily in my stomach, I felt ill, and for the first time in my life, I fainted. Mussolini was a bit shaken by this, but when he realized that there was nothing seriously wrong, he began to tease me. 'What shame to faint like that, and a young Italian girl too!' Another time, he was involved in the 'torture' of Marcello who'd come home on leave and was invited to join us at Terminillo. My brother was 1.84 metres tall,* had an athletic build, and an uncommon physical strength. Nevertheless, after three hours of that 'hard, miserable existence,' he was exhausted. 'What's this, don't people eat around here?' he'd ask me quietly every so often; then he'd complain to himself: 'This is enough! I'm not going through this again!'

"Mussolini would realize that Marcello was somewhat disgusted. 'I see that you are not taught to ski in the Navy,' he said. 'Exercise, improve yourself. With a body like yours that shouldn't be difficult.' Marcello was on the point of answering him that in the Navy he was taught to eat at regular hours but naturally, he held his tongue. Then, realizing that we just didn't have the strength to continue, Claretta would suggest a pause for a snack. Suddenly Mussolini would announce that he had to return to

---

* About 6 feet.

Rome. 'If you wish, signora, you can join me later,' he'd say, and off he'd go. We'd drag ourselves to the restaurant where we'd down an incredible amount of polenta with sausage."

The Duce had to be the best even on the ski hills. If he took a tumble—and he had some—it was never his fault, but due to the too icy snow, of the too mealy surfaces, because of the skis, the poles, or the boots. There was hell to pay if Miriam, for example, passed him. He had always to be the first to arrive at a certain point. For the same reason, he had to win at card games with the young sisters and the faithful hotelkeeper during afternoons when the weather was stormy.

Sometimes when he happened to come to Terminillo and he had to return to Rome the next day, those nights were unforgettable ones for the young mistress. After supper, Signor Giocondo would load up an old Victrola and they'd dance for at least an hour to waltzes above all, and polkas that Ben and Claretta loved so much. When she was prisoner in Novara in August 1943, she would remember those far away magic moments this way: "Do you remember Ben, that night, at sunset when the snow was crunching and flying, all light and fluffy, like tiny, bright crystals? And the fire in the fireplace that gave off its warm, healing heat? And then ... Remember? When I was being pulled along because my little weak heart couldn't take the quick steep climb and you would give me sugar bathed with cognac ... and you'd apportion it like a happy child... and the war was still far away? And the ride back to town by car together?... Remember?"

No less joyous, though more ephemeral, the meetings at the seashore on the Adriatic, or near Riccione in summer where he and his family would vacation in a small villa, or on the beaches of Rimini where Claretta would holiday with her family.

Not being able to show himself publicly at the shore amidst all the people (Il Duce's appearance in bathing trunks unleashed uncontrollable hysteria amongst the bathers: there were even some who'd jump into the water fully clothed), Ben and his girlfriend would arrange to meet a few hundred metres from the water's edge. He'd go there by motor launch with the protective operatives who would discretely make themselves scarce beyond the waves; she in a rowboat, alone or with Miriam. These were innocent and hurried meetings, and to see each other for longer, more intimate periods, they had to wait for night fall when they would head off into the countryside by car, or to a nearby pine grove, like a young, newly engaged couple.

However, sometimes, at dawn, they would be on the beach, by the fishing boats. "I love her, I love this child, I love her, yes, I am not ashamed to shout this because I adore her," he'd declaim to the waves … "I adore you, my little Clara. You are the loveliest part of my life, you are my soul, my spring, my youth, and I need you, I need your fresh, good, stormy, absolute, bold love, just as my love is violent, demanding and jealous, because I am envious of you. I tell you this by the sea that I worship, after not seeing you for so many days, that you may always remember these words, said to you at the breaking of the day, in the unforgettable purity of the hour, just being caressed by the rising sun. Remember Clara, what a man tells you in the sunset of his life, in the downward spiral of age, these are the most profound, the most intense of feelings: I love you, and whatever happens, I love you, I've loved you and I shall love you always. You are the only woman that in my tumultuous, difficult and tormented life I have truly and deeply loved. Yes, I have loved and love only you, darling, my little darling one, given to me by destiny and to whom I cause involuntarily so much misery."

The very same words uttered when they visit the Gradara Castle, and the famous room of Paolo and Francesca, where they leaf through the "book of illicit love," before climbing up into the tower.[20] To those words, with equally impassioned emphasis, Claretta will respond, more radiant than ever while she gazes at her Ben "straight, hands on hips, head held high," seeing in him "the long-time owner of the manor, who is observing his lands with the look of a ruler."

But even when they were away from each other, at least during those happy years, they felt themselves amazingly and marvelously close. In 1937, when he travels to Sicily and she could not be with him, she goes to Naples, spending two weeks in a hotel, staying in a room that she never leaves, always in anticipation of his call.

He telephones her up to four times a day, as in September of the same year when he is in Berlin. After his resounding speech, punctuated by waves of applause and torrents of rain at Maifeld, before two million Germans, he will ask her: "Were you able to hear me well?"

"I heard you very well. You were terrific. You speak German perfectly, with a clear pronunciation, even in the subtle expressions. I am suffering a great deal. I think of you being close to another woman. Who knows how many have adored you today. Tell me who is in your room with you now?"

"I beg you to leave me at peace," he replies, suddenly changing tone. "Don't you realize that at this very moment a thousand persons could be listening to us? I called you so that you could let me have your reaction to my speech."

But the stubborn Claretta persists. "I'm crazy for you. I'm jealous. Tell me, who was with you today?"

"I told you to let me be. Good night." And he hangs up.

She'd break down in tears now, but the next morning, being penitent, she'd write him a long, contrite letter full of excuses.

Mad with jealousy, she'd decide to be not only her own inspiration, but also her own salvation, as she'd note in her diary: "I feel as if sent by heaven to help him and to defend him from the riffraff he has around him ... I am necessary for him because he is alone, and all human beings need someone to be near them, someone with whom they can talk, feel happiness, or suffer."

Perhaps she was really necessary to him, but she was wrong to reproach him for infidelities, since these, in essence, did not exist. She didn't understand, or didn't want to understand, that sensuality is not to be confused with real feeling, since he could enjoy the favours of one of his new visitors every day, but she would remain his only true love—as asserts Navarra.

If she were completely his—she'd continue to ask herself tormentingly—why shouldn't he also be completely hers? If she only lived for him, why shouldn't he also live only for her? Becoming completely dejected, she'd now send him a message and a rose. "I hope this flower will fade on your desk in the same way that my love withers little by little. With each blow the petals fall off, without air and without sunshine ... If the great shadow of sorrow that perhaps you cannot understand because you have never loved so deeply, and have not suffered so much, had not dimmed the light of my love nor upset the impetus, the still living and renewing rapture of my love, never would a tear or bitterness have broken our joyous love. If you could be as I've dreamt of you since childhood, and as I've loved and believed you, if you'd have succeeded in being all mine only, and not contaminated the perfect gladiator's body whose every part I love, every corner of it more precious; if your self-denial were absolute and whole like my love for you ... great love of mine, my joy would be sublime and divine, and I would have achieved the most perfect happiness."

He had quite a time getting angry, denying, or promising since he wasn't believed even if she'd listen to his outbursts and self-justifications now and then. But only at that moment, because later, with Miriam or Zita Ritossa, her brother's companion, or with her friend Donadio, she'd carry out frantic "investigations" at night by car to those spots where, according to her own informants, her faithless lover was disporting himself with other women. "If one of 'his' cars was parked by one of the entrances, there were problems," relates Miriam. "The next day, when he'd telephone, I'd have to answer, and the story was always the same, every time, exactly alike. 'Why are you answering the phone?' 'Claretta does not want to take it.' 'Why not?' 'Because last night you went to visit such-and-such a woman.' He'd get annoyed. 'I do not give anyone permission to follow me. I've already told you that I do not tolerate being shadowed.' I'd remain calm. 'But you went.' 'You understand nothing, you little idiot. I had to leave a file there, that's all.' The 'files' really existed. Mussolini gave them out generously to all women who reappeared often from his past. I'd take advantage of the situation to try to get an explanation from him. The formal 'you' would show up punctually, and the bickering would continue. 'You don't understand, signora. I have work commitments, office duties and, if you'll allow, personal obligations also. I cannot change the past.'"

Claretta often persisted, continuing to question him, giving peace neither to him, nor to herself. At this point, losing his patience, he'd burst out; "Signora, stop it! You're exaggerating, signora. I've done nothing, I assure you. You know that I love only you." Finally, thanks to Miriam's intervention, she'd throw her arms around his neck, a smile would return to her lips, and the romance would continue.

Until, that is, a new escapade of his would provoke a new reaction on her part. One day, she confides to La Ritossa, "I am prepared to overlook everything, but not to be deceived. I don't keep track anymore of all the things Ben does to me." Seeing her in such a state, Zita suggests that she break off the relationship. "If he loves you, he will be the one to look for you." To which she replies, "If I leave him, not only will he let me go, but he will no longer allow me to see him."

This was not quite true since even he loved her and he would not have thrown her over. If only she'd been less jealous and possessive, if only she'd have tolerated his straying a bit. But otherwise it couldn't be. He was stronger than she; she was so weak in comparison to him. "If you only knew what evil you are doing to me ... torturing me like this ..." she poured out on the telephone to him one night.

"Do you think you are the only one to torment yourself?"

"But you find the time for distraction ... However, all that I can do is cry! ... What you tell me is an abject slander, while you ..."

"What are you trying to suggest?"

"Nothing ... Except that I am very sure of what I'm saying, despite your promises and your vows. I know with certainty that in the last little while you've been seen often with your lovely Romilda."

"But are you crazy?"

"Lying is useless. I even know that she takes the same road I do. My God! She even sits where I sit ... on the same sofa!"

"But you are delirious!"

"Would that God had wished that! But you no longer love me ... you no longer love me as in the past."

"You must believe me ..."

" I say the same thing to you, Ben of mine, you must believe me."

"I believe you,"

"Then let's not talk about that anymore."

"Okay."

The year 1939 was quickly moving along, and ever darkening clouds were thickening over Italy, Europe, and the world. Few people knew about Ben and Claretta, but the morsel was too delicious, the secret too spicy for these people to keep this to themselves. In short, the Rome that counted, that was closest to the Regime, became the malicious holder of the secret. Only Rachele, enclosed by the walls of Villa Torlonia, continued to remain in the dark.

Nine

Italians! To Arms!

"**F**ighters on land, sea, and air! Black Shirts of the Revolution and of the Legions! Men and women of Italy, of the Empire, and of the Kingdom of Albania! Listen!

"The hour proclaimed by destiny is sounding for our country. The hour of irrevocable decisions is at hand. A declaration of war has already been handed to the ambassadors of Great Britain and France. We are taking the field against the plutocratic and reactionary western democracies, which for long have blocked the march, and often plotted against the very existence of the Italian people ...

"Our conscience is absolutely clear. Like you, the entire world has seen that the Italy of the Littorio has done everything humanly possibly to avoid the torment that convulses Europe, but everything has been in vain ...

"Proletarian, Fascist Italy rises up for the third time, strong, proud and united as never before. There is one order, and only one, categorical and obligatory for every one. It overcomes and seizes our hearts from the Alps to the Indian Ocean: to conquer! And we shall conquer...!

"People of Italy! Rush to arms and show your tenacity, your bravery, and your valor!"

A loud roar of approval rises from the crowd. Improbably full, in the sunshine of a warm spring, soothed by a westerly breeze with the various fora providing a monumental backdrop, Piazza Venezia is an extraordinary theatre pit. In his black uniform, wearing a beret, military decorations, sword belt, praised as a divinity or as an heroic being, arms akimbo, his chest swollen, his lower lip jutting out, eyes wide open and rotating, voice teacher-like and loud, his tone menacing and reassuring, his sentences syncopated and imperious, the Duce has declared war. This is his war.

The date is 10 June 1940, but the powder kegs of the Old Continent had already caught fire, lit by Hitler whose brazen wickedness had invaded and squashed Poland in September 1939.

Mussolini had conceived the resounding proclamation in his frugal and stately private office where, for a period of more than ten years, he'd lived in the shadows and in the company of a myth diligently created, amidst fawning courtiers, including the flattery of his ambitious and disloyal *gerarchi*, and the heated deference of his awe-struck citizens.

This had not been an easy task. Every word had been pondered and weighed again, brooding while pacing the room, pausing thoughtfully in front of the window, absorbed under the chandelier, running his hand along the molding of the armchair, caressing the frame of Mamma Rosa's picture, or the knickknack given to him by Claretta, whom he'd telephoned the night before.

"I was worried," she'd answered to his unmistakable 'pronto.' "I was reading and waiting. You are working too much, Ben. You need to rest."

"Of course," he'd agreed tersely.

"But do you feel sick, my precious?"

"Sick, no. But I don't feel at ease, that's all."

"My love, I'm desolated, but I wouldn't want you to have other worries. Swear to me that you are mine ... only mine. Don't torment me like this, Ben dear."

Bothered by that sugary sweet imploring, he'd remained silent, but she anxiously returns to the fray. "Treasure of mine ... What's the matter?... Why don't you talk to me? Perhaps you don't love me any more? You are no longer mine?"

He'd now lost his patience. "But is it really necessary to talk of such stupidity... when the fate of Italy will be in the balance in a few hours, when only one action, just one word could bring victory, and a glorious future, or also the most horrible end?"

And he hung up, provoking in Claretta a violent fit of sobbing.

Then regretting what he'd done, he calls her again.

"Excuse me, darling ... you'll understand."

"There's nothing to excuse, Ben of mine. I was stupid, I realize it now, to talk to you of our love, of our good times, of my jealousy, without thinking of what is going on in your brain at this terrible time. I've been an absolute simpleton and I hope that you will be able to forgive me because of my very great love for you."

"To our great and infinite love."

"Good night, my treasure."

"Thanks, love."

"Try to rest if you can... I am with you, my precious darling."

In the afternoon, he'd called her again, before presenting himself to the Romans with his declaration of war. Claretta was not in and he had spoken with Miriam to whom he confided. "In an hour I shall declare war. I am forced to declare it." His little "in-law" as he'd renamed the younger Petacci girl, who knew all about the love affair, astounded at the indiscretion, limits herself to stammering, "Will it be a short one?"

"No. It will last long. Not less than five years," had predicted, like an oracle, the Founder of the Empire. Hanging up, he peered from behind the window drapes to eye the piazza crammed with supporters, bristling with flags, banners, pennants, and scattered loudspeakers.

This was a setting worthy of Caesar, and enough to make Napoleon's mouth water. Not a detail was missing. Here was a treat for the eye. Never had the blacksmith's son savored his personal power so much, in this matter only a step behind that of the Führer.

But Hitler was his ally. The victories of the Braunau dauber would be his as well, the glory of one would rub off on the other. The Italians realized this possibility, and because of this they applauded him with such unanimity and with such enthusiastic acceptance.

The Regime had played its hand well; the puppeteer had held the strings tightly. Naturally, not missing were those who had understood what was going on and had not allowed themselves to be dazzled or duped by the tirades of the official propaganda, but most had been bewitched.

In reality, Fascism had already touched its zenith, the lictorial tree had already yielded its best fruit with the lightning war in Ethiopia and the founding of the Empire. The downward spiral, microscopic but inevitable, was already underway in a world always more restless and divided which, if it did not want war, didn't want peace either, and betwixt and between, tottered full of doubt and without foresight.

Actually, from the adroitly manipulated polls, results were issued showing that the majority of Italians were not averse to a war against France and Great Britain. The lower bourgeoisie supported the Duce in the illusion that a settling of accounts would be achieved quickly, and that the country would obtain its fair share of booty.

Although more disenchanted, the upper middle classes were not quite as optimistic, but this did not exclude the feeling that in the wake of the German tanks, the game, in the end, would be won. Labourers and peasants rolled with the punches. Big business was allied more for profit than because of conviction: Fascism was good for business as long as the commissions were guaranteed. Force-fed by the Minculpop,[21] the press backed Mussolini and his "UNALTERABLE CHOICES," publicized in capital letters.

Even the intelligentsia was drawn up about even, with some slight differences and the usual reservations based on the real world. They didn't want to lose the crests, honours, and sinecures so labouriously acquired at the price of so much bowing and scraping. There was always time to be a turncoat.

And how about the *gerarchi*?

This was the painful spot since the opposition to the Regime and its haughty Chief had been covertly traitorous, and disguised. If Starace and Farinacci seemed to have sold their souls to Hitler, Bottai, Balbo and Ciano fed on irresolution. Especially the last named, then Minister of External Affairs, who jots down in his diary for the 10th: "Declaration of war. First I received Poncet,[22] who tried hard not to show his emotion. ... 'Perhaps you already know the reason for my calling you.' He answered: 'Although I may not be very intelligent, this time I've understood.' Then he smiled for just a moment. After having heard the declaration of war, he replied: 'This is a stab in the back to a man who is already down. I thank you, nevertheless, for using a velvet glove.' He continued saying that he had foreseen everything for the last two years, and that he'd given up hope of avoiding war when the Pact of Steel was signed. [23] He was not resigned to considering me an enemy, just as he could not view any Italian as such. Anyway, when it would be necessary to find again a structure for European co-operation in the future, he hoped that an unbridgeable chasm would not have been dug between Italy and France. 'The Germans are hard taskmasters. You'll also become aware of this.' I did not reply. That did not seem to me to be the time to argue. 'Make sure that you don't get killed,' he concluded, indicating my Air Force uniform, and he shook my hand. Sir Percy Lorraine was more terse and impassive. [24] He received the communiqué without batting an eyelash or growing pale. He limited himself to writing down the exact words I used and he asked if my statement was to be considered a warning or a real and actual declaration of war. Being told that the latter was the case, he withdrew with dignity and courtesy. At the door, we exchanged a long and cordial handshake. Mussolini is speaking from Palazzo Venezia's Balcony. The news of war doesn't seem to surprise anyone, and doesn't awaken excessive enthusiasm. I am sad, very sad. The adventure is beginning. May God help Italy."

Count Ciano, the spouse of Edda, Il Duce's favourite daughter, was sad, but not sad enough to condemn honestly his father-in-law's action, and resign. He grumbled to himself, and to a few intimates, no less unhappy than he was by the bellicose evening's announcement, of the hand extended to a Germany that seemed to need no one else just then.

No less vague was the high command, the prominent generals, beginning with Pietro Badoglio, the most important—and the least significant—of all. On 26 May, accompanied by Balbo in a conference with Mussolini, he'd declared that the country was "unprepared militarily." He actually had the courage to state: "We don't even have a sufficient number of shirts for all the soldiers. How is it possible to declare war in such circumstances? This is suicide." But he was lacking the more heroic dimension of handing in his resignation. He'd never been a fierce warrior and he'd never give up his decorations and military stipend. He loved to command too much: almost as much as to disobey and, when needed, to betray. And if, as Teruzzi, he hadn't sown his own military stripes on his own pyjamas, he was fonder of his marshal's baton than of his own honour.[25]

With war decided upon, he won't lose any time blessing the participation, and to be sarcastic about the huge assembly of the 10th of June, which he himself, as chief of the high command, attended. "A wretched spectacle. 'A common herd,' jammed between *gerarchi* and the 'scum' of the party, who had been given orders to applaud every word of the speech. But with the event over, the crowd melts away in silence to attend to personal matters. Because of all the vileness of that all-powerful system of coercion, public opinion feels the grave dangers of that step, and of the hard results that this would bring to the country. Mussolini was ecstatic. He accepted all the very high praise that the most powerful *gerarchi*, in competition with each other, piled upon him. I found myself in the corner of the room, as if hidden. Someone came up to me and said, 'Now it's over. This is not the time for recriminations. May God have mercy on us.' "

Badoglio wasn't the only one to sermonize well and to scratch about badly. But he was certainly the most blameworthy because of his very high rank. If Mussolini committed an extreme foolishness by going to war, in accepting to become his strategist, Badoglio assumed in the worst and most equivocal way the personal duty of an officer.

What about the Royal house? And the Church?

Vittorio Emanuele III was in full agreement. His fate was linked to that of the Duce. The message that he sends to the Armed Forces was not, in fact, less pompous then the dictator's. "Soldiers on land, sea and air. Being the Supreme Head of all the Land, Sea and Air Forces, and in line with my feelings and with the traditions of my Royal house, I am returning to you as I did twenty-five years ago. I am placing in the hands of the Head of the Government, Il Duce of Fascism, First Marshal of the Empire, the command of the troops fighting on all the fronts ..." There is something not quite clear here. "Supreme head of all the forces," how could he entrust the Prime Minister with the command of all the Forces "on all fronts"? But no one was paying any attention to this.

Pope Pius XII was upset, but his repeated efforts to keep Italy outside the conflict had failed, his appeals to Mussolini had fallen on deaf ears. All that he could do was pray. And he prayed.

Besides, the Duce seemed not to hear any of the entreaties. On the eve of the declaration of war, when all did not seem to be lost, President Roosevelt had written to him in a last ditch effort. "You who are called *Condottiero* by the great Italian people, have in your hands the possibility of stopping the spread of this war to a further group of two hundred million souls in the Mediterranean region ... No man, no matter how omniscient, can foresee the outcome of such a conflict either for himself or for his people."

And yet, according to Ciano's diary, that inexhaustible mine of news and gossip, the Founder of the Empire had agonized long before striking the tocsin of war. His love-hate relationship with the Führer, the attraction-repulsion for his former disciple, but now teacher, the fear of ending up in a blind alley, across a diabolical trap, in case of a German victory, and to see his own position diminished, his prestige severely curtailed, tugged at the Duce. He twisted and turned: first he wanted to, and then he'd pull back. Today he was for war; tomorrow he'd change his mind. On the 4th of September 1939, after the predatory German attack on Poland, "... he seems to be tied to the idea of neutrality which allows both economic and military development at the same time ... But it's a momentary idea. The notion of intervention on the side of the Germans attracts him." On the 25th of the same month "... more than ever is he convinced that Hitler will rue the day because of his pulling the Russians back into the European heartland." On the 9th of December, he is once again for the Führer, while on the 26th he hopes that he'll be thrashed. And so on, month after month, buffeted by those who would range him with Hitler, some against, others for neutrality. This last is a word that he does not like because it would make of Italy a Switzerland "multiplied by ten."

Mussolini meets Hitler, the winner of dazzling victories, for the fourth time at the Brenner Pass on 18 March 1940. It's as if he's enslaved: he hangs onto his every word, and he no longer doubts that his personal fate is to be at Hitler's side. He tells Claretta about this, but she doesn't know, or doesn't want to know, how to make him see what is going on. He dreams about an army like the German one, trained and disciplined, but he realizes that this is all an illusion. He frets over this fact, and confides to Eugen Dollmann, head of the SS: "I would like to have here the rigours of snow, from the Alps to Mt. Etna, to be able to transform Italians into a race of warriors."

His feelings towards Hitler were changeable, reversing themselves from a monotonous dance to a lively jig, from ill temper to warmth. From proclaiming himself his best friend, to holding him peevishly at arms length, from vowing that he will win, to that he will lose. But, down deep, he feared him: if Italy were to align itself with the French and the English, Germany would overwhelm the country. He was certain of that.

His ideas were confused on the possible length of the conflict. Although he predicted to Miriam that the war would last five years, to Badoglio who was complaining about the unevenness of the Armed Forces, he would reply cynically on May 26: "... in September all will be over... I need a few thousand dead to sit at the peace table to be accepted as a cobelligerent."

So much shilly-shallying is confusing; so much indecision casts doubts about the political fitness of a man who leads a nation of more than forty million people for twenty years, and to whom he has presented an Empire. And yet, at Munich in September of 1938, he'd been an important leader. Thanks to him and to his good offices, the war had, more or less, been postponed.

According to Bottai, "a number of offensive statements in the English, French and American press, and some attitudes of open hostility towards Italians in foreign countries and to the Italian merchant marine, also weighed heavily on Il Duce's decision. Mussolini received daily reports, and, no doubt, this served to reenforce the feeling of finding himself in a snare, between a west that pushed Italy aside, and a Reich that from one hour to the next might no longer need him."

For Federzoni, the Duce who had snubbed the Führer in the past, "was building in himself an inferiority complex. The German victories irritated him. He felt himself dispossessed, put in the shadows, and he was convinced that he and Fascist Italy would share the same fate. Besides, he knew that some people in Berlin were already imputing to him the wish to repeat the 'betrayal' of 1915, and this rumour hurt him." [26]

According to Grandi, he himself shared the opinions of Mussolini, "for whom historical claims had an enormous importance, and he could not but be impressed that, after the fall of France, Italy's frontiers were open to Hitler's troops; and open without the least hope of resistance on our part. This, and not the greed of victory, was the reason that pushed Mussolini to enter the war. He was embracing the victor in the wish not to be smashed."

But he would not have been squashed, nor been attacked if, after Ethiopia, he'd not yielded so much to Hitler, giving way to mad, ambitious follies. The declaration of 10 June is the obvious, disastrous result of a policy based on three clear points: the Rome-Berlin Axis, the Munich Conference, and the Pact of Steel.

When the Duce appeared on the Balcony of Palazzo Venezia, he was supreme, at least at that moment, convinced that the "corrupt " and "cowardly" western democracies would soon be liquidated by the strong and warlike Nazi-Fascist forces; that the "demo-plutomasonic" powers would finally receive their well-deserved just rewards. The dice, however, had been cast. There was no going back now.

In those days, Claretta was closer to him than ever, even knowing that to pay the price for the new events was likely to be their idyllic love. He would always have less time for her; her waits in the Zodiac Room would get ever lengthier, and the already short meetings would be shorter still. No more weekends at Terminillo, goodbye to picnics by the sea, to motor launch junkets, and to horseback rides on Via Appia. And who knows how many other things she'd have to give up.

But of what importance could any of these things be if he continued to love her, and to be loved by her? This was the only thing that counted for her since only this made her happy.

Ten

A Sad Love in Rome

A ccording to Miriam, the first person to sniff out the love affair between Clara and Ben was a Roman woman who had noticed maliciously the glances that the couple gave each other on a warm day in May, at a horse meet in Piazza di Siena. A short time later, all of Rome's upper crust knew about this romance. "All who had a slight suspicion now were certain of it. Everybody who had been aware of something going on now felt themselves free of the obligation to be silent. Reports made the rounds of Roman salons, and evil tongues jumped into the fray."

The silliest rumours were spread, the most poisonous impertinence, and suppositions of the most unlikely sort. Some stated that Mussolini and his mistress had met at a dance; others, instead, swore that Edda, the Duce's first born, had introduced them; some said Starace was the catalyst; others that it had been no less than Buffarini Guidi, the Undersecretary at the Ministry of Internal Affairs.

But the gossip didn't stop there, coloring itself either pink or yellow [being either romantic or nasty], and challenging the very limits of propriety. There were even those who rushed to categorize, fantasizing the gifts that Il Duce had given Claretta since their meeting: hundreds of dresses, dozens of furs, rare perfumes and priceless jewels. According to these not entirely disinterested blood-hounds, blind with love, the Founder of the Empire hung on to every word of his young lover, granting her every wish and fancy. He'd telephone her continuously, and he even suspended his meetings in order to see her. But these were only inane tales. He might have given her some dressing gowns, but he hadn't swamped her with furs or loaded her down with gems.

Even if the reports of the relationship did not reach Rachele's ears, though she also employed very well informed spies (she was not advised so as not to wound her), the children were not so spared. Vittorio writes, "I'd heard of Claretta almost from the beginning, and my sole worry was for my mother who should not have to add this additional torment to the many serious ones that she already had. Nevertheless, I hoped that this affair would end quickly as had happened previously; but I should have realized that, with the passage of time, the attachment of that woman to my father was really strong and that this was a special case. What vexed me most in all this business was that my father's enemies would have a way of causing him more difficulties by shouting about the scandal. A certain type of politics relies extensively on these means, and I was beginning to realize the importance that the Petacci affair was assuming under the impetus of some groups and of the hypocritical camouflage being used."

These were not unfounded fears since, to Mussolini's ambitious and meddlesome entourage, the proximity of a woman, that particular woman, to the Head of the Government, gave many headaches. Her power over him—as contended some persons— could transform her into a sort of Pompadour who would not have been satisfied merely to advise, but who would have influenced his political choices.

It is true that no one, except for Rachele and La Sarfatti, had successfully conquered Mussolini's heart. But it is also equally true—and it didn't take much to realize this fact—that this time the fire for La Petacci was unprecedented.

This doesn't mean that Claretta had absolutely no power over him. The few times that she tried to express a not strictly personal opinion, he'd quickly shut her up with a "Don't talk nonsense." Of her usually unselfish suggestions, she could, at most, prevail in private and individual cases.

She sought to be his Héloise, not his Egeria; he, perhaps, her Abélard—before the treacherous mutilation, of course—not her Numa Pompilius.[27] All that Claretta was looking for was love, and she was ready to sacrifice everybody and everything for this. The Cianos, the Balbos, and the De Bonos needn't have troubled their heads. As long as they remained loyal to Il Duce, she would have ignored them contemptuously. To accuse her of plots and intrigues is wrong, therefore. She never profited from Ben's position, and if she ever asked for favours, these were not for her but for those who were close to her such as relatives or friends, and always against her will.

Instead of making her proud, the discovery of their affair wounded her deeply, making her even more wary. How many women would have wanted to be in her place, being party to such privileges! What others thought they knew and speculated about offended and humiliated her. What right did they have to make a display of her feelings and those of her man, to feed public prurience on her privacy? "Our love is a sad one," she'll complain to a friend. "We are even denied the pleasure of walking about together on nice moonlit nights, something dear to all lovers. If we go out by car some rare time, we have to stay hidden as if we were fugitives. Many times, after having waited for him all day in the unhappiest loneliness in that gloomy room in Palazzo Venezia, I succeed in seeing him only when he comes to say goodbye just before returning to Villa Torlonia. And often, his goodbye is so fast that if I have something to tell me, I'm forced to write it down for him the next day. Every so often, he visits one of his former girlfriends who holds him bound to her with the pretext more or less true that one of her children is his. My love is a very sad one, full of hurtful silences and of repressed tears. If I were overcome by fatigue, weakened by the impossible struggle, and I would stay away from him, believe me, in his infinite goodness and, let us even say his artlessness, he'd become the object of a thousand extortions and he'd fill up the gossip pages of tabloids the world over. I don't defend him only for me, but for all Italians. No one is grateful to me for my lengthy suffering, however ..."

She had, in the meanwhile, (late summer of 1939) moved from Via Spallanzani with her family, and had settled into a vast, modern villa on Monte Mario baptized La Camillucia, after the street of the same name.

Sig.ra Giuseppina had wanted the new house since she considered the old abode not quite worthy of the status of the Petacci family. Francesco Saverio held a prestigious position and had eminent friends; Marcello had received his medical degree with distinction; Claretta was Mussolini's lover. Three good reasons, especially the last one, to site the household gods in more worthy quarters.

The cost of the Camilluccia surpassed all estimates, forcing the Petaccis to seek a real estate loan of 350 000 lire from the Banca Nazionale del Lavoro, repayable in twenty-five years, with 1 350 000 lire added, 225 000 lire for a half hectare of land, paid in two installments of 135 516, and ninety thousand lire; the remaining sum deposited in trust for construction work handled by a small building enterprise and managed, without charge, by Monaco and Luccichenti, two friends in architecture.

Sig.ra Giuseppina had supervised the work personally, going to the site everyday, giving orders to the master-builder and to the masons, checking the material so that nothing would be wasted.

The construction took many months and when the Petacci family moved in, the house was not yet completed. Thus they were forced to occupy a few rooms just freshly plastered and without furnishings.

The villa had thirty-two rooms, on two levels, a first and an upper floor, the second overhung by a terrace, used to hang out the wash and, if required, as a sunroof.

The first floor was for receptions, containing a vast entrance hall, punctuated by white marble columns, and a salon with a marble floor as well, partially covered by Persian carpets; in the center, a statue of a female nude, also in marble, and at the corners, a harp and a piano. On the right side was a bar with a white silk half-moon shaped sofa in front of it, as well as two tall bar stools and a gaming table.

Still on the ground floor, next to a winding staircase made of reinforced cement covered in marble but without a banister, was a drawing room in Venetian style that led, through a sliding door, to the so-called Room of Mirrors. The walls were lined by mirrors and reflected Clara's large bed. The wooden base of the bed was hidden under gray fabric, and covering it was a magnificent rose-colored silk quilt, the same color as the telephone on the bedside table. Entrance to the bathroom, whose walls were of multicolored mosaic and contained a sunken black tub, was through a small doorway.

This was the little apartment of Mussolini's mistress, desired for her by her mother, but which Claretta rarely used. She preferred the bedroom on the second floor, near that of her parents, of Miriam and of Marcello, the latter having moved to Milan where he'd met Zita Ritossa, the lovely model, with whom he was living.

Always on this floor were found the dining room, Dr. Saverio's library-office, the servants' quarters, the kitchen, and the utility rooms. There were also various cellars where, after the outbreak of war was fashioned a bomb shelter containing sand bags and gas masks (at every alarm, everyone descended the stairs of the villa, preceded by Sig.ra Giuseppina holding in one hand her Rosary, in the other a bottle of cognac). The premises also included a tennis court and a pool, which were Claretta's domain, and a garden and a hen house that her mother looked after.

Access to the villa, located on a panoramic hill that overlooked the City of Rome, was made through a massive, wrought iron gate and along a graveled, ascending small roadway. To the left, next to the gateway, were the custodian's quarters; on the right, a sentry box reserved for surveillance by protective service agents who took turns standing guard at what someone had spite-fully named Claretta's "smooth box of candy."

The villa's construction occurred at the same time as the affair of the former Signora Federici and Mussolini came to public attention. There were some who murmured that within its walls, in the mirrored room, Claretta, Ben and other guests drunk with champagne gushing from the golden taps of the bathtub, surren-dered to Tiberian debauchery. If in the chic salons of the Capital, frequented by the more worldly *gerarchi*, beginning with the most mundane and fatuous Galeazzo Ciano, no one paid any attention to the vile rumours, there were some, however, who thought that Mussolini had wanted, and paid for, La Camilluccia. This was a slander that hurt Claretta no less than the repeated cheating that Ben inflicted on her.

The Camilluccia represented for the Petacci family not only a sign of a very envied social advancement, but also the daily goal of all the seekers of every sort and rank who implored the paramour to help, either being unwilling, or unable, to approach Il Duce directly.

Every day the postman delivered piles of letters addressed to the "Blessed Lady Clara," to "Her Excellency Petacci," to the "Charitable Fairy Queen," to the "Enlightened Grace of God," to the "Maiden with the Great Heart," imploring help, advice, can-cellation of penalties, or revocation of exile.

Helped by her mother and her uncle Stefano, at the time head of the INAM,[28] Claretta sifted carefully through the corre-spondence one at a time, pausing before those that were deemed worthy of reply. The mail included every situation: women betrayed and girls raped; adulterous husbands who wanted to recapture their wives' affection; people anxious to know their per-sonal future (with this in mind, some enclosed birth certificates and photos). But most were on firmer ground, oppressed by real and urgent needs: the evicted seeking new lodgings; those out of work seeking work; the sick begging for medicine; and students requiring books. There were even those who proposed business deals, offered patents, or sought hearings with high officials.

"My sister," writes Miriam, "considered only three types of letters: appeals from the poor; requests from the clergy; and the complaints from persons who claimed that they were the victims of some injustice or of some irregular procedure. These letters were handed on to Mussolini's secretarial office which looked them over quickly—the only privilege allowed her by him. Then, the authorities prepared an inquest, gathering information and, if the petitioner was recognized as being worthy of help, received a subsidy from the relevant assistance fund. Claretta could do nothing else beyond this point: not even a single lira passed through her hands since it was up to the political secretary to carry out the payment. This was also the case for sewing machines, orthopedic equipment and the donations that were arranged directly through factories. She'd insist on getting a receipt from the person concerned, more than anything to be certain of the outcome of the assistance. But she never even saw the money. Only once did she have a sum in hand, and this was when Mussolini gave her nine thousand lire to distribute to the poor of the Tiburtino district. The distribution was done in the presence of, and under the control of, several hundred persons, but this was not repeated because Claretta did not like that sort of "publicly advertised" form of charity.

That La Petacci received money once from her lover, or through an intermediary from him, is mentioned only by Miriam, contradicted on what basis we don't know, by Ciano who asserts in his diary (24 December 1941): "(Buffarini) ... would give, under the guise of charity, a further hundred thousand lire monthly to La Petacci, which a certain Donadio deals with, whose role is not very well defined ... Serena[29] says that a group of Petacci adherents has formed around Il Duce, manipulated in the shadows by Buffarini and helped by De Cesare, who acquires influence every day and works in a sinister way."[30]

Ciano hated Claretta, her family, and her friends, Buffarini in particular. His affirmation, even if in the conditional ("would give"), is best taken with a grain of salt. More reliable, perhaps, is that of Donadio, an intimate of the favourite, who reduces the monthly allowance given personally by the Duce to La Petacci to twenty thousand lire. The passage of so many years, and the lack of evidence make this contention impossible to prove.

Nevertheless, one thing is certain: neither Claretta nor her parents ever profited from the funds put at their disposal by the dictator (if indeed he ever did such a thing). They donated the money, up to the very last coin, to the more than forty thousand needy, as document the receipts from these people, preserved in six large bags, two of which fortunately escaped the raid on the Petacci property.

If Claretta obtained anything from Ben, it was the promotion, and in very rare cases, the torpedoing of this or that *gerarca*, of this or that civil servant, requested not for advantage, but because of affection or aversion, usually shared as well by the Head of Government.

That very bad blood existed between La Petacci and the Duce's personal secretary, for example, was very obvious and so when Sebastiani was replaced by De Cesare, a regular visitor to La Camilluccia, every one saw in that replacement the hand of the mistress. The same thing happened with Galbiati, aspirant to the office of Chief of Staff of the Militia, and with Visconti Prasca, who coveted the higher command of the forces in Albania. With Claretta's assistance—as Ciano noted in his diary entry for 12 November 1941—was the actual naming also of Arturo Riccardi to the position of Chief of Staff of the Navy.

But, La Petacci detested General Roatta and Marshals Cavallero, Badoglio, and De Bono because they had ignored her when coming face-to-face at Palazzo Venezia (in revenge for the affront, she started the rumour that the white-haired Quadrumvir would enjoy making love to his mistress, a well-known aristocrat, on a black velvet coverlet).

Much different were the relations between Claretta and Guido Buffarini Guidi, Undersecretary at Internal Affairs, an ambitious man from Livorno, a busybody, cunning and crooked, who had a finger in several pies. Confidant of La Petacci and toady to Sig.ra Rachele, he flitted about from La Camilluccia to Villa Torlonia where he'd arrive carrying bottles of vintage wines, boxes of early fruit, tins of *marrons glacés*, or chocolate confectionery (when he'll fall into disgrace and everyone gives him up for lost, Claretta will be the one to rescue him at the last moment, thus allowing him to keep his seat in the Grand Council).

La Petacci's pressures on her lover occasionally did not have the right effect. If in a few cases she succeeds in having someone assigned, or removed from, important tasks, at other times she has to bend to a superior will. As when, in September 1941, a relative in the Air Force receives orders to proceed to Africa, and her uncle Stefano pleads with her to intercede with Mussolini to have the order canceled. Giorgio, Stefano's son, recounts, "We were dining at La Camilluccia when my cousin who was moved emotionally by the military assignment, assured us that she would do all that was possible in the matter. She returns to table with the Duce's reply, which was a categorical no. 'Do you want to know what his exact words were?' asks Claretta. 'Here they are: 'Bruno died while doing his duty.[31] He was my son. If necessary, others must also know how to die.' Having uttered that statement,

Claretta doesn't say anything further. All of us finish eating in silence. Carlo Mastrofini, my cousin, leaves a few days later for Libya, and there he is made prisoner by the English."

La Petacci knew her man too well to insist. If, sometime later she'd return to the endeavour and he satisfied her, it was only to be forgiven for his repeated philandering.

The more he'd betray her, the more she'd philosophize. "Many women," she'll confide to a friend, "despair when their man breaks away and abandons them. Very few have the courage to recite the *mea culpa*. Love is the most delicate flower that exists and has need of careful and continuous care. Day by day, every hour, a woman must build around the man of her heart a structure in which he finds himself prisoner, without his realizing it. She should favour his habits, giving him the impression that what he does or says, is right, or if it is the case, contradict him but without ever wanting him to admit that he is wrong; letting him overcome his whims with a short-lived adventure from time to time, but reserving our fire more efficaciously when the danger of a 'relationship' lurks. Because of this we must keep our eyes open and our ears cocked, in silence, but ready for battle, with tears or smiles, according to the situation, ready to take back our man. I want to tell you, in conclusion, that many women wouldn't cry 'afterwards' if they had worked 'before,' laboured so that the moat around their loved one would be secure and insurmountable. Because believe me, even love, as everything else in this world, is work and toil."

Even he was jealous, although she never gave him reason to be so. If at the theatre, or the opera, or during a public event where they had to pretend not to know each other, he saw her talking to a man, or smile at him, using the formal "you" the next day, he'd reproach her dryly. "Signora, where were you last night?" "But you know that even better than I do: at the reception. We saw each other. You told me to be there." "But I didn't tell you to wear that low-cut dress and to linger with strangers. Who was that man who talked to you? What did he want?" At this point, if she were there, Miriam to whom we owe this anecdote, would intervene. "Excuse me, Duce, but other than the fact that Claretta's dress was less low-cut than anyone else's, I want to tell you that the person was so-and-so, an acquaintance of mine, and he'd stopped to talk to me." Then using a different approach, with eyes wide open, inquisitorially, Mussolini would force her to swear to the truth. Challenging his look, she'd obey, at which point he'd burst out laughing, calling her "little idiot."

But, despite passing quarrels and inevitable outbursts, the relationship seemed to become an ever-closer one. Italy's going to war did not substantially alter the habits of the couple. Claretta continued to go to Palazzo Venezia every afternoon, using a taxi now — always the same one — because of fuel rationing.

Naturally, the atmosphere was no longer the euphoric and festive one of times past. If the announcement of the declaration of war had been greeted favourably by a public opinion entrapped by propaganda, this same public opinion quickly took note that the war was lasting not weeks, or months, but years. While it is true that the Germans were reaping many victories, it was also true that the theatre of operations was widening immeasurably and frighteningly. Neither Mussolini, nor the *gerarchi* or the generals could now have any more illusions about the state of the Italian troops.

Mussolini now had less time for his mistress. Their meetings, after the end of hearings, were ever shorter, not uncommonly ending in brief battles, followed by hasty departures. Seeing him tired, unhappy, and worried, she'd hold him to her, she'd tell him the latest joke, the most recent gossip; above all she'd reassert her great love for him. But things were no longer as at the beginning. Something had changed, routine had got the upper hand.

To shake Claretta, even if only for a brief period, was her pregnancy, an event which put her life in serious peril.

All this began on 18 August 1940, at the Grand Hotel of Rimini where, every summer, the Petacci family spent their vacation, thus allowing Claretta also to be close to her Duce. Only her family knew that she was with child, other than Mussolini, of course, who'd warned her not to talk about this to anyone: "This matter must remain secret even from my Chief of Police."

Claretta was stricken by unexpected, atrocious abdominal pains that no sedative succeeded in alleviating. Because of this, it was decided to take her to Rome, not to the clinic, but to La Camilluccia, to that mirrored room set up for special occasions.

Here she was seen by Dr. Noccioli, the noted gynecologist, who diagnosed an extra-uterine pregnancy, with danger of peritonitis. Were more time to be lost, the young woman would not survive. On 27 August, the room was transformed into an operating theatre and Dr. Rubbiani, assisted by his colleague Ciminata and by Dr. Saverio, carry out the difficult surgery.

That the Duce was present, in surgical gown, a sterile mask

covering his face, as someone has written, is to be discounted. Not only because Miriam—the most reliable source—doesn't make mention of this, but because the situation is very unlikely. The physicians who rushed to Claretta's bedside would have been in a considerable quandary in the presence of the dictator, who in any case would have felt absolutely ill at ease.

Ben limits himself to going to her bedside right after the operation that had shaken him so much. Pleased with the outcome, he seats himself on the side of her bed and, taking Claretta's hand while she is still groggy from the anesthesia, feels her pulse, smiling silently to himself, with the look more of a father than of a lover.

The condition of the mistress was improving, her fever went down, and even the pains began to abate. However, after not even a week, on the first of September, there was an inexplicable relapse. The crisis lasts for only three hours—from six to nine at night—but they were three terrible and endless hours. Ben suspends his hearings and rushes to La Camilluccia. "I'll never forget it," recalls Miriam. "He remained seated in a corner, absolutely still, with his eyes wide open, staring into space. He didn't hear what was said to him, and he also didn't notice that my father and Dr. Noccioli were proceeding towards the room of the sick one. He seemed to be a piece of marble. 'You know that I prayed for you that day' he'll confide to Claretta later. 'It was a strange thing. At one point, I was surprised to hear myself saying: Lord, don't have her die on me. That was the second time in my life that I prayed.' "[32]

When the doctors finally issue their prognosis, he embraces Dr. Saverio and pleads, "Swear that I am not going to lose her, that she'll make it, that she'll live. Don't hold back."

Never had Claretta felt him to belong so much to her, and never had she felt so much his. These were marvelous and terrible moments that caused her so much suffering, but which also gave her so many dreams that she would never forget. How often in the few years left them to live will she repeat the words that he had whispered to her while she was grappling with the pain, or from the letters that he'd written to her while she was mending: "My dear little one. I suppose that you will have to climb the 'Holy Stairs' of good health. You've already covered twenty steps. This week that is forecast full of sunshine, you will ascend twenty more. Then you'll get up and the climb will be so much faster. In a few moments I'm going to go into your room, which is the way you left it and it is waiting for you. Everything else also awaits you.

Books, music, violin, dressing gowns. And Ben is waiting for you, so happy with his role as your nurse. Tell me what will speed up your healing. Today I'm coming back to you. Ben hugs you with the tenderness that you know." And again: "My darling little one. What sunshine this morning! And how unhappy to see you still abed, after the last gray night. I'm so happy to have brought you so much liquid. I'll bring you another supply today. I'm sending you "Nestrovit," a mixture of four vitamins. I'm also taking this. It is an excellent tonic. It exists in tablet and liquid form. Take it immediately in the prescribed doses. No solid food, only liquid today: very sweetened water, coffee, chamomile tea. You have been in bed for one month today. Now's the time to heal up. I send you, with my hugs, all my deepest tenderness. Ben."

She was blooming again and the hour of her return to Palazzo Venezia couldn't come fast enough, to resume the old romantic goings-on. But only Ben, with his messages, succeeds in soothing her impatience. "Little darling. One month has passed since the day that you submitted so courageously to the knives of the surgeons. There were highs and lows during these very long days, but by now the fullness of life begins to flow in your flesh and, above all, in your inner being. This splendid season helps you and, perhaps even my love has aided you a little bit. As soon as you receive this note, prepare to get up. Have yourself brought outside to the fresh air because you will have a great restorative boost. Life is really beautiful, even when this strong sun in such a deep blue sky is missing. And it is worthwhile to fill up life with a great love such as mine is for you. From Monday the 30th and continuing, I expect you here. Everything is awaiting you here, including, naturally, Ben."

Not being able to move about just yet, he'd visit her, while Sig.ra Giuseppina, her fragile heart in turmoil, ordered all the servants to remain in their own rooms and not to come out until the mysterious guest had left, although everyone knew who he was. The only exception is made for Pia the cook who is given the task of preparing a small snack consisting of cured prosciutto, stuffed, baked tomatoes, greens and fruit for the guest with no appetite.

Claretta would wait for Ben in the mirrored room, or in the salon where they'd play chess if he weren't in a hurry—but he was always in a rush. (One day, to show her the true Fascist belief, she finds a decapitated white king that he's included.)

Between moves, they'd talk of their love, she'd ask him one hundred, one thousand other times what she'd already asked him, and he'd answer what he'd already told her one hundred, one thousand other times.

To upset these sweet get-togethers was the disturbing news from Greece, which Italy crazily attacked on 28 October.

How many times Ben told her that the campaign, designed more to teach Hitler a lesson for having acted too often without his ally's knowledge, was really a strategic necessity, and would be like a victorious walk! But how those hasty predictions were to prove wrong! The adversaries showed themselves to be much harder nuts to crack than foreseen to the point where Italian troops would have found themselves in the sea with greater ignominy without the providential German intervention.

This is the first real humiliation for the Regime, so much more intense because it was so unexpected, but also by having the defeatist effect of showing how unprepared the Italian military machine was, and the thoughtlessness of the heads of the armed services. This turn of events has a disastrous effect on the dictator's health, worsening his dormant gastritis.

When Claretta finally gets well and she resumes her visits to Palazzo Venezia, she finds another Mussolini. He has become a touchy and silent man, who asks no questions and answers only in monosyllables those she directly poses him while she tries to elicit a smile at least from him with anecdotes and funny stories.

As if insensitive to so much devotion, he continues to philander. And with the first woman to come along, the first one who offers herself to him—according to her—the usual shriveled up old whore who worms money out of him and distracts him from his important duties.

Here then is Claretta, reproaching him for his adultery shamelessly consummated under the very roof, while in the Room of the Zodiac, she was counting the hours, the minutes, the seconds. Violent but also pathetic scenes ensue, punctuated by the inevitable reconciliations. Only once does she threaten to leave him, to disappear, to depart from his life forever.

On a January 1941 night, a quarrel breaks out over a certain Sig.ra R that Ben is supposed to have received the day before, keeping the other woman unusually long, and more than necessary. As always, he denies everything; she calls him a liar; he proclaims his utter innocence; she levels her charge, after which she returns to La Camilluccia in tears.

She encloses herself in her bedroom with her mother who tries to calm her down frantically, holding in her hands her inevitable Rosary. Before too long, two black cars stop before the gate. The one containing the police agents waits at the caretaker's lodge, the other proceeds up the driveway to the entrance of the villa.

Mussolini, in civilian clothes, gets out, his hat low over his eyes; the collar of his coat turned up, and Dr. Francesco Saverio welcomes him ceremoniously. He asks if he might speak to Claretta, who shows up shortly, cheeks reddened, her face convulsed with tears. They proceed together to the salon next to the mirrored room. After a quarter of an hour, they come out. Ben takes his leave, and gets back into the car. The next day Claretta returns to Palazzo Venezia.

She forgives him once again. That visit of his was his way of affirming that he could not live without her. And, for her, that was what counted..

A much more dramatic replay occurs on 7 August 1941, when she is on vacation at Rimini and she learns of the death of Bruno, the Duce's favourite son. He was only twenty-three, a test pilot at Marina di Pisa, where during a landing, the plane shook frighteningly, and slammed into the ground.

Mussolini is told about this while he was making his way to an elevator—it was about eleven in the morning. A civil servant approaches him: "Duce, a short time ago your son crashed, and he is in very grave danger." "He's dead?" asks the dictator. "Yes." His face becomes ashen, he leans against the door jamb, closes his eyes and, for a few moments remains silent in that position. Then he asks as if in a daze and in a weak voice, "Where?" "Pisa."

From then on he is no longer himself. A part of him departs with his son, and that which remains is stamped forever by a deep loss, by an inconsolable mourning. This is the beginning of a sad decline which external events, the military reverses, the political and diplomatic humiliations, the crumbling away of a myth speed him towards his final collapse.

Claretta returns to Rome quickly, and, instead of going to her lover, she writes: "Ben, my beloved Ben. After this enormous disaster that has struck you I think that I should return to the shadows to leave you alone with your tremendous pain. There is no further room in your lacerated heart for me. I can no longer return to you. I must remain far away. I feel that this is my duty, and I am ready if you so desire, to sacrifice myself for your love and to honour the memory of your poor, dear Bruno."

If he'd asked her to do this, perhaps she'd even have done so (with what cost to her, however). But he does not make such a request: he says that never does he need her as much as he does at that moment, perhaps because neither Rachele, nor his children, overcome by the tragedy, can provide him with the solace that he seeks.

However, their meetings will no longer be those of lovers. The link between them established when she was convalescing and receiving him at La Camilluccia, had mutated, the roles had reversed: now she is the mother, whereas a few months previously, he'd been the father. Ben talks to her as if Bruno were still alive; he recalls meetings that never took place; he tells her about absurd visits. "He wants to convince himself and he wants to convince me that it is not possible that he will never be able to see his son again," she'll confide to a friend. "Today he noticed my effort not to cry and he embraced he: 'If you cry, that means that you really think that he's lost.' Every night, before sitting down at table at Villa Torlonia, he passes his hand in a furtive caress on the back of Bruno's chair, still unused, at its usual place, as he did, since this son was the closest one to his heart. And I, you understand, must smile, and tell him that his son will return. You don't know, perhaps, what it is like not to be able to cry when your eyes burn and when you have a knot in your throat that is suffocating you. I feel like screaming, but instead, I must remain quiet, stifle the sobs and smile."

However, once alone, she'd burst into tears and a gloomy void would overcome her. Had the spell been broken? Had the ecstasy vanished? Had the flighty and inscrutable Fates decreed the end of their happiness? Naturally, she would not be able to prevent this, but of one thing she was certain: she could never give up that love.

Eleven

Dying for Love

With its high and low swings of fortune, the war soon takes on a bitter twist. The sudden, or very foreseeable, failure of the Greek campaign opens the eyes of many Italians, who now begin to doubt the infallibility of the Head of Government.

But, more than ever confident in the magical rectitude of her very own man, Claretta attributes every reversal to the perfidy of the *gerarchi*, to bad advisers, in constant suicidal competition among themselves. She says to Navarra that she is the only true, disinterested ally of the Duce, the only one who would never betray him.

But how would this all end? What would become of the two of them?

Why not consult the stars, perhaps seeking the advice of Mustafà Omari, who is mentioned so often in the salons of the Capital.

Undersecretary at Internal Affairs Buffarini, and Eugen Dollmann, the powerful SS officer who had invited the astrologer to Rome, and two other companions, come with him to La Camilluccia. Marcello bids the group welcome, and leads them to his sister's salon.

Knowing Claretta's birth date, but being unaware of her identity, Mustafà seats himself beside her and, taking her hand, prepares to read her palm, raising his eyes every so often to scrutinize hers, she being anxious to find out her personal future. At a certain point, he turns to the SS officer who is acting as interpreter, asking him if he may speak. Dollmann to whom we owe the narrative that follows—the historian Susmel is the one who relates this episode in *Gente*—replies that this is why he is there, at which point Mustafà begins to prophesy: "In a few years, very few perhaps, you will find yourself in very grave danger, signora. And even Venus, even the very planet that watches over you, and Jupiter, begin to grow dim. Saturn casts his shadow on your life, menacing it with destruction. But Saturn comes to you from another heavenly sphere, because you are not alone. Your stars

97

show this, confirmed by the signs in your hand; your destiny wishes you to be linked forever to another for the rest of your life. If I'm not mistaken, no, I can't be mistaken, you are linked to the life of a Leo ... This man to whom you've tied yourself with an oath of loyalty, signora, has found himself confronted by a very dangerous decision, perhaps the most perilous and the most demanding of his life. And yours too, signora, because your destiny is linked permanently to that of your man."

The young woman never had any doubts about this link, but what did Saturn's shadow mean, at what point would it endanger her relationship with Ben?

With his eyes fixed on Claretta's palm, the astrologer continues relentlessly. "The spring of 1943 will bring about a crisis similar to the one I've mentioned, a crisis that will involve you as much as your companion, the one who shares his fate with you. There will be attempts to separate one from the other. Jupiter will distance himself from you, and Venus will be held prisoner by Saturn."

"Saturn again," interrupts Claretta. "Will he prevail?"

"No," answers Mustafà, "you will win out, signora, but at what a price! You'll recapture your happiness, but it will be the last happiness, destined to last for a short time only."

"Until when?" she asks.

"Autumn and the first months of 1944 will be the last felicitous moments for you, and the same will occur for the man with whom you share your destiny. The great period of the Lion is getting ready to set; from month to month, at the end of this configuration, a moment is coming closer when choices about your life and death will be decided. You will have to protect yourself against a tragic, impending doom."

Having said this, he releases the young woman's hand, remains quiet for an instant, then resumes. "Give me your hand again, signora, and gaze steadily into my eyes. Now I can give you some advice, the only valid one: free yourself, give up everything. Go back to where you came from, to your former life. Be happy with the simple, every day middle class one. However, I read in your hand, and I see written in your eyes: you cannot, and do not want to take this decisive step."

He certainly read well, and he saw well. Her happiness was with Mussolini, and only with him. Nothing and no one would ever separate them. She'd always be by his side, no matter what she'd have to give up, ready for any sacrifice. Even the extreme one: her life.

"Tell me, tell me, what must I do?" presses Claretta. "What must I advise him, my man, because of the evil times that you have predicted for me? He doesn't listen to me, he doesn't want to listen to me. He talks to me about everything, but he never wants to hear of his future, of his destiny."

"Signora, you know that the stars don't force, they don't impose conditions; they merely advise. You, then, and only you, can find the correct way. Try to throw water on the fires of self-love, on the supposed infallibility of your Leo, because these are the blemishes that bring to ruin those born under the stars of August. The most disastrous example that comes to mind is Napoleon. You will succeed in surviving to spring 1945 only on condition that you think solely of yourself and about your health. If you do this, you will live long, quietly and without shocks, until the tomb. But, I repeat, only if you follow this advice."

Renewing the warning to her, he gets up and heads towards the door. Here he says goodbye to Claretta, after telling her to get in touch with Dollmann, in case of need.

Does the favourite talk to her lover about this, or does she choose to keep him in the dark, knowing how easily he was affected by superstition? We do not know. Of course, did things really happen this way, did Mustafà, in fact, draw up such a horoscope, did the German officer reconstruct that prediction at a later date? This causes so much confusion. It is a pity that no one else mentions this event.

The gloomy predictions do not dissuade Claretta from dissolving her marriage, not a simple step at such a time. As we've seen, in 1936 a separation was obtained, thanks to which she was able to leave the conjugal roof, though continue to use the Federici name. But being married, her loving another man rendered her unhappy. This is the real reason why she now sought an annulment.

Perhaps, someone may interpret this gesture as a first step towards a future union with the Duce, who, however, would never have left his wife. At least three reasons can be found for this: even while he was betraying her, he still loved his wife; he adored his children; as Head of Government, especially after the Lateran Pact, he was forced to provide a good example, even though this was a pure formality.

All this differs from what Miriam writes in her memoirs. "Claretta was the one to dissuade Mussolini from the idea of leaving his family that had come to him in a moment of annoyance, which possibly had contributed to the speeding up of the plan for the 'little divorce' already being considered for some time in the Palazzo Venezia office. Claretta involves herself because this was a matter that regarded her directly, and was against her own personal interests. Perhaps Mussolini would have come to a different idea on his own, but, without doubt, he was impressed by the woman's words, who while she should be encouraging him, was telling him instead: 'Don't do it, you can't … a scandal in your family would harm you enormously. The effects could be disastrous.' It is easy to imagine how damaging this would have been to him."

Perhaps Miriam does not know what her sister confides on the eve of the judicial hearing to Gino Sotis, her personal attorney, author of a detailed diary on which we've drawn. "When I talked to him the first time about my desire to have my marriage annulled, he (Ben) became gloomy: perhaps he feared that I was incubating a secret project. I explained the reasons to him in detail; he seemed to convince himself, without enthusiasm, without a hint of emotion. 'Do it,' he agrees with a touch of annoyance. And he adds, as if wanting to cut off one of my supposed hopes: 'For me, divorced or separated is the same thing. Remember that.'"

Claretta goes to see Sotis, the most fashionable lawyer of the time specializing in marriage breakdown, with the consent of her lover. She appears in his office one afternoon in March 1941, giving her name as Persichetti and she identifies herself correctly only upon departure, explaining: "A lawyer is like a priest. He must not be lied to."

She had in her purse a packet of letters from Ben that she handed over to the attorney to whom, in a moving and passionate tone, she outlined her personal position: "Unfortunately for me, there is no divorce in Italy. The law recognizes that a marriage may be a mistake, and even worse than a mistake, but it does not free a person, does not even allow an individual the moral rectitude of the personal self. Legal separation keeps one in a constant false position, often an immoral one, if not for others, at least for oneself. I want to get out of this situation, Sir; I want to get out of it. I want to go back to what I was before."

Sotis understands immediately that without valid reasons, a church annulment, or a civil one would not be easy, at least in Italy. However, an attempt could be made outside of the country, perhaps in Hungary where the Roman lawyer had a colleague, an attorney called Felës. But Federici's consent was required and he was advised of his wife's request by telegram at his Tokyo post.

Riccardo replies from the Japanese Capital that he was in agreement, and he permits Sotis to begin the arrangements.

But another difficulty arises: the annulment has to be granted by a Hungarian court, which means that this can only be done in the presence of the lawyer and his client in the court of that country. Claretta is ready to leave, but her lover hesitates: "He wishes that this be kept as secret as possible," says the mistress to her lawyer. "He worries about the backlash that might resound from abroad that would give an evil and gossipy interpretation to this procedure."

Sotis asks Felës if a way could be found to avoid such a trip, but the answer was no: either Claretta went to Hungary, or there would be no annulment. About ten days pass and, finally, the dictator gives his okay. Beaming, the favourite calls her lawyer: "Let's go. Prepare the bags and the passports."

La Petacci and Sotis (who travel separately as far as Tarvisio) are not the only two to leave, however, but also Miriam, Princess Alma Matteucci Cattaneo della Volta, a Hungarian and German interpreter, and a number of escort agents.

The group stops briefly at the Imperial Hotel in Vienna and, in the afternoon, accompanied by an Italian diplomat, tour the city and the Castle of Schönbrunn. At noon the next day, they continue to Budapest, where they are met by Felës.

All of them stay at the Hungaria Hotel where the Petacci sisters are assigned the largest and brightest room. As she always does, even before taking off her fur coat, Claretta pulls out of her bag a framed photograph of Ben and, after kissing the picture, she places it on the bedside table.

That night they go to a restaurant, to a fashionable gypsy spot (when the small orchestra discovers that they are Italians, they play the Italian *Royal March* and *Giovinezza* in their honour).

During this supper, thinking that he would please Claretta, Felës refers to her as "this century's lovely Pompadour." But she was not flattered at all by this, and later, she explains the reason why to Sotis: "If he only knew that to pay for this trip, my father obtained from *Il Messaggero* an advance on his salary for one year, his view would be much different.[33] Everyone has his own way of doing things. I realize that every one sees me and thinks of me in his own particular way. When I think of the opinions of people, I seem to see myself in one of those trick circus mirrors which deform a person, making her thin, or short or twisted. Pompadour?

Why not Cleopatra, or Walewska, or Cavour's unidentified woman? What do they know of me? Did you ever ask yourself what my truth is? Perhaps a little miserable truth like the one I've already told you? Did you ever imagine the advance of salary sought by my father? Mussolini covers me with gold, chokes me with jewels; all I need do is ask, dig my hands into coffers filled with money and precious stones. That is the way that the people think of me, right? Don't say no to me: I cost the state millions. I love Mussolini, or pretend to love him, because he enriches me, because he allows me a luxurious life. I am not even spared this accusation. They don't know that I am poor, that I am forced to argue for a fraction of a lira. He doesn't think about this. He's got an absolute insensitivity to even my smallest needs. Oh, not because of wickedness or avarice; but because he just doesn't think of it."

At this point, after a brief pause, she raises her eyes almost in a challenge of defiance to Sotis, and then she continues. "Every so often, absentmindedly, as if about a person far away and unknown, he asks me 'How do you keep yourself alive?' I answer that my father helps me with his professional earnings, with his salary as Vatican physician. Once I told him that I'd sold two paintings; he became furious, looking at me as if I'd insulted him, shouting at me that I was a silly fool. I don't dwell on this, that's all. I like it this way, I prefer it to be this way, I want it to be this way. One day my truth will be known: Claretta didn't love for money."

She then raises a hand and, indicating the ring on the other one, says: "See this? My mother gave it to me. It is the only jewel of value that I own. The others I wear for show. I've read all that's been written about La Pompadour; she wasn't like me. Before leaving, tell Felës. He'll be disappointed, perhaps, but what I've told you is the truth."

Another pause, and another confession. "I'm afraid of life, as if I were walking at the edge of a precipice, always with the fear of falling over, of getting smashed down below. As a child, a gypsy woman predicted that I would die for love ... I will die for love. I'll kill myself, or I'll be killed, I don't know. Or I'll die worn out by pain, because he'll abandon me, he'll no longer want me. No, that's impossible. He and I are one together. Against everything and against everybody. His family hates me. They don't understand me. I am taking nothing away from them: neither time, or money, or affection. Mussolini told me once: 'The family for me is untouchable, unchangeable; to destroy the family is to commit suicide. I don't like suicides, I have contempt for them, they are cowards ...' Nevertheless, everything will end badly for me. And for me, who dreamt since childhood of a simple love with some unknown man, one of the many who walk along the roads without anyone commenting: that's so-and-so. To take a walk arm in arm at Villa Borghese, to the Pincio, and on Saturday or Sunday nights, stop to have some ice cream in a café, at outside tables, in full view, in front of everybody, free to love, to quarrel, to suffer as everybody else."

Her eyes had moistened and her voice become hoarse. "Yes, dear Sotis, 'the sweet Pompadour of our century' is crying. The favourite who is crying, a lovely title for a love story, like the ones that secretaries read on the bus. With a smile or a caress, I should be able to open up the showcases at Bulgari, I'd have my friends rise to power, I'd obtain all the advantages that a woman loved can desire. Aren't these the advantages of a mistress? A luxurious car idles nearby for me, takes me comfortably stretched out on soft cushions to the mysterious and scented love nest at Palazzo Venezia, where Mussolini waits for me, forgetting the ambassadors, generals and politicians who crowd his waiting room. The hours pass, I hold him back in my arms and ... send Italy hurtling toward ruin. Today they whisper this, one day they will write this. All that doesn't matter to me. God sees and he will judge. Most times, the luxurious, eight-cylinder car is the sidecar of a motorcycle, and I reach Palazzo Venezia dusty or shivering or wet, according to the weather. And there, in the Cybo apartment, nine times out of ten, I wait for him until nine-thirty at night to see him for a few moments. 'I am going home,' he says, 'at last there's no one else, and my desk is clear.'

"Mussolini is changeable and erratic. With me he swings from moments of wild frenzy and violent jealousy, to periods of frozen indifference and near wickedness. And yet I feel that he loves me, more than the others, not like the others. The others exist. They aren't fantasies of mine. Life is a constant struggle against them. I always fear that someone will succeed in stealing him away from me ... He says that he likes women in their 'natural' state, and that he hates refinement and style. But if I come to him with my hair uncombed, and wearing the same dress I've worn four times, he becomes cross, almost as if my self-neglect offends him personally ... He's alone, at the top of a mountain. At times, unexpectedly, I find him different from what he is like usually; I think that he is hiding something from me, some anxiety, a worry, some bad news. He becomes insolent to me, he becomes irritated because of the tears that I have trouble controlling; or, giving me the formal 'you', he teases me, or even worse. Do you know what he said to me when I talked to him about the need for this Hungarian trip? 'You want the divorce for the trip, not the trip for the divorce.' And he was laughing, having fun at my pain and my bewilderment. But this is not a wickedness of his, it is nervous tension that exasperates him. And I have no greater satisfaction than to see him eventually cheer up and return to what he is really like. He takes his violin and plays. He's quite a performer, he's as convinced about that as I am, and we laugh together. For him to play music is like taking a sedative."

Sotis who had gone to see the Duce before leaving to report to him on the procedure for the annulment, tries to console her, telling her that in Mussolini he'd seen a man sincerely in love, even if in his own fashion. A smile breaks out on Claretta's face and, for the rest of the stay, she remains in a good mood, even if that night she wrote in her diary before going to bed: "You are Caesar ... I don't hear you, you don't think of me. All feeling is dead in you. I look for you vainly in me. You really don't love me anymore ... Perhaps the position of Icarus is right for me. The great sun has burned my wings."

She had something melodramatically masochistic in her. She suffered not only because the Duce caused her to suffer; but also because of her apprehensive and questioning nature. She'd have wanted Ben all to herself, just as she was all his, away from all sharing or deals. Resisting arbitrary compromises, she saw and lived in a special state, and only from love that was reciprocated and totally devoted could she draw an ethical ideal.

The court of Balassagyarmat where La Petacci presents herself with Sotis and the Hungarian attorney grants the divorce, thanks above all to Felës' skill. The ceremony is a strange one, Claretta not knowing either Hungarian or German, the languages spoken by the judge who, on his part, doesn't know French. The obstacle is overcome, in any case, by resorting to Latin.

On 29 December, the former Sig.ra Federici thus obtains the annulment that she had desired for so long because of *impotentia coeundi*, or 'irreconcilable differences with her husband.'

Finally she was free.

Just at that time she gets the impression that she might be pregnant once again and, in the middle of the night, she tells this to her Ben:

"How are you, love?

"Always the same."

"Any news?

"Nothing new, at least until now ... If everything goes well it might be possible to bring something really good to a conclusion."

"And you aren't happy about that?"

"Yes and no."

"You really can't be made happy. Perhaps I should tell you something very important for the two of us."

"You are making me curious."

"I don't know how to begin ..."

"Out with it."

"Perhaps I feel that I might be having a baby."

"Is that all?"

"You are displeased?"

"On the contrary ... But why didn't you tell me earlier?"

"You're so involved in other things ... then, it isn't absolutely sure. I can only be certain about this in a while."

"We'll see then."

"Would you prefer a little boy or a little girl?"

"I've no preferences, as long as it's healthy, strong, and pretty."

"The important thing is that this mustn't displease you."

"Why should I be displeased?"

Twelve

No Peace at Home

As we've seen, Claretta had a brother and a sister.

Born in 1923, Miriam is the only survivor of this so very fortunate, but yet so very unlucky family.* Eleven years younger than Claretta, her inseparable confidante and the affectionate keeper of so many of her secrets, she was a lovely girl: energetic, self-confident, and full of verve. She was not tall, but attractively built, having light chestnut hair, very bright, shrewd eyes, a fine nose, an ever-smiling mouth, and a somewhat prominent chin. She had not attended school any more than her sister, with whom she shared a love of sport (she was an expert swimmer), of Russian literature, and music, above all classical, particularly of a lyric variety. But her overwhelming interest was in theatre where, at the age of five, she had made her debut in the role of Cinderella in a little comedy for children.

She loved to please, she was pleasing and she knew this. And even Sig.ra Giuseppina who watched over her, perhaps more than was necessary, just as she did over Claretta, also appreciated this quality of hers. Although less well behaved than her sister, even she, in the end, bent to her mother's wishes, however. At thirteen, she made her debut in society wearing an evening dress of iridescent taffeta, which earned her the nickname of "Botticelli's Spring."

Mussolini meets her in 1937, on the ski trails of Terminillo, and he comes to like her very quickly: not merely because she was the sister of his lover, but also because of her youthful bluntness (if she didn't agree with him, she'd tell him so to his face).

Every time that Ben and her sister quarreled, she'd act as peacemaker, siding with Claretta without fail.

Someone has written—actually many have written this— that without the Duce, Miriam would never have become an actress. We can reject this contention, although admitting that she really didn't have the stuff to be a Duse, nor perhaps did she have the modest talent of an Alida Valli or of a Clara Calamai. She did not lack flair, however, especially in comic roles, suitable to her

---

* She died in 1991.

extraverted nature and to her glowing personality.

Her first steps in the cinematic world, despite so many important acquaintances, were not easy ones. Failing a screen test for *I Promessi Sposi*, she doesn't have better luck with De Sica, then popular, who after an interview at the Teatro Eliseo, dismisses her with a cryptic, "We'll see."

Actually, she decides to exploit her main bent for the operatic stage, encouraged by Toti Dal Monte, the noted soprano, an old friend of the family. The girl didn't have a great voice, but she used it well, and there was nothing wrong with her stage presence.

Her baptism of fire comes in *La Locanda Portoghese*, an operetta by Cherubini, in which she plays the part of a waitress. The performance at the Teatro delle Arti in Via Sicilia, was advertised extensively, not only by the impresario, but above all, by the indefatigable Giuseppina, who had asked one of Claretta's friends who was close to Crown Prince Umberto di Savoia to request that Marie José, his wife, attend the première.

But here, about this incident, we have Zita Ritossa's rather bitter account. "The Teatro delle Arti was extremely full when, a quarter of an hour before the beginning, Marcello and I enter the hall. Clara was seated in the first row: she'd preceded us with some friends. Sig.ra Giuseppina had been at the theatre since morning, to supervise the final preparations in person. We'd only just sat down when a friend came to give us the great news: 'Marie José is buying her ticket ...' Miriam and Sig.ra Giuseppina were immediately advised, and their nervousness climbs to new heights. But a few minutes later, the drama begins. 'The princess —the same friend tells us—was about to enter but then glancing at the placard hanging over the wicket, and seeing in large letters Miriam Petacci's name, turns around and leaves.' Miriam bursts into tears, while this is a shock for Sig.ra Giuseppina. Her anger risked bringing on an attack of hysteria. She even tries to blame us and she begins to shout at us like a possessed being: 'Run, stop her, have her come back at whatever cost!' "

We doubt that things actually happened that way. If Marie José actually went to the theatre, she could hardly be unaware of Miriam's performance since this is why she'd gone there (improbable also the purchase of a ticket at the booth since, because of her station, the princess would have found an invitation for her there).

The operetta achieved some success, but less than anticipated, even though the Duce ordered, through his personal secretary's office, that the EIAR broadcast it.[34]

Perhaps because she was frustrated, or because she preferred the silver screen to the lyric stage, she tries film once more, in agreement with her mother. Again according to La Ritossa—a controversial source, therefore untrustworthy and to be taken gingerly—Sig.ra Giuseppina sets up Viralba Films, a veritable production company "for the exclusive benefit of her daughter."

The company was actually formed, but Miriam was not the only one to profit by it. Yes, she does obtain one part, and even an important one at that, in the film *Le Vie del Cuore*, based on *Cause ed Effecti*, a comedy by Paolo Ferrari, but this is not enough to sustain the idea that Viralba was to serve the Petacci family exclusively.

The film which went into production in February 1942, directed by Camillo Mastrocinque had, as was predictable, a favourable reception. Every one had good things to say about it, and some even had very good things to say. Miriam, who had renamed herself "di San Servolo," a name taken from the castle of an ancestor, and not after the Venetian mental institution as Monelli asserts, was especially praised.

The picture had the honour of being shown at the Venice Film Festival that September, present besides Miriam was the restless Giuseppina. Even here there was applause, partly because amongst the spectators were dozens of sailors purposely recruited by Marcello, at that time an officer in the City of the Doges.

Also enthusiastic were the critics. "As for Miria di San Servolo, a great originality of the film," wrote Dino Falconi in *Il Popolo d'Italia*, "this being her first appearance on the screen, she performs with a free and easy assurance, and versatile ease." For Francesco Pasinetti, writer for the review *Cinema*, managed by Vittorio Mussolini, the actress reveals "fresh comic gifts."

In fact, two other pictures follow that one, the first of which was titled *L'Amico delle Donne,* and *Sogno d'Amore*, which perhaps the Duce himself screened in his film room at Villa Torlonia (even the beloved borrowed films from the Ministry of Popular Culture and looked at them at La Camilluccia).

Not even her marriage to Marchese Armando Boggiano, son and heir of a former Italian consul in Egypt, the very rich grower and exporter of cotton, disrupts Miriam's artistic career.

Boggiano and the younger Petacci girl had met at Cortina in December 1941, during a festival. According to La Ritossa, it was the proverbial lightning strike for both of them, something that consoled Miriam after a recent romantic disappointment. But this differs from what the person concerned will write many years later. "The marriage was one 'concocted' in the worst sense of the word, and I was wrong by reacting in the way that I did to the arrangement with a combination of extreme pride and spite. From a list of 'suitors,' more or less rich, and more or less pleasant, I chose randomly the name of someone who'd courted me recently, and said: 'Okay, this one. Anyway, he'll do as well as anyone else.'"

This is not a very convincing version and doesn't do much credit either to Miriam or to Sig.ra Giuseppina, in any case, the latter being the frenetic mover from the sidelines behind the unlucky marriage.

The wedding took place on 22 June 1942, in Santa Maria degli Angeli, the Roman basilica, jammed with flowers and ornaments, attended by patricians, politicians, industrialists, and artists. Miriam wore a splendid dress with train, and Boggiano a tuxedo. Claretta looked very elegant in a dress of violet silk, with gray lace and blue fox trimming and attracted the eyes of all the guests.

The reception in the ballroom of the nearby Grand Hotel was no less sumptuous, and it continued until late to allow the guests to taste the dainty morsels at the buffet tables, and to admire the wealth of gifts. Everything was there, especially furs, but what attracted the most attention were twelve silver plates, without a note. These were Il Duce's gift who, according to Ciano, confides to a *gerarca*: "While we're talking, the marriage is taking place at Santa Maria degli Angeli. Good in an economic sense, damaging for the art of the girl who finally had a cinematic future. I hope that the papers will have the good sense not to refer to this happening. Only *Il Messagero*—for which the girl's father writes—should report this event in their gossip column."

That same night, the couple leaves on their honeymoon, destination Budapest. "Twenty-four hours of married life were enough for me to realize that I had made an irreversible mistake. Armando was an intelligent and sensitive man, but he was a real gentleman above all, and this fact prevents me from talking about his faults. I spent a few happy hours with him perhaps, but many months of wretched unhappiness. Then, everything ends and I experience such great sorrows preventing me from dwelling too much on my private mishaps."

Equally unlucky, but for other reasons, is the common-law relationship of Marcello and Zita Ritossa.

The eldest child of the Petacci family, born in 1910, had a difficult disposition. Impulsive and violent, restless and arrogant, effusive and superficial, he was the initiator of aggressive activities, almost always wrong, and whose ideas were generally impractical.

By hook or by crook he wanted to be the centre of attention, something that he often succeeded in doing since he was endowed with an extraordinary physical vigor. Tall, strong, with blond hair, sporting a goatee as Flemish painters wore, he possessed an exceptional energy inherited, perhaps, from his mother; an unusual intelligence; and a devil-may-care boastful talkativeness. Unlike his sisters, he had done regular and complete studies, succeeding with the highest grades. At twenty-two, he'd obtained his medical degree, attaining three lectureships thanks to dozens of scientific papers he'd prepared. He also won a competition to be a medical officer in the Royal Italian Navy, becoming second lieutenant in 1936.

While still very young, he is transferred to Milan to practice in Dr. Donati's university clinic where, in 1937, he meets the woman who was to become his companion in his short and tragic life.

Zita Ritossa, from an Istrian family, had come to Milan, Lombardy's largest town, to attend painting classes at the Brera Academy. An independent and strong-willed woman, she worked as a fashion model in a tailor's shop during her free time after her art lessons.

The meeting with Marcello occurs on the eve of a tonsillectomy that Zita underwent that same year. "Dr. Petacci," we read in her memoirs, "was talking with some colleagues. When I went by him, our eyes met. But, at least on my part, this was nothing resembling the classical lightning bolt ... If I must be truthful, I even didn't like him. His typical Roman accent bothered me. And then, he was presumptuous and he liked to boast about his success with women, over and above the limits of good taste. In essence, an insufferable type."

Having left the clinic, Marcello begins to bombard her with telephone calls, up to four a day. "The more I pushed him away, the more he persisted. Finally, I decided to accept his invitation, promising myself that at the first immoderate action, I'd teach him a good lesson. But, instead, he was faultless. Reserved in his speech, gallant and extremely correct, I not only change my mind where he is concerned, but I fall absolutely in love with him. Only a few months later do I discover the violent and obsessive sickness in him: jealousy."

Their relations will eventually be poisoned by just this jealousy, besides his foolhardy and ruinous commercial operations, and to the very bad blood that arises from the very beginning between Zita and Sig.ra Giuseppina.

Marcello's mother and her would-be daughter-in-law never succeed in forming a bond. Sig.ra Giuseppina had a weakness for that singular rogue and high-spirited son who over-reacted and overdid everything, and because of this he was so much like her. She would never have resigned herself to the possibility of another woman grabbing him away from her, distancing him from her not always beneficial influence. She would have preferred her children to be only hers, forever by her side and under her protection.

In fact, she had succeeded in this with Claretta and Miriam, even though the latter lived in Milan. But the younger daughter spent long periods in Rome. With La Ritossa, however, the approach soon reveals itself to be catastrophic.

Zita was not the sort of person to tolerate any interference, either in her own life or in that of Marcello's, and this brought on endless quarrels, aggravated by the unhealthy possessiveness of her companion: he imagined lovers and betrayal everywhere. Not even the birth of sons Benvenuto and Ferdinando bettered the family connection between the women, as well as between the "mates."

One day, fed up to the gills, Zita decides to dump Marcello. Taking advantage of one of his visits to the Naval Ministry, she flees to a friend from whose house she then telephones him. "Life has become impossible in your house. Only bitterness and disappointments exist for me. Your mother doesn't give me an instant of peace." At this point he begs: "You must return, you must return at whatever cost, for me, for the children, only for us, for no one else ... I'll do anything you want, we'll go where ever you want to go, but you can't leave me."

They move to the Grand Hotel that same night, to the Imperial suite, and leave the next day for Merano.

Between quarrels and jealous scenes, Marcello devotes less and less of his time to his medical practice, and more and more to the improvised one of business affairs.

That he saw in this activity the road to riches, so much easier as the brother of the favourite of the Head of Government, has been asserted and written about by many. Certainly, pushing his family name, he obtains some advantages, even if perhaps, not always lawfully. But, more often then not, what he did he tried to do for the greater glory of Fascism of which, until the end, he is a fanatical adherent. As an example, the bizarre memo sent to Mussolini after the African rout. "My Duce, if a general today were to try to recapture Tripoli by going from west to east, I'd say that he was a daydreamer and a fool. I recall the words I wrote in a memo sent to you quite some time ago: victorious armies always march from east to west, going as does the sun, not against the sun! Unfortunately, history repeats itself for us ... One thing is to be done: a strong line of resistance at the Tunisian lakes, but you don't need a great general for that. All that is required is to prepare the defensive installations of the towns, and make sure that you have sufficient time to position them. In my view, Tripoli must not be reconquered by troops and fighting; it must fall because the English abandon it! ... We shall have to talk about all this, Duce, and at length, since I especially want to see my Head of Government in difficult times." And, every so often they saw each other, and they talked, even about business affairs.

In the first months of 1942, Marcello tells the Duce in great secrecy that an importing company would be able to acquire in Spain large quantities of tuna and sardines, and a considerable sum of gold sterling. As payment—he explains—would be used certain frozen credits in the Iberian territory, and that the heads of the firm would be repaid in lire. The only problem: a license.

According to Miriam, Mussolini who interested himself very little in such business dealings and who didn't trouble himself with such matters, appoints an investigator to examine the proposal: "Now Marcello makes an error. He thought the meeting at Palazzo Venezia was enough to smooth over everything, and communicates to the import company (of which he was not a part) that it was possible to proceed at once, without further delay. The merchandise and the gold were acquired and delivery was arranged almost immediately. But when everything was ready, the bomb explodes: there was no license, and one would never be obtained."

Very different is the version that Ciano enters in his diary on 24 June of the same year: "The question of the Petacci gold becomes more acute. Riccardi talks to the Duce about this matter, while Buffarini had already tried to latch on to it.[35] According to Riccardi, Mussolini is very indignant about this event and he gives orders to proceed against the perpetrators using the full terms of the law, without special considerations and without pity; according to Buffarini, however, he became vexed with Riccardi for having created a scandal over such a problem that really deserved a private or different investigation. To complicate this situation, the notorious Dr. Petacci has come out of the shadows to send to Buffarini, Riccardi and the Duce a violent letter in which he claims for himself the 'Fascist and National credit for this deal,' and covers with very bad words everyone who is hindering this project. The thing can't end too happily: it will be interesting to see who will come out of this in one piece."

When Claretta is informed of this matter, she falls from the clouds. She adored her brother and she would have sworn on his honesty. But she loved Ben even more, and the mere thought that he suspected her of being in a conspiracy tortured her. Grave problems were affecting the Duce at that moment: he didn't need more from Marcello. If he'd really been guilty, then and there, she herself would have to pay for it. And, with her, her own, or more precisely, their love.

Thirteen

Ready for Anything

For a while now, the love affair seemed to be in danger because of various circumstances. Not really due to Claretta's doing, engrossed as on the first day to her passionate cult, but due to the general situation, to the dramatic downturn in the war. Without warning, Hitler attacks the Soviet Union on 21 June 1941, until then an ally. As usual, Mussolini learns this as a fait accompli, since not even this time has he been consulted by the Führer.

Even on the African front the war is going badly. The English had dealt some very hard blows to the Italian troops, taking the fortresses of Tobruk and of Bardia, destroying five hundred airplanes, neutralizing the Tenth Army, and capturing 130 000 soldiers. The Duce is forced to remove the useless Graziani and, with considerable reluctance, to ask the Germans for aid. But without this, the Italians risked being thrown back into the sea. Hitler dispatches Rommel, his best general, to give a hand, along with two divisions—one armoured, one motorized—and this reverses the military debacle in that zone in a few weeks.

Towards the end of the year, on 7 December 1941, the treacherous Japanese attack the American base at Pearl Harbour, resulting in the drawing of the United States into the war. This is a fact of immense and decisive importance, but discounted by both Mussolini and Hitler, at that time being at grips with the Soviet Union, a much better battle-ready enemy.

Though he is bound to the German war machine, the Duce is biding his time impatiently. Every time he finds himself in trouble, the Germans have to come along and pull him out of the lion's den, thus creating another obligation on his part. The news of a further defeat throws him into an indescribable dejection; the announcement of a victory—no matter how minor—renews his confidence, opening up his spirit to new dreams.

Claretta also has her own worries, her own anxieties, and her own uneasiness. She wanted to be Mussolini's only friend, companion, and comforter, and if he didn't open up his heart to her, she felt as if she'd been defrauded of the right to help him. The idea that her love, so total and so blind, was not enough for him convulsed her.

As a result of her pressure, he seemed to withdraw into himself, almost as if he didn't need her anymore. And this was the worst type of condemnation. Was someone else bewitching him?

No. He still loved her, even if not with the same heat as previously. They continue to see each other, but their meetings are more discomposed than ever.

This is a fatal course for a relationship that has lasted more than five years, but that is beginning to weight down heavily upon him. For her, instead, it is still as it was on the first day, the first week, the first month, when she'd write him those interminably, sweet letters, filled with a resonant devotion. She could not perceive, or she didn't want to realize that, if he was everything to her, she for him was merely one part. If Ben filled up her heart, she had to share him with Rachele who as her husband he would never leave; with his children who as their father he would never give up; and with power, which was his very life.

This was something that Claretta could not understand. This was her limitation, as well as her strength: only in this way, amidst so many crises and unexpected disasters, could she keep alive the flame of a resolute and unbending passion.

If only the events of the war were not so adverse, and internal matters so dramatic and disturbing. But, instead everything was going badly.

He'd become affectionate and gentle only when he received news of successes. Then, he would go to the telephone and call her. As on that 24th of June 1942, after the victories of the Axis, which were really the victories of Rommel in North Africa.

"My love, you are well?"

"Very well. Above all I'm pleased with the lovely news from Africa."

"Even I am most delighted. But there's something new."

"Don't keep me on pins and needles."

"I'm leaving. I'm going there."

"But it's madness!... Aren't you thinking of the dangers you'd be exposing yourself to? Aren't you thinking of your life?... It's sacred!"

"I think of that ... I think of my responsibilities, but it's necessary that I do so, to stir up the troops. Then, I find it very important that I be at the victory parade. Understand?" (He didn't want that the honours be only for Rommel and the Germans.)

"But the victory parade can be held even if you aren't present."

"Do you really think so?"

"And you are always the prime mover for everything. Then, did you think of the dangers of the crossing? Can't you imagine how many enemy planes you can meet along the route?"

"Have no fears about these things because all the precautions will be taken. The flight will not be a direct one."

"Aren't you aware of what my anxiety will be during those days?"

"Danger exists for me anywhere."

"How many days will you be away? The time will be an absolute torture for me."

"If all goes well, about ten."

"May God look after you. May I at least hug you before then?"

"Yes, but I can't promise."

We do not know if they saw each other. The trip that was to end gloriously was a clamorous failure, however. Arriving in Tripoli on 29 June, Mussolini continues to Derna, where, according to plans, a ship was to take him to Alexandria. In that city, in the uniform of a Marshal of the Empire, the illustrious Sword of Islam hanging from his side, he was to ride on horseback through the streets of that town.

But the thwarted rendezvous with Rommel who was at El Alamein, expecting to enter Cairo and Alexandria, having come and gone, the Duce's dreams also become vainglorious: he has to content himself with visiting the troops and the prisoner-of-war camps hundreds of kilometres from the lines of battle. The shame could not be greater.

He returns to the Capital, telephones Claretta, who welcomes him back joyously.

"Finally, Ben of mine! ... You've relieved me of my agony. When did you arrive?"

"A short time ago."

"Imagine how tired you must be ... Good news?"

"Not exactly. Also Sciarretta, my attendant, was killed."

"Poor thing! ... By the English?"

"No. He was in the baggage van in the camp at Bardia when he was knocked down by a fighter that was landing, due to an unfortunate error."

"He was such a good man ... And what else?"

"A real disaster... And just to think that if the equipment had been available, the objective would have been attained, without doubt."

"So it's a lie that a sufficient amount is being sent?"

"On paper ... I'll have to look into this matter. Then, the accursed enemy know to the minute when our convoys leave, and they quickly send them all to the bottom with clock-work precision: especially the ships carrying tanks and fuel."[36]

"What do you think of all this?"

"There's something that doesn't gel ... But I don't know what."

"I understand."

"The men are magnificent, however. But that isn't enough, especially since even in the 'higher echelons,' there exists a stupid feeling of envy that rebounds fatally on the entire course of operations."

"Of course. Now get some rest. When are we going to see each other again?"

"I'll let you know."

Rarely had she felt him to be so down-in-the-dumps.

Learning then that, during the trip, afflicted with violent intestinal pains, he'd lost seven kilos, she requests that she visit him very soon. But he replies that the doctor has prescribed complete rest, so the meeting was postponed.

Those are very anxious days and weeks. Ben's health becomes a nightmare for Claretta, made worse by the difficulty of communicating with him. She doesn't leave her home any more, not even venturing into the garden, awaiting his call. Once she tries to telephone him, but when she is asked her identity, she hangs up. She finds out a few things from Buffarini, from Navarra, from his personal secretary, but the news is vague, and has the effect of alarming her more than of reassuring her.

Sometimes she blames his silences on his worsening illness, at other times to a real or imagined disinterest in love, which causes her to suffer more than her man is wracked with his stomach ailment. She cries continuously, she hardly touches her meals, she doesn't sleep at night; even she loses a lot of weight.

She seems to revive only when Ben returns to work, and she is once again in the Zodiac Room whose threshold she hasn't crossed for so long. Seeing him again that torrid August afternoon, she hardly recognizes him. He is pale, his eyes sunken and lifeless, his cheeks loose, his voice a monotone, his gestures weary. He tells her that he is getting better, but that he is not yet well, that the pains have diminished, but they haven't disappeared.

"What if the doctors made a mistake?" she asks him. He shakes his head, at which point she suggests that he see someone in tropical medicine.

Dr. Castellani diagnoses an ameba and orders certain injections. These not only prove to be worthless, but worsen the general state of the patient's health. He is saved, in the end, by the famous Frugoni, according to whom the Duce is merely suffering from gastritis.

He is immediately subjected to concentrated medical therapy whose efficacy contradicts those who, like Marcello, impute the illness to a plot.

His good health having been restored, but not his humour, Ben begins to receive Claretta at Palazzo Venezia once again, but not with the regularity or the diligence of times past.

How things had changed, even if she went up to him as always upon hearing his footsteps, throwing her arms around his neck, and pushing him towards the sofa as in the past! But those caresses, those sighs, those tears, those obsessive declarations of love now seem to annoy him, no less than the inevitable jealous scenes. Why had he deceived her? Why had he gone to visit Angela Curti Cucciati, his old girlfriend?

Claretta couldn't understand, or perhaps overcome by love, she did not want to understand, that the vilified, defeated and humiliated Ben of the end of 1942 was no longer the one of 1932 when they met, or of 1936 when they became lovers, or even of 1940 when sure of winning, and winning quickly, he declares war on France and Great Britain.

The passion of love was over for him, even if he still felt tenderness and attraction for her. Could she possibly not be aware of this? Was it possible that after so many years she still wanted from him what he was no longer able to give her? The flame had grown feeble, reducing itself to embers; it continued to burn but no longer to blaze. Is it possible that she who pretended to know so much about love was not aware of the cyclical nature of this emotion, mutating without necessarily going out, and that the rhythms change when they can no longer excite? She doesn't notice such transformations in herself, complicating an already difficult romance due to the interference of the *gerarchi*, jealous of such a privileged intimacy.

The first signs of this uneasiness emerge at a conference of

Party secretaries held at Lucca where, as tabled by Vidussoni, the young Party Secretary, the Petacci case is discussed as an affair of state. The question that the delegates try to resolve was: "Should we, or should we not, ask the Duce to put an end to this indecency?"

When the dictator is informed by Senise, the Chief of Police, he hits the ceiling. He calls Vidussoni and he remonstrates with him. Politics, he says, is one thing; his private life is something else, and no one has the right to try to control it. For the sake of conscience, he adds that statesmen no less illustrious had also had their lovers, citing Napoleon, Cavour, and Giolitti who, at eighty, suffered the pangs of requited love for a lady called Rosa.

The incident comes to an end, but where the affair is concerned, now known by too many, talk continues to the ill-concealed embarrassment on his part, and her growing apprehension. She is alarmed at the idea that to quell the rumours, Ben might have to break off the relationship.

A Sicilian princess, an old flame of the dictator, confides to Ciano just at that time, that the Head of Government "has had enough of Claretta, her brother, her sister, and with everybody else," but that he couldn't "get rid of them because they are very bad people, ready for blackmail and scandal." "Talking with the same princess ... the Duce is supposed to have said that, though he'd loved the girl in the past, now she'd become 'an emetic' for him."

At this point, the Minister of Foreign Affairs asks himself this question: "How much truth is there in all this, and how much is ancient, but still active, female jealousy?" And he concludes: "The princess attributes all that is going wrong in Italy to the Petaccis, even including the Duce's illness. All of which seems to me to be a little exaggerated."

We are in agreement with this assessment, but that doesn't detract from the certainty, more or less allowable, that Marcello's intrigues had really irritated Mussolini, provoking dramatic flare-ups with Claretta.

With this subject in mind, the ever vigilant Navarra relates: "One day, the bell from the Cybo apartment clangs and I, entering the Zodiac sitting room, was surprised by an unusual spectacle: the Duce, panting, his face contorted, was trying to drag the limp body of the 'signora' to the couch. He asks me breathlessly to help, and I quickly grab Claretta's feet and we place her on the sofa. The Duce explains to me strangely that she had felt ill, and orders me to call her father right away so that he can come to have a look at her. Having said that, Mussolini returns to the Sala del

Mappamondo to continue with the audiences. Meanwhile, Claretta revives and she relates to me what had happened. During a quarrel about her brother Marcello, Mussolini strikes her with a violent punch that sends her crashing into the wall, and causing her to faint. Dr. Petacci whom I'd telephoned, arrives quickly. Having given some aide to his daughter, always with me present, he asks her what had happened. 'Because of Marcello,' answers Claretta. 'He gave me a punch.' 'The punch will pass!' exclaims Dr. Petacci, while patting a little cotton batting, dipped in cologne, on his daughter's temples.

To this and other altercations, pathetic reconciliations would follow: repenting, Ben asks to be foregiven; Claretta grants this willingly, but he continues then with accusations against her and her family

Even the retreat of the Duce to convalesce at Rocca delle Caminate becomes a reason for inexpressible pain to her. He was faraway; she, ever more alone, would sink still deeper into herself. Fearing now that all might be lost, she'd occasionally find a glimmer of hope, and the gleam of a smile. It is true that the war was going badly, the Armed Forces were in retreat everywhere, the number of dead was astronomical, the exasperated population was grumbling, but, perhaps thanks to the Germans, the game wasn't over yet.

What discomforted her the most, however, was the duplicity of the *gerarchi*, beginning with the ungrateful Ciano who hated her at least as much as she hated him. Mussolini's own true enemies, as she never tired of repeating to Ben, were those whom he'd too generously covered with rank and honours. These were the privileged who sabotaged his decisions, plotted to depose him, ganging up against the one who loved him the most.

One can easily imagine, therefore, the joy with which she receives the Duce's telephone call of 15 February 1943:

"Good evening, darling."

"Ben, sweetheart, you sound so much more at ease."

"Of course."

"Anything new?"

"Several things. I've decided on a changing of the guard."

"At last you've come to a decision."

"It's not easy at a time like this, but there have been a few events ..."

"I can very well imagine ...Which ones are going?"

"Riccardi, Di Revel, Venturi, Buffarini, ... the two 'cronies' ... Pavolini ..."

"Buffarini also? I'm sorry about him."

"But just imagine that even my son-in-law is in the group ... in other words, they're all going. As for Buffarini, Venturi and Pavolini, I'm also sorry. But it's a necessary procedure now."

"And your son-in-law?"

"He won't be unemployed. At first I thought of dispatching him off to Berlin to replace that good-for-nothing who only knows how to come to Rome to consult, but it's obvious that even my son-in-law is afraid of Ribbentrop and he begged me to find him a quieter spot: the Holy See."

"Quieter so that ..."

"So that he'll be able to rid himself of his famous 'fetid fish' ... Anyway, the thing isn't settled yet."

"Who will you appoint at Foreign Affairs?"

"I'll assume the post. I'll use the services of Bastianini whom I've already tried out."

"So that you'll really increase your responsibilities, while what you need is rest."

"I'll take care of myself when I have to."

But the shuffle is only window dressing, effective for the moment, and only of psychological value. The removal of a treacherous minister, or of a disloyal *gerarca* would certainly not alter the outcome of a war whose results were already determined. When the very dictator had the courage to peer at reality squarely in the face, it became obvious to him that the Axis would collapse sooner or later, sweeping the Regime away with it.

In her ever-shorter meetings at Palazzo Venezia, Claretta seeks to cheer up her inamorato, but rarely does she succeed. He'd smile faintly, only to sink quickly into a brooding silence, which she interprets as a sign of impatience, or of downright intolerance. She'd tell him that and he'd have an outburst of rage, almost as if everything were over between them, and their passion had become a mere futile, capricious game.

She'd then return to La Camilluccia in tears and, sadder than usual, she'd write to him. "Ben, only a few words because I feel utterly terrible. The painful tension of the last few days and tonight's dramatic ones have broken me ... If my love is a joke, you are right to treat me this way after these disputes; if my suffering is just sport, it is right that you humiliate me the way that you do, and that you don't understand me. You are right: it is not modern to suffer the way that I do, it isn't pretty, and above all, it's useless. When I think that up to a short time ago, I was the dear, delectable young girl worthy to be adored, and a little later, everything becomes tomfoolery, despite my still living the same idea, I ask myself if I'm crazy, or if I'm heading that way ... You were lying, then, in your tenderness, and in your comforting love, and yet ... One thing is certain: even if you consider it a ridiculous thing, my love is still in its strongest stage, so that I can't even stand the sweet nuances in your voice for someone else, and I am jealous of the air that caresses you, and that in this excruciating moment my heart is breaking. I'd rather die instantly than feel that you can betray me, that you could no longer love me."

The usual refrain had become a great torment: the presence of another woman who would take, or was about to take her place. "The hour of my replacement is at hand; I've been thinking about this for a long time ... and I can't struggle. I have done nothing for you, I am nothing for you, I've only given you grief, I've only brought you bitter times, I only remember times when the dreadful pain of your cheating overwhelmed me ... But you, you are right: time passes and everything becomes old-fashioned, a person needs to bring herself up to date ... unfortunately, I believe that you will free yourself of my silly, great love before I stop loving you and merely feel for you a friendly and conciliating love."

But would she really ever succeed at that sort of feeling for him, not to love him anymore? She who, since her eighth year, thought only of him, dreamt only of him, suffered and enjoyed only for him? Naturally, she could have left him, but at what price? To give him up would mean the dumping of all her personal dreams, of her private hopes, of her own past and of her own future, of herself, of everything. Was it really true that he wasn't aware of this?

No, perhaps he understood, but those indictments vexed him. So much self-denial, in such difficult times, amidst so many reversals, brought him painful uneasiness.

If Claretta had been able to keep herself aloof a little more, if she hadn't assailed him so mournfully, on 1 May 1943, perhaps he would not have treated her as he did, inflicting the worst of humiliations on her.

That afternoon, at the usual time, in the usual taxi, she presents herself at the usual door on Via degli Astalli, surprisingly blocked by a policeman. Peering into the small window, she doesn't even have time to ask the officer for an explanation before the latter, using a cold, officious tone, forbids her to cross the threshold. "What? What's going on?" she asks astonished. "I said that you cannot come in. Go back," retorts the officer insolently. "What for?" "Orders from the Duce. I can't say more."

Having heard the exchange, the taxi driver throws the car into reverse, asking Claretta if he should drive her home. "No," she replies. "Let's go to see Navarra." The car continues for a few dozen metres, stopping in front of the usher's house, in the main part of Palazzo Venezia.

Navarra isn't home, but his wife is, and even she becomes upset by the apparently inexplicable exclusion. She tries to reassure her guest saying that there must be a misunderstanding that could be cleared up straightaway. But Claretta is so upset that she can't remain seated. She paces back and forth in the room, biting her lips, fluttering her eyelids, and clenching her fists convulsively. Finally, overcome by the tension, she throws herself into an armchair, giving way to fits of crying, her head in her hands, in a sobbing monotone: "Why? Why? So it's true you no longer love me? So you really don't want to see me anymore? So it's true you love someone else?" She wasn't giving herself any peace, offended and anguished by that drastic blow.

Taking the telephone, Navarra's wife summons her husband, who rushes over. "I met the woman and tried to calm her down," he will write later, "and I promised to speak with Mussolini about this. Never, however, had I seen Claretta in such a state: she'd been overtaken by a real and actual hysterical crisis. She soon asked me insistently that I let her talk on the telephone to Edda, to settle that 'question' once and for all. Claretta knew what opinion the Ciano household had of her, and she linked the Duce's decision to a stratagem of his daughter. Naturally, I do not acquiesce to the request. She continues to cry without stopping until my wife opens her purse to take out her handkerchief to dry her tears; but she remains frozen, and she looks at me, showing me that the purse contained a pistol. 'What's this?' I ask Claretta, referring to the weapon. 'It is the gun that will bring me peace.'"

Since she continued to weep, Navarra telephones Dr. Francesco Saverio who is by his daughter's side fifteen minutes later, and he gives her an injection of a cardiotonic. As soon as she feels better, they return to La Camilluccia

Sig.ra Giuseppina is not home, and even Marcello is away: the first is at Meina, visiting her daughter and son-in-law; the other is at Merano where he'd moved with Zita and his small sons. Without even taking off her jacket, Claretta telephones her mother, relating the incident so dramatically that the very same night, Sig.ra Giuseppina rushes back to the Capital.

The next day the family gets together to consider the matter. In everybody's opinion, the best thing to do is to bring the whole matter into the open. Claretta rings Mussolini, but the dictator's private number, which very few people knew, squeals in vain. She tries the switchboard, only to be told that there are strict orders not to forward her calls.

She then begins to write letters, some begging, others resentful, some desperate, others hopeful, all with no results. One morning, in the depths of unhappiness, she decides to confront Ben when he left Villa Torlonia to go to Palazzo Venezia. But as luck—or ill luck would have it—he wasn't feeling well that day, and he stayed home. Therefore her action came to nothing.

Finally, after a week that seemed to Claretta to be a century, in fact, an eternity, either because he wanted to put a stop to the flood of letters, or because he regretted the long silence, he phones her. "I'd decided not to see you again," he begins in an indifferent tone. "I'd realized that. But why?" asks Claretta, even she feigning detachment. "I have my reasons," he replies dryly. "And you didn't want to give them to me? You let me stay without an explanation, something that is accorded even those condemned to death? What did I do to you?" "You, nothing," Ben reassures her, "but grave accusations exist against a member of your family." "What sort of accusations?" pursues Claretta. "Trafficking in currency and smuggling gold. Come to see me and I'll show you the report," replies the dictator curtly.

She goes to Palazzo Venezia and he shows her the document, which, without mincing words, actually in very crude terms, accuses Marcello of illegal trading in currency. While admitting that the charges are grave, Claretta casts doubt on their validity. "But look here, you know everything and yet you believe these people? Why don't you say that Marcello came to see you, that he told you about this?" At which Ben replies, according to Miriam, "that the matter was presented to him in a much different light and, consequently, he'd felt the need to examine it well before giving an opinion. He does not tell her that he was exasperated, above all, by the fact that this matter had given the *gerarchi* a pretext to censure his private, intimate life. To compensate, he does something rare for him: he apologizes."

They proceed to the Zodiac Room, where an equally bitter surprise awaits the beloved: her paintings, her vases, her books, her records, even his picture, are no longer there.

"I tore it up in a moment of anger," Ben defends himself while she stares into space, dismayed. His picture destroyed! What an atrocious thank you, after so many years of blind self-denial! But when he asks her to forgive him a second time, she doesn't have the strength to say no to him.

The reconciliation is short-lived, however, especially since, both in, and out of, the country things were crashing down, the Fascist state was in complete decay, the dictator more alone than ever.

At a particular point, Ben suggests that the visits be limited until better times, about which she writes him indignantly: "Having begun a dramatic phase, perhaps the most dramatic of your life, you have only one thought, only one goal: to throw me out ... Not even with your thieving and vile associates have you had so much fortitude and firmness ... Everything is finished. Not because of the war which I have been living with you for four years. Not because of the bombs which fell as recently as yesterday ... Everything is finished in you. When I entered my room and saw that nothing of mine was there anymore, that you had taken away all my belongings, my photograph, I felt like dying. This is really the end ... And since the end of your love is the end of my life, today I am ready for anything."

Having received the message, Ben telephones her: the decision—he says—is a heavy one even for him, but the latest events (the Allied landings in Sicily on the night of 9 – 10 July, the bloody air raid on the Capital on the 19th of the same month, his recent meeting with Hitler), had made this necessary.

"I'm tired," replies a resentfully altruistic Claretta. "I hope that you will have nothing to do with women who are unworthy of you, to have no problems, to be supremely happy, and to win out ..."

But on 23 July—on the 22nd Palermo had fallen—Mussolini wants her again at Palazzo Venezia. The meeting is brief, moving, almost secretive. He seems defeated: the gastritis doesn't give him any respite, but above all, the Anglo-Americans don't give him any either. How different he was from the man of their first meeting within the same walls when, hand in hand, eyes only for each other, while dusk was falling outside, and the swallows were tracing their fantastic patterns in the air, he declared his love for her, and she, as if in a dream, ecstatic and sighing, surrendered herself to him. The sacred spell had now dissolved, the cycle of destiny had turned, mutated; Clotho and Lachesis, the fickle children of Night, were no longer smiling on them, but instead, their faces were transmuted into very menacing ones.

Before saying goodbye, Ben tells her that Grandi has requested a meeting of the Grand Council, and that he is not opposed to this. She replies that in this way, he is legitimizing the Fronde, risking of finding himself in the minority. In order to reassure her and, perhaps to reassure himself, he explains that this is merely a consultative vote about which there is nothing to fear, the King being on his side.

The same day, the eve of the prophetic meeting, she phones him.

"Am I disturbing you?"

"Secretary Scorza just now left, and I am getting ready for tomorrow night."[37]

"But didn't you tell me that Grandi asked for a postponement?"

"Yes; but given the pressure of events, the sooner it's done, the better it is."

"I want to tell you that, in conformity with your promise, I have a great desire to go to Castelporziano on Sunday."

"Just imagine how much I want that too, how much I feel the need ..."

"Well then?"

"I think it will be very difficult, if not impossible."

"But why are you giving so much importance to this?"

"It's not a matter of giving it importance or not. This time I'm afraid that things will be much less easy than you imagine."

"You are frightening me ..."

"There is little to fear. I know that they will ask me for an accounting of all my work."

"And you?"

"I have documents ready showing what they were, and of what they have become; but I think that this may not be enough."

"You will see that even this time your benevolence will prevail."

"Wish it for me. As for the beach, we'll postpone it to the near future."

"Ciao, Ben dear. At least, phone me ..."

"As soon as possible."

"Good work now."

"Thanks."

Never had she been overcome by so much agitation. She wanted to do something, but what? She mulls it over for a long time; she talks to her mother at length and, late in the afternoon of 24 July, with the session already underway, sends Miriam to

Navarra with a brief message for her lover.

Her sister's meeting with the usher takes place in the roadway beside Palazzo Venezia. "How's it going?" asks Miriam anxiously. "Badly, very badly," replies Navarra who seems to be in a great hurry.

By now, the hand had been played, Fascism's hours were numbered. And with them, those of it's leader.

Fourteen

Duce, Don't Go!

The twenty-eight members of the Grand Council, comprising eight ministers, the Presidents of the Senate, of the Fasces and Corporations, and various privileged *gerarchi*, had not met for four years. A vote in the Council was not binding and, perhaps because of this, the dictator hadn't even bothered to convene it on the declaration of war. But now that the war seemed lost, this body took on a decisive importance.

In the Sala del Pappagallo, on the second floor of Palazzo Venezia, where the supreme body of the Regime met to carry out its duties, the Fascist Fronde finally had found a place to preach its message. It is true that according to the Charter of the Grand Council, which the Duce himself had drawn up, he was not obliged to give an accounting of the choices he'd made to anybody. But it is also true that, the way the wind was blowing, a non-confidence motion would have shaken his prestige fatally, and threatened his leadership. This was an examination fraught with consequences, from which Mussolini didn't want to, and couldn't, extricate himself. He didn't want to because he couldn't imagine the outcome of the meeting. He couldn't ignore Grandi's request for a meeting, an expression of the ever-widening discontent because to do so would have accentuated his own isolation.

The Councilors begin arriving at about 4:45 in the afternoon of a torrid Saturday, stuffed into black bush jackets, feet and calves tight in officers' boots, exhausted by the great heat. Their pace, and more so, their looks, betray an acute tension. An unusual calm prevails in the palace, rendered suspect because the Duce's bodyguard, that is, his Praetorian Guard, is absent, having gone to clear away the debris from the San Lorenzo district, in disorder after the bombing of 19 July (a special police unit is called in to take their place). Perhaps without reason, some of the members think that the Duce intends to shorten the length of the session of the Council (amongst other things, this is the first time that the Fascist ensign is not fluttering from the flagpole of the palace).

Duce, Don't Go!

The sitting begins a little after five. Mussolini, at the centre of the table, flanked by veterans De Bono and De Vecchi on the right and to his left, Secretary Scorza, seems more tired than worried. For more than two hours, in a hoarse and humdrum voice, he explains his political and military choices, revealing that in October 1942, after the umpteenth, most violent gastritis attack, he'd come very close to retiring from the political wars, but his sense of duty and his obligations to the State had induced him to remain ("A ship is not abandoned in a storm," he said). Then, he sums up the failures of the Nation, complaining about the scarcity of arms, munitions, foodstuffs, and raw materials.

The *gerarchi* listen to him in bewilderment, almost as if his fate, whatever he'd say, whatever excuses he might advance, were already decided. At last, they arrive at the Grandi Agenda with which the Assembly is familiar, its author already having distributed the proposals. "The Grand Council," it read in substance, "affirms the necessity of the moral and the material unity of all Italians ... Declares that, with such a goal, the complete restoration of all State functions is necessary and urgent, assigning to the Crown, to the Grand Council, to the Government, to Parliament, to the Corporations, the tasks and responsibilities established by our Statutory and Constitutional Laws ... invites the Head of Government to beg His Majesty the King ... so that He can, for the honour and the salvation of the Nation, assume, with the active command of the Armed Forces on land, sea and air, according to Article 5 of the Constitution of the Realm, that supreme initiative ..."

This is not an invitation or an appeal. This is an order. Never, in twenty years, had anyone dared speak to the Duce that way, in that way accuse him, and in that way seek his head.

Piling it on further, eyes fixed on the man, those whom he'd covered with so many honours (ministers, ambassadors, members of that very Grand Council), Grandi adds madly: "You think that you have the devotion of the people! You lost that the day you tied Italy to Germany. You choked the very being of everyone under an historic and perpetual dictatorship. You think that you are a soldier. Let me tell you Italy was lost the same day that you put marshal's stripes on your cap! ... Tear off that ridiculous military insignia and return to being what you were: our Mussolini, the Mussolini that we obeyed and followed."

At this point, the Duce objects indignantly that the people are still with him, but undaunted, Grandi persists: "In the last war, six hundred thousand Italian mothers mourned the deaths of their sons, but they knew that they had died for the King and their Country. In this war, we've had to date one hundred thousand dead, and we have one hundred thousand mothers who cry aloud: 'Mussolini has murdered my son.'

"That is not true," the Head of Government replies angrily, "that is not true!" But by now the implacable accuser has let the cat out of the bag, leveling the field for whoever wishes to continue in the same vein.

The few siding with Mussolini, although with different emphases and ideas are: Farinacci, the pro German, who calls for a major German presence in Italy; and Galbiati, furious over the denunciation of the dictator, who suggests an adjournment until the next day.

Party Secretary Scorza scrawls down the request on a piece of paper and hands it to Mussolini who agrees to this. But Grandi rebels, fearing that with this delay, the Duce would gain time to mount a counterattack. "No, no! When the matter under discussion was the Labour Charter, you kept us here until seven in the morning. Now that the subject is the very existence of our Nation, we can remain here to discuss for a week, if need be. Our soldiers are dying while we are speaking."

Indifferently, the Duce doesn't insist and, after two other speakers, suspends the meeting for fifteen minutes.

Gloomy and silent, he returns to his personal office where, to find relief from his atrocious stomach pains, he drinks a glass of milk. Then, he glances at the note from his mistress, and he rings her up. "Only three or four are with you," she says, putting him immediately on his guard, "all the others oppose you. If you come to a vote, they will throw you out. If you allow them to leave Palazzo Venezia, everything is finished. You can rely on Galbiati. Order him to arrest them and you are safe."

With a voice seemingly calm, he replies that the situation is under control, the King wouldn't betray him, the Fronde would be tamed, the rebels punished. But she repeats her own fears, and with such stubbornness that, finally, losing his patience, he says goodbye, telling her that he would call her again later.

The session resumes at 12:25 in the morning with another talk by the Duce who, hoping perhaps to move his listeners, in the main so hostile to him, re-evokes the long political militancy, the achievements of the last twenty years, and the benefits of Fascism. In his speech there is a touch of clumsy nostalgia, almost as if the cycle had turned, the allegory exhausted. He refers to the "magnificent adventure," reconfirming his intention to retire.

But the monologue raises pity, rather than solidarity. The demi-god has lost his former astuteness and the old sulky look. The remarks and the pauses are no longer the ones of the past, neither are the scowls or the poses those of former times. He reaches the height of pathos, however, when "with the look of a child who asks a riddle," announces "I could tell you some great news about a very important fact that will reverse the war situation in favour of the Axis. But I prefer not to tell you just yet."

Then, he reasserts his personal loyalty to the King, and that of the King to Fascism, implying that he who wasn't with him was against him, and he who was against him was against the Crown, that is, the Nation. The maneuver had all the appearance of a bluff, which in actual fact it was, since the conspirators were not disregarding the sentiments of the Monarch, anxious to get rid of that Prime Minister who had inflicted so much humiliation upon him.

At 2:40 in the morning, in an atmosphere full of suspicion and fear, the Grandi motion finally comes to a vote, which Scorza proceeds to tally. "Nineteen, yes; eight, no; abstention, one."

Having heard the verdict, Mussolini gathers up his papers quickly and angrily, adjourns the meeting and takes his leave rancorously. "You have brought about the collapse of the Regime."

The Councilors head quickly for the courtyard where their cars and drivers have been idling for ten hours. But, the Duce returns to his private office where he telephones Claretta again.

"How did it go?" asks his mistress apprehensively.

"How did you expect it to go?"

"You are frightening me."

"There is little to fear. We are at the conclusion ... at the greatest turn in history ..."

"But what's the matter with you, Ben sweetheart?... I don't understand you."

"The star has dimmed."

"Don't torture me like that ... explain to me."

" Everything is over. Even you must try to take cover now."

"And you?" she asks.

"Don't think of me. Move quickly."

"But what if nothing is known"

"You will know in a few hours."

"This is really one of your ideas ..."

"Unfortunately, it isn't like that."

"What then?"

"Do as I've told you, or else things might be much worse," he cuts short and hangs up.

It was as if a lightning bolt had reduced Claretta's heart to ashes. Or a knife had eviscerated her. She breaks down into bitter weeping and when she looks at herself in the morning, after a sleepless night, she almost doesn't recognize herself. The tears have not only puffed up her eyes and blanched her cheeks, but they had muffled her spirit. She wanders about the house like a robot, mechanically repeating the words that Ben had said to her, and what she'd replied to him. She was particularly upset by that "or else things might be much worse." And yet, the drama had barely begun.

On the morning of the 25th, she waits fruitlessly for her lover to communicate with her, after which she tries to call him, but without any luck. Finally, at about noon, he re-emerges, to assure her that the Sovereign sides with him and that the Grand Council vote would only have a reshuffling of the Government as a consequence, as well as the assumption of the supreme military command of the Armed Forces by Vittorio Emanuele.

He seems more relaxed and optimistic than a few hours before, and when he tells her that he would see the King in the afternoon, he is absolutely euphoric. "Don't go," begs Claretta. "If I were you I wouldn't trust anybody... Be especially wary of Badoglio." On hearing that name, he exclaims insultingly: "But no, Badoglio has other things to do. He's playing bocce." "I would not want him to play bocce with your head," Claretta comments. And with this exchange they say goodbye. Once again she is the more farsighted of the two.

After leaving Palazzo Venezia following an audience with the Japanese ambassador whose government—according to the Fascist leader—was seeking to convince Hitler to make a truce with Stalin, he tours the Roman districts destroyed in the recent bombing, entering Villa Torlonia at about three.

He is the only one who eats, chatting with Rachele, who later will recall the conversation this way: " 'I'm going to see the King today, at five,' Benito said to me. As if stung by a wasp, I jump. 'Don't go, I beg you!' 'I must go. We have a pact that ties us to the Germans and we must respect it. The King signed it just as I did, and we must decide together what we must do. But whether I remain as Prime Minister or resign, the King will have to allow me to arrest all the defeatists, the cowards and the traitors. You know, we are crossing the blackest moment of our lives and of that of Italy. Remember Caporetto? That seemed the end, but remaining united as we did then, we will come out of this with honour, you'll see.' "

At that moment the telephone rings. The Royal Palace is calling. The audience set for five that afternoon is confirmed (normally these consultations took place on Mondays, but the results of the Grand Council meeting have forced Mussolini to ask for, and obtain, an advance of twenty-four hours).

The Duce remains with his wife a little longer, then he goes to change his clothes (usually he'd wear a military uniform, but that day, because of the Sovereign's wishes, he is to dress in civilian clothes, something which causes Rachele to become suspicious). He chooses a dark blue suit, while his wife seeks, desperately and uselessly, to delay him, to keep him from setting foot outside of the villa—she said—or he would regret it bitterly. But he is obdurate, certain of the Sovereign's support (how little he knew the latter. And after more than twenty years too!).

At a quarter to five, with the familiar bowler hat and the no less ubiquitous gloves, accompanied by his private secretary De Cesare, he leaves for Villa Savoia, which he reaches before five. He is immediately ushered into Vittorio Emanuele's office, while one of the Monarch's aides-de-camp takes charge of his associate.

On the historic meeting we have, essentially, similar versions by the two participants. Mussolini begins. "Your Majesty is aware, no doubt, of last night's trick ..." "What a trick!" corrects the Sovereign acidly. "Majesty," continues the Duce, "the Grand Council vote has no validity ..."

The King objects that this is an Organ of State, sought by Mussolini himself and given legitimacy by Parliament, after which, falling back on its legendary irritation, votes for dismissal. "Dear Duce, things are no longer going the way they should. Italy is under pressure, the Army's morale has been run into the ground, the soldiers no longer want to fight, the mountain regiments sing a song in Piemontese dialect in which they claim they no longer want to wage war for Mussolini." Not satisfied, he repeats the refrain: "Down with Mussolini, murderer of the Alpini."

The guest doesn't bat an eyelash, and his host takes advantage to spew out more poison. "I have been assured that Farinacci and Buffarini, those two bums you had close to you when it was not certain whether I would or would no sign the decree by which you wanted to assume the command of the Armed Forces, said: 'He will sign, or else we'll kick his behind.'"

Then he turns to the Grand Council vote. "The vote is terrible. Nineteen votes for Grandi's Agenda. Obviously, you cannot now delude yourself about the state of mind of the Italians where you are concerned. You are the most hated man in Italy at this moment, and you can't rely on even one friend. I'm the only one you have left." "In that case," Mussolini blurts out, "I should resign ..." "And I tell you that I would accept your resignation without conditions," answers the Sovereign curtly.

For the Duce of Fascism, this is almost like capital punishment, rendered even more merciless by the dissembling tone of his adversary. The King is now the referee; on him now depends the fate of a man who had used Savoy power to conquer and reinforce his own position for so long.

Mussolini understands that even for this, or above all because of this, to insist was useless, that the one before whom he found himself, even though declaring himself his friend, could never reaffirm his trust in him as Duce. He merely exclaims, shaking his head: "Then my collapse is total." At which the malicious Monarch fires a last, overwhelming shot: "I have come to the conclusion that the only person who can remedy the present situation is Marshal Badoglio. Badoglio is the man of the hour. He will form a military government and continue the war. He has the complete confidence of the Armed Forces and of the Police." How his women had been right! If only he'd paid attention to them! But now the trap had sprung!

At the moment of dismissal, Vittorio Emanuele takes hold of his guest's hand, and with insincere solicitude, reassures him: "Have no fear for your personal safety. I will issue orders to protect you." It was 5:20.

Followed by De Cesare, Mussolini doesn't even have time to descend the stairs before Paolo Vigneri, a captain of the Royal Carabinieri, comes forward, salutes him militarily, exclaiming: "Duce, by orders of the King, we must protect you against the possible violence of the mob." "That's not necessary," answers the dictator, heading towards his car, but seizing him by the arm, the officer diverts him to the other end of the villa, to an ambulance, with fifty Carabinieri surrounding it. He repeats that this is an order and finally, Il Duce obeys, settling inside the ambulance with his secretary, some escort officers, and the same Vigneri. In only two hours, the vehicle had been transformed into a paddy wagon.

The ambulance heads for the Carabinieri's Podgora Barracks where no one is expecting such an extraordinary visitor, and everyone springs to attention. When the astounded Commander Linfozzi sees Mussolini, he blurts out: "Duce, what an honour!" At which Vigneri explains: "The Duce is our guest. I beg you, Colonel, to have the Officers' Club opened so that he can stay there."

Mussolini is taken to a small Empire-style sitting room, along with De Cesare, who asks if his Chief could use the telephone. "No," replies Vigneri, courteously, but emphatically. Then, Major Scivicco, another officer, approaches the set and cuts its line. Only at this point does the Duce understand: he isn't a guest, but a prisoner, even if a respected one.

He felt tired, frustrated, sluggish, as he'd never felt before, not even when he'd learned of Bruno's death at the elevator of Palazzo Venezia in August 1941.

He does not remain long at the Podgora Barracks as his arrival has provoked some alarming excitement. Better to move him to a more secure spot, perhaps to the residence of the student Carabinieri in Via Legnano.

Here he is examined by Major Santillo, a doctor, who finds him "very pale and with a deathly look." The events of the last few hours have dismayed him, his gastritis is acting up and making him suffer terribly.

He is allowed to rest on a couch but, at one in the morning, a colonel wakens him and leads him to a nearby room where he receives a note from Badoglio.

The new Head of Government informs him that everything was being done to insure his safety, menaced by "a serious conspiracy," since "from various quarters," had come "definite signs." He offers him, then, "a safe conduct, with due regard, wherever you've decide to go."

Even if the message came from a man whom he hated, and who hated him, it reassures him. He replies to him thus: "I wish to thank Badoglio, Marshal of Italy, for the attention that he has sought to accord to my person. The only residence that I can use is at Rocca delle Caminate, to which I am prepared to move at anytime. I wish to reassure the Marshal of Italy, even in remembering the work that we did together in former times, that on my part, I will not create any difficulties what-so-ever, but that you will be extended all the possible help ... I am happy about the decision taken to continue the war with the Ally, since this is what honour and the interests of the country require right now, and I express a hope that success may crown the serious work for which Marshal Badoglio prepares himself, by order of, and in the name of His Majesty the King, of whom I was the loyal servant for twenty-one years, and which I still remain. Long live Italy! Benito Mussolini." A declaration of loyalty dictated, perhaps, more by the knowledge of having had his day, rather than hoping to win over the new boss.

The Founder of the Empire had a great desire to return to his Romagna, far from the noises and the responsibilities that had oppressed him for twenty years. At Rocca delle Caminate, near his children and Rachele, he would find again his own strength, and the serenity that he needed now more than ever. His thoughts also turn to Claretta, but more with gratitude than with desire or nostalgia. Would he see her again?

While he is going to see the King, as a mouse to the trap, in the old love nest in Palazzo Venezia, in the Room of the Zodiac, where they had spent so many unforgettable hours, his prescient woman is anxiously awaiting him. However, when at five o'clock Navarra confirms to her the visit to Villa Savoia, she leaves the apartment hurriedly to return to La Camilluccia.

Here she receives a call from Marinelli, Galbiati's aide, a friend also of Marcello, who informs her of Mussolini's arrest, exhorting her to leave the villa quickly.

But to go where?

She talks to her parents and together they decide that the best thing, for the moment, would be to move to Donadio's house. First, however, she wants to safeguard Ben's letters and the copies of hers to him (all this while her parents gather together some personal effects, and a little money). "Sig.ra Giuseppina and the others," will relate Zita Ritossa, "got out of the car as if they felt that they were already being pursued. They were pale, and their eyes were full of fear. Mamma Giuseppina had a large bundle in her hands. Barely in the house, she puts the package on the table and she removes the wrapping paper very carefully. It was a pan full of baked tomatoes which she had just barely finished cooking and which she had not been able to serve because of the news of Mussolini's arrest."

But Donadio's house, even if welcoming, couldn't house all the Petacci family, who then move on to driver Gasperini's more spacious one in Prati.

Claretta doesn't close her eyes, being more worried about

Ben's fate than about that of her parents or herself. What had become of him? Where was he at that very moment? Where might they have taken him? Was he thinking of her? She telephones many friends and acquaintances but she learns nothing more than she already knows; also, many who had been friendly to her until the day before, now disavow everything, fearing to be put in danger.

No use even talking about returning to the Camilluccia. In fact, when the next morning, a Monday, Gasperini visits the house, he finds the place surrounded by Carabinieri. Marshal Antichi, their commander, tells him that everything is in order, and that not even a hair of the owners would be touched (but he was very quickly proved wrong by an eruption of vandalism at Dr. Francesco Saverio's office on Via Nazionale).

This induces the Petaccis to flee to Meina, where Miriam's husband had a lovely and comfortable house. Before leaving, however, the head of the family is received by the new Assistant Secretary at Internal Affairs, who tells him that he would put three trucks at their disposal for the move, and assign two escort Carabinieri (but the convoy will never reach its destination).

On the 27th, Claretta and her family—minus Marcello— leave Rome.

"We did not suffer any of the 'manifestations of popular hatred' that the Badoglio government stated should be feared after the attack at the [Dr. Francesco Saverio] office," recounts Miriam. "But all the same, the trip was an anxious one, and even today I remember it with anguish in my heart. The most fantastic rumours assail us all along the way: there were those who said that Mussolini was dead, others said that he was a prisoner of the Allies. Almost everyone believed that the war was practically over. My mother was in a desperate state because we'd received no news of Marcello since the night of the 23rd. Claretta, who had overcome an attack of quiet crying, remained still, looking fixedly in front of her. At times, she didn't even respond to our questions.

"At the Futa Pass where we stop to eat, one of the escort Carabinieri sees Mussolini's picture on the wall of the trattoria, and says that the picture would have to be taken down. The innkeeper replies dryly, 'While I am still here, that will remain at its usual spot,' and he turns his back to the officer. We didn't know yet that we had been witnesses to a very rare happening for those times, but we should have guessed so much as, during the night, when we were crossing the deserted streets of Milan, we were greeted by the echoes of gunfire that emanated from the outskirts of the city. The pavement was covered by burnt paper, shattered Fasces, and busts of Mussolini smashed to bits. The public was getting rid of the Twenty Years of Fascism. Finally, at dawn, we reach Meina."

Fifteen

A Revolver, Please

The announcement of Mussolini's arrest and the ambiguous declaration by Badoglio ("The war continues") unleashes a wave of tumultuous enthusiasm everywhere. If it is true that few Italians expected such a brutal dismissal, it is also true that the problems of the Regime had been in the air for a long time now: the latest military failures had merely accelerated this event. What was stupefying about all this, really, was the opportunistic ideological conversion of many Italians who from one day to the next, in fact, from one hour to the next, discover themselves to be anti-Fascists. No one continues to wear uniforms. No one sports Black Shirts. No one shows the Fascist lapel pin, and no one carries the Fascist card. Everyone, or almost everyone, reviles the deposed tyrant who had dragged the country into the abyss, but many praise the two-faced and haughty Badoglio. As Collier reports,

> In Via Veneto, a barrel-chested demonstrator begins to shout: "See? I can yell 'Mussolini is a pig' and no one arrests me." At which a more or less devil-may-care fellow who is standing near by, suggests: "Try shouting 'Badoglio is a pig' and see what happens to you."

Even Rachele is about to suffer the consequences of the changed situation as she learns of her husband's arrest that night from a radio report (in late afternoon her suspicions were aroused by the absence of the security guards and the arrival of some military transport trucks which discharge a company of Carabinieri in front of Villa Torlonia's gate).

After hearing the news, she sends Raffaele Fratoni, a family friend, to warn Vittorio who is typing in his office, wearing only shorts: "Your father has been arrested ... I think it would be best for you to find yourself a safe place." Putting on his trousers hurriedly, the young man gets into his personal car, and slips out of the secondary entrance on Via Spallanzani.

Then Rachele calls Romano, at that time in Riccione with his sister-in-law, Bruno's widow, and his sister Anna Maria. After this, she tries like Claretta to have other news of Il Duce, but no one is willing to supply any.

The only thing she succeeds in learning the next day, the 26th, is about her husband's relationship with La Petacci. Irma, her maid, reveals this to her and she receives a slap from her husband in Rachele's presence. Later, she will learn the salacious and fantastic details of the affair from the newspapers.

She finds out something about Benito the morning of the 27th, thanks to a letter from Princess Mafalda [daughter of the Italian King], reassuring her of the state of health of the prisoner. A few days later, General Polito delivers a message to her: "Dear Rachele. You know what the condition of my health allows me to eat, but don't send me much: only a few suits because I don't have any, and some books. I can't tell you where I am, but I can assure you that I am well. Stay calm and kiss the children for me."

The officer also gives her a letter from Badoglio who, in a sophomoric rather than chivalrous tone, urges her to send money for food as the government cannot, or does not want to provide this directly. All of which provokes in her an understandable outburst of indignation. "For twenty years Mussolini received no salary, giving to the State all the precious gifts received from Italians and foreigners. And this from the very Badoglio who enriched himself through my husband's government but now refuses to provide Mussolini with a piece of bread?" In one parcel, she carefully packs fresh tomatoes, fruit, eggs, a can of oil (which gets lost) and a book, Ricciotti's *Life of Jesus Christ*.

Even she will leave Rome for Rocca delle Caminate on 2 August, escorted by Polito who smokes stinking cigars during the entire trip, rudely uses the singular "you," and tries to molest her with obscene advances. "My violent reactions stop his motions abruptly," Rachele will write later. "If he'd tried anything else, believe me, I'd have killed him. I don't know how, but I would have done it."

Mussolini is transferred to Gaeta at first, and from there to Ponza on the night of 27 – 28 July (this despite Badoglio's promises).

When he is disembarking, he cannot hide his unhappiness since, on that island were confined others he'd sent there: Zaniboni, his attempted assassin, and Pietro Nenni, his old friend, but now implacable enemy (he fears that on meeting them, he will have to submit to their sarcasm).

He is lodged in a two-story shack, furnished rudely, with a swaying bed, without sheets, and with an iron washbasin.

This is where he spends his sixtieth birthday, which occurs on 29 July, far from his wife, his children, and Claretta already at Meina and without any news of her Ben. He is, without doubt, thinking of her less than she is thinking of him.

He feels that he is a finished man, drastically and irrevocably outside of history. For almost forty years he'd trod the political stage, for twenty he'd ruled Italy. Now he had only one wish: to retire and be forgotten.

He remains on Ponza until 7 August when, fearing that the Germans would come to free him after finding out his hiding place, Badoglio has him moved to the Sardinian island of La Maddalena. Here he is housed in the more protected and comfortable Villa Weber that has a solid bed, a nice bathroom, a sitting room with sofa, four chairs and a table.

To kill time, he reads, he writes his memoirs, collected later in the volume *Storia di un Anno,** plays cards, and talks to the custodians. On the 19th, coming especially from Rome, Admiral Brivonesi gives him the *Collected Works of Nietzsche*, in twenty-four volumes, one of his favourite authors, courtesy of Hitler. He knows the works already, but he re-reads them, between a gastritis attack, and a gloomy feeling of hopelessness.

He eats little, goes to bed at dusk, rises at dawn, takes short walks in the pine forests, or stretches his legs in the garden. One day he asks to get together with the parish priest of the island with whom he has at least four meetings. It seems that he even attends Mass, and there are some who aver that he would absolutely have converted—something that we find hard to believe—had the authorities not taken him away from La Maddalena to transfer him to the more difficult and remote Gran Sasso.

At four in the morning, accompanied by a lieutenant and a marshal, he leaves in a seaplane for Lake Bracciano where Inspector Gueli, responsible for his safety, awaits him. He gets into an ambulance ("Always an ambulance," he says), which takes the road for Abruzzo. Reaching the departure station of the funicular railway to Campo Imperatore, he finds temporary shelter in a nearby small villa, to be taken on 2 September to a height of 2112 metres, to the only hotel available.

---

* The book was issued in English later with varying titles. In New York the volume appeared as *The Fall of Mussolini*, while the longer British edition was *Memoirs, 1942-1943*.

He is assigned Apartment 201, with bedroom, bath, and sitting room, and he is also allowed a maid, a Lisetta Moscardi, residing in a nearby town.

The air is healthy, and the prison keepers—cordial, deferential, and attentive—grant his every request. He eats in the sitting room next to the bedroom, and always the same things: boiled rice, eggs, vegetables, and fresh fruit, all washed down with mineral water. In the afternoon, he takes a brief walk with Gueli, and at night, after his very frugal meal, he plays a card game with the inspector and his aides. If someone turns on the radio, as happens regularly, and mention is made of Hitler, Vittorio Emanuele, or Badoglio, he continues to play impassively, while the others anxiously cock an ear. He isn't even disturbed by the news that the King and his new Prime Minister have fled to Pescara, something which causes his guardians to fly into a panic (From whom would they get their orders now?).

One night, more than usually depressed, perhaps fearing that he might fall into enemy hands, he sends Lt. Faiola this note: "I will never submit to such an insult, and I beg you to send me your revolver." The officer rushes to his room, finds him in bed, wielding a shaving blade. The soldier snatches the blade violently, after which he demands all the objects with which the prisoner could hurt himself. Then the officer leaves, promising solemnly not to hand him over to the Allies.

In that pathetic performance, there is all the indolence of a man now tired of life, but too apathetic or too cynical to end it all. Nothing seems to interest him anymore, and in any case, if liberation were to jolt him from that torpor, it would also have the effect of putting him face to face with problems that he would not be able to resolve. As we shall see when Hitler, his destiny's referee, will put him in charge of the puppet state at Gargano.

The job of extricating him from his prison guards is entrusted by the Führer personally to General Student, flying ace of the German Air Force, organizer of the Parachutists' Corps, even if the honour for the operation, at least in the public's opinion, goes to Captain Otto Skorzeny, a huge Viennese, with a scarred face, and a great expert in commando action.

The kidnapping takes place on 12 September 1943, four days after the armistice signed at Cassibile by General Castellano representing Badoglio, and by his counterpart, Bedell Smith, head of the General Staff of Eisenhower, the Supreme Commander of Allied Forces in Europe.

Claretta as a toddler.

Claretta and her father, Dr. Francesco Saverio Petacci.

Mussolini in an Alfa Romeo in 1929, a gift from the carmaker.

Mussolini and female admirers.

Claretta and Riccardo on their wedding day
in Rome, 27 June 1934.

Claretta's painting, *La Strada Bianca* (1935/36).

Claretta in a large hat.

Claretta vacationing at Rimini in 1939.

Claretta, photographed by Elio Luxardo (1939).

Claretta in festive dress.

La Camilluccia, where the Petacci family lives,
from summer 1939.

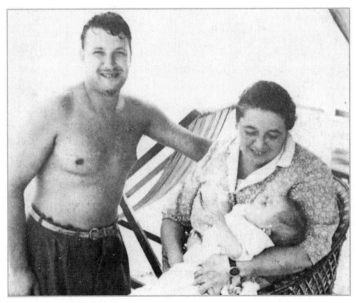

Marcello Petacci, and his mother Giuseppina Persichetti
holding Benvenuto, Marcello's first born son,
at Rimini in 1940.

Claretta at the piano (1940).

Mussolini riding a horse.

Mussolini on a motorcycle.

One of Claretta's letters to Mussolini.

The locket celebrating their meeting: Mussolini's gift
to Claretta, dated 24 April 1941.

Villa Fiordaliso, the Petacci family home,
beginning in autumn 1943.

A last photo of Claretta, September 1944.

Claretta's bedroom at Villa Fiordaliso.

The bedroom in which Claretta and Ben spend
their last night together.

A Revolver, Please

It is a very sunny Sunday which makes the action easier, perhaps, but also riskier, for the flight of the ten gliders and as many airplanes, with ninety parachutists on board, which had taken off from Pratica di Mare.

At the Gran Sasso, as Il Duce will mention in his memoirs, "reigned a strange atmosphere of uncertainty." The armistice had spread contradictory feelings of fears and hopes in the country. The move of the Royal Family, of Badoglio, and of so many high ranking officers of the General Staff to Brindisi, sneaking away from Rome the morning of 9 September, had all the appearances of a disgraceful flight, which is exactly what it was: a flight from responsibility and from the inevitable Nazi reprisals.

The descent is supposed to be a surprise, and a surprise it is. Landing on the stony plateau of Campo Imperatore, the Germans, machine guns and pistols in hand, rush towards the hotel while several Italian soldiers are readying two of their own machine guns from which no shots are fired. Running to the prisoner's room, Skorzeny presents himself: "Duce, my Führer has sent me to set you at liberty. You are free." "I knew that my friend Adolf Hitler would not abandon me," answers Mussolini, embracing him. But when he learns that his Ally wants him in Germany, he protests. "Captain, I feel an absolute need to remain here with my family." Skorzeny objects that the orders are to ferry him to Pratica di Mare, and from there to Vienna in a tri-motor plane.

The take-off is miraculous as the very small two-seater aircraft contains besides Il Duce and the pilot, the bulky SS officer who insists on climbing aboard. Only the exceptional ability of Captain Gerlach and perhaps, lots of luck, prevent the plane from crashing into the crag below.

After reaching Pratica di Mare, they switch to the more comfortable Heinkel that leaves for the Austrian Capital without delay. They land in the evening, receiving all the honours upon arrival.

From Vienna, the former prisoner is taken to Munich where his wife and the two youngest of his four children, Romano and Anna Maria, are waiting for him. One dramatic adventure is over. But a much more tragic one is about to begin.

Sixteen

The Little Slave

The trip from Rome to Meina is an exceptionally difficult one
for the Petacci family. The most exhausted of all is Claretta,
but even her sister and her parents seem worn out.

Armando, Miriam's husband, arrives in the Capital just as
they are leaving it. They know nothing of Marcello, and if this isn't
enough, they feel spied upon: the continuous visits by policemen
and Carabinieri in civilian clothes offering to carry secret messages to Il Duce confirm this for them. Actually, the intruders
merely wish to extract some information from them, something
that the Petacci family could not supply in any case.

Claretta keeps the radio turned on all the time in the hope of
hearing news of Ben, but Marshal Badoglio's instructions were
categorical: nothing, for whatever reason, is to leak out.

She does not leave the house, enclosing herself in her own
room to re-read what her lover wrote her in August and
September 1940, when he was worrying about her health. Even if
she does not know where to send them, she pens long missives
affirming her eternal love for him, declaring herself ready to die
for him, asking herself, and him, as was her fixation, if she was
being supplanted by some other woman: "My beloved Ben, I've no
ink and the town is far away and I can't wait to tell you about a
sudden thought that has overcome me violently since last night,
rushing the blood to my heart and taking my breath away. You will
say that there is nothing outside of this tragedy that has over-
turned the world, all things, existence itself and, above all, will
overwhelm the universe; but things don't end this way, and that is
certain, because I am, and thus I feel love, and therefore I live,
because of this ray of sunlight, this love which gives me the
strength to survive with a mad hope: I talk to you, I talk to you so
as not to go crazy, but I shall end badly nevertheless, even while
conquering the blackest pain and with the thought that I shall
draw you closer to me, especially in the ever-present memory of
every moment of your life and of our lives together ...[38]

"No, love conquers time, rises above it, dominates it, fills it, making it alive and worthy to be experienced. Forgive my worries, Ben. In me, in my head, is a double exposure, like a picture super-imposed on a negative by someone without any photographic skill, and all is an interplay of light and shadow that I succeed in deci-phering and disentangling, then everything becomes confused in a white cloud ... Sometimes, imagine how ridiculous I am, Ben, sometimes I am seized by a sudden jealousy, a sudden rebellion against all the women who've crossed my life of love, all the women who have taken from you what I considered to be mine alone, and many bouts of tears, of the hurt that you caused to my feelings, still tear apart my flesh and my spirit. How you made me cry, but how you could have made me entirely happy had you been satisfied with my devoted, pure, and complete love! Bitter hours that I shall never forget. Many tears fell leaving an indelible mark; others have remained hooked to my heart like the shaggy black claws of poisonous insects, and still today, in this drama, they take my breath away ...

"Why can't I be near you, Ben? Why don't they allow me to be with you, wherever you are? I'd even sleep on the floor, I'd do even the most menial of tasks, be your handmaiden, your drudge, any-thing so that I could see you, anything to be able to stay with you, also to share your torture with you, and to give you my tremen-dous, undying love as always! Ben, my love, let me come to you, let me stay on my knees before you, to look at you and to listen to your warm, singular voice. No one else in the world has your voice, your eyes, your hands. Call me to you, Ben: I am your little slave. Take my life, but don't suffer so much, don't feel so alone. My love is with you ...

"Pray, Ben, pray to Saint Rita—even you were once a believer—pray with me even if your outraged, gloomy and tormented spirit no longer believes in anything or in anyone. My beloved Ben, give me a sign of you, give me a sign of life, help me not to die. Without you, all is finished, everything ends, everything is spiritless, without light, without a reason why ... My love, for the love that you have felt for me and which, down deep, I think you still feel for me, a signal, just a word: I can't continue, I can't stand this anymore."

Only one thing did she want—and how she desired it!—to join him, no matter where he was. But who could help her? The German ambassador? The commander of the military police? She tries to get in touch with both, but each effort is useless: no one wants to hear her out.

Nothing happens for a week, other than the usual visits from the usual strange policemen. Then, one day, a captain of the Carabinieri shows up, requesting the passports of everyone. The documents are in proper order, but rather than giving them back, he asks their owners why they hadn't fled to Switzerland. They reply that they hadn't thought of that, having nothing to hide nor anything to be ashamed of. At this point, shaking his head and throwing his hands into the air, the officer leaves.

From that moment on, their surveillance becomes more acute to the point where Miriam decides to speak about this to a Roman friend, an officer in the Carabinieri. She telephones him, but as soon as he hears her voice, he says that he knows nothing about anything, and that there was nothing he could do for her and her family. Not only this: he warns her not to call again.

A short time later, Miriam herself learns that her husband has been arrested at the Grand Hotel where he usually stayed. It becomes clear at this point that, sooner or later, they would also suffer the same fate. Any excuse would have done very well, but that of "aggravated embezzlement and theft" seemed first-rate.

Aggravated embezzlement of what? Theft of what things? The warrant for the arrest sent to the Carabinieri of Meina by the Internal Affairs Minister doesn't make clear: the charge was vague. Details would be available only later.

This is what the trouble was about. The previous May, a certain Marchese Ugo Montagna who will re-emerge many years later implicated in the infamous Wilma Montesi scandal, had offered a pile of Persian carpets to the Petacci family for half a million lire. They weren't his, but of someone else who wanted to get rid of them. He was only the middleman, and would receive a commission. The deal was deemed to be a profitable one by Dr. Francesco Saverio and his wife—the merchandise seemed to be of quality and was also in good condition—therefore they decide to acquire the carpets. The payment was to be effected in various installments. But the collapse of 25 July, the hurried departure to Meina, and the pillage of La Camilluccia, prevented the issuing of regular payments.

At this point, Badoglio has no difficulty in passing off missed payments as theft, and proceeds to have the Petaccis arrested. And so, on the night of 12 August, St. Clare's Day, the usual captain of the Carabinieri, and some corporals, show up at Villa Boggiano with the order to bring them all to Novara. When Claretta asks the reason for this, he answers: "For a brief questioning, purely a formality." No one, at that moment, envisages jail, even if the unforeseen trip should have raised a few questions. Whether they wanted to or not, the Petacci family had no choice but to gather up a few of their things and do as they were told.

The only problem—not a simple matter to resolve—were the identity papers, other important documents, and above all, the thirty-six letters from Mussolini which Claretta was unwilling to let out of her sight no matter what the cost. The small purse containing the letters, held together by a pink ribbon, was not a safe place: in case of a search, the rummaging would begin there, before any place else.

Miriam suggests that they be left at Meina in a hidden case, but Claretta doesn't want to hear any of this: the letters and the pendant she wore around her neck with its inscription "Clara, I am yours, you are mine, Ben," were the only things of his she had left in her possession, his only momentoes. Since keeping them in the purse was risky, why not hide them in Sig.ra Giuseppina's dress?

Arriving in Novara in the middle of the night, they are directed to the Carabinieri barracks for the "brief questioning, purely a formality." But this turns out to be neither brief, nor pure. After a half hour they are shoved into a large "filthy" room, then taken to another room where mother and daughters are to be searched.

A woman tells them to take their clothes off, a request that Sig.ra Giuseppina executes reluctantly, both because of natural modesty, and fear that the letters would be seized upon discovery. This, in fact, happens.

Silent and powerless, Claretta has to witness the cruel confiscation: she'd rebel, but she understood that to do so would worsen her position, and that of her sister and parents.

From the barracks they are taken to the local jail, an old, run-down castle of the Visconti era, where they are searched again with the same crudeness as previously. Besides their clothes, their watches, their wedding rings, even their fountain pens are confiscated. This time Claretta does not restrain herself, which brings down upon her the violent reactions of the warden who tells her menacingly to be quiet.

In the meantime, the alarm bell had sounded so that instead of being moved back to their cells, they are sent to the bomb shelter already filled with the other detainees: hundreds of dirty, smelly, sleepy men and woman, of varying ages.

Claretta feels such disgust that she requests to be permitted to go up to the overhanging staircase landing, across a stairway from the putrid detention room, and containing a small window. While she is here, daydreaming, thinking about the sky full of stars (the date is August 12), a bomb explodes a few hundred metres away. She is overcome by the resulting rush of air that hurls her against a wall, causing her to roll down the stairs. She loses consciousness as a result of the blow, and it is not easy to bring her to. When the alarm sounds ending the emergency, with her father holding her around the waist, he leads her up to the threshold of the room.

Crossing this with Miriam and her mother, she is stricken with horror: how could she live in that three-metre square mouse warren, walls corroded by mildew and by humidity, with a very low ceiling, the floor fissured with cracks, ideal nooks for mice and cockroaches? In the corner, a filthy toilet with a single roll of coarse toilet paper and two folding cots, more like litters for animals than suitable for human bedding, lean against a wall.

As soon as the guard leaves, Claretta breaks into tears because of disgust with the revolting shelter, because Ben is far away and she has no news of him, and also because she feels responsible for her family's present situation. "I am the one who got you into so much trouble; I am the cause of your suffering" she'd repeat desperately, while her sister and her mother try to free her of that absurd feeling of guilt.

Finally, she quietens down and tries to fall asleep, without removing her clothes, with her head on her fur coat which she's folded in two like a cushion, but when dawn breaks and the rays of the rising sun strike her eyes, she stirs back to her surroundings. She sleeps badly for a short while only, and when she wakens, her first thought is to search through the pockets of her fur coat, looking for a pencil, miraculously having escaped the seizures. She has a great need to write and take up her diary, but where to find paper? She could ask the jailer, but after what happened, he would surely refuse.

The only writing surface she can use is the toilet tissue and, since necessity is the mother of invention, she appropriates it for such a purpose for the entire period of her detention, confiding there her personal thoughts, her own fears, and her hopes.

"My bones get weary," she will note in one of the beginning pages. "My kidneys bother me. My back is entirely bruised. I don't look like a human being anymore. We're afraid to look at each other. Fever grips me. Mama is not well. Mimi seems in a daze.[39] We'll die in here ..."

Apart from the filth and the stomach-turning rations, the

guards do everything to poison the lives of the prisoners. Not only do they seize their furs the second day, but they warn the food distributor not to refrigerate the milk, the only sustenance that the heart-ailing Sig.ra Giuseppina can consume. Then the toilet breaks down, and the three women suffer for an entire week before someone condescends to fix it (the smell is such that the plumber has to don a gas mask).

If only Dr. Francesco Saverio were able to be with them! And yet, they are not even allowed to see him during the half hour outside—from three to three-thirty in the afternoon—that the warden had ruled that the women could be in the yard after the men had re-entered. All this made the detention even more cruel.

The prison guards watch their every move from the ramparts and, from time to time, they even say a word or two to them. One day, a guard tosses a bunch of grapes to the women, only to follow this action quickly with scolding words: "What do you know, they're millionaires, they eat what they like because they can pay." Claretta is forced to stifle her anger with some difficulty, replying that the grapes are for her mother.

A graver crisis than the usual ones—remembers Miriam— overcomes Sig.ra Giuseppina in the shelter on another night. "My father was with the men, a few steps away, but to have him rush in, Claretta and I had to beg the King's public prosecutor and Celia, the captain of the Carabinieri who were in that cellar. They give their permission only when they fear that my mother might die, from one minute to the next, right under their eyes.

"This was a dreadful moment. My mother was as white as a sheet, and hardly breathing; Claretta and I were holding her hands while tears flowed down our cheeks. Near us, Father Pozzetto was praying; and all the internees, on their knees, joined in. In the dim light of the dungeon, the sing-songy voices had a tragic, hopeless sound. A young girl had an attack of hysteria, and she had to be taken away bodily. Then finally, they called my father. He gave mama some injections and, little by little, the crisis passed."

Even Claretta and Miriam did not feel well, although they were only slight, temporary ailments. Miriam had trouble with her stomach, and Claretta was affected by migraines, brought on by the humidity in the cell. Seated on a straw mat, roll of toilet paper on her knees, the dictator's mistress recorded fastidiously what was happening in the jail, and in her very self. "Oh, Ben, my soul, today (31 August) I can't control my tears and burst out into sobs, without having anymore strength. I fear, I am afraid that I shall go crazy. Fifteen days ago we asked for things with which to cover ourselves, to change clothes. Nothing came. Today they had the housekeeper in here, but they did not let us see her. She brought two sweaters, and two kerchiefs surreptitiously; the nun sneaked them in to us later."

She rages against "that old blockhead traitor," the King, and "that damned" Badoglio, source of so much trouble for her and for her family, and for Ben for whose health her mother, her sister, and she pray every night.

Gradually, as the days slip by, she asks herself for how many more days would she rot in that filthy jail. And if they would all be tried. But for what crimes? For having supported Fascism? For having believed in its Leader? Because she'd loved him?

One day, a guard tells her that she's been condemned to death, something that does not seem to disturb her in the least. The same night, in fact, she'll note in her diary, technically directed to Ben: "With the speed of thought and imagination that you know in me, while I listen, I see what is happening around me, and I think about and record what might happen ... I will not allow them to blindfold me, that is certain, and I shall yell so loud that all will hear 'For my Duce, my one and only love.' "

And so, the 8th of September comes, and the expected armistice that Claretta greets as the worst of abominations: "This is the end, the very end! The second collapse after the 25th of July. Eternal dishonour! Infamy! There was only one Man who could have discussed peace: YOU. And where are you? What are they doing to you? What will they do to you? Where are they holding you? They will hand you over to the English, I feel it, I feel it. That's the shameful pact, the infamy ... Damned!"

Confusion and perturbation reign in the jail: orders and counter orders cross each other, the warden not knowing which way to turn, the custodians whom to obey, the internees are creating disturbances, cursing, threatening, and throwing their cots against the walls. At a certain point, a rumour is rife that the Germans are in the area, and in a short time they would take over the prison.

When things settle down, she sends a heartfelt message to the Germans through the intermediary of a religious sister and a Salesian monk. "I understand and believe I heard that other Fascists have been released ... How about us? Why are they still hiding us here? Is it possible that the Chief of the local

The Little Slave

Constabulary is going to play a final dirty trick on us?"

That night she falls asleep very disturbed, and for the entire night she is assailed by nightmares. "I had a long dream of you, but you were deceiving me and you didn't want me anymore. You were doing so with a certain 'Bianca Biancardi,' in fact, a strange name, a non-Italian one, and I was told that you saw her everyday. Then I understood why I didn't hear from you, why you weren't helping me to get out of this place. But in the previous dream, however, I saved your life by putting my hand at the discharge point of a gun, and I was wounded. This was during a sort of a great gathering in a small theatre made over into a hall. Soon afterward, I speak to you and I tell you 'I am going to the hospital,' and you answer me 'Go, I'll join you soon.' And while you are talking, your wedding ring falls off your finger, and you put it back on right away. Then they tell me that you are having a tryst with this person. In essence, Ben, I cried, oh how I cried! I woke up in tears. Everything was really over for me. Everything ..."

And, all day she is sad, as she'd never been before, since the beginning of her incarceration in that squalid prison. What if another woman had really taken her place? Had she only become a memory for him, she who "for twelve years" (really only seven) had been his "possession?" She didn't want to think about this since "the intertwined strands" of their "souls" were "an undeniable and clear reality." But the doubt persists: only "HE" could disperse this, soothing the fury that was torturing her, reconfirming his love for her, and vowing everlasting loyalty. Ah, if "transformed into a white swan, like the very sweet Lohengrin," she could swoop down on him and "snatch him" away, "while the divine prelude to Act One accompanied their "liberation!" But even this was a dream that would never come to pass.

The day of her liberation was approaching, however, and her hopes begin to rise when she reads in a newspaper given to her secretly by a detainee that Ben is safe, and that he is in Germany with Hitler, his friend.

The release from jail was not an easy one, in any case. And, if it hadn't been for Marcello, also imprisoned, but who had made a daring escape, who knows how much longer the wait would have been! The young man, with the help of Boggiano, freed after fifty days, had presented himself to the German Command, asking for, and obtaining, freedom for his family.

That night Claretta will write on a sheet of real paper. "We get out, pale and trembling, not having to climb again the grimy, dark stairs. As soon as we are outside, amidst tears, and as if in a cloud, we see Marcello. He seems to have grown smaller and he is pale and ashen. We hug each other while sobbing. When mama embraces him, Marcello points to the dark, slim German officer who is also moved, but stands apart, saying, 'He's the one you should kiss, mama. If it weren't for them, you would not have come out of here again ...'

"Marcello tells us that orders to free us were issued five days before, and that the Carabinieri were not giving us our freedom while waiting for orders from Rome for our execution. They hoped to get the job done first, or at least to succeed in keeping me as a hostage, and they were working very hard towards that contemptible goal. They wanted to send me to Badoglio, the pig, by air, or put me on display at so many dollars per viewing, or for some other unknown reasons! So, just in the nick of time! "

On coming out, they find themselves confronted by a small crowd, gathered together, according to Claretta, by the wife of the chief guard, "a treacherous, sharp-tongued hag," to deride and insult them (but not a single voice is raised against them, perhaps because of the German presence).

They go by car to the German Command set up in a city school where they are fed prosciutto sandwiches, anchovies, and served glasses of spumante. After this, they head out to the lodgings that the liberators have put at their disposal.

Il Duce's lover settles into a double bed with her sister, but neither of them sleep for the entire night. Claretta can only talk of Ben, certain at last that she'll be able to kiss him again soon. The next afternoon, still by car, they leave Novara, heading for Merano in the Alto Adige, to Marcello's castle.

Before departing, Claretta had sought news of her lover, but she finds out nothing more than she already knows: that he is in Germany, under the Führer's protection, and that he would return to Italy soon. Therefore, she still has to wait, after almost two months of absence, thirty-seven days of imprisonment (from 12 August to 17 September), and that atrocious suffering. But what else could she do?

The car breaks down on the road between Bergamo and Brescia, forcing the driver to try to get help from the nearby airport at Ghedi. While waiting for the repairs, the passengers are accompanied to a shack where they sit on makeshift benches (they are even given cognac). Seeming to be a bit tired and seeing a cot, Claretta lies down. In a corner, an old radio plays marches and other rousing music.

Suddenly, the music stops, and a deep voice announces a transmission from Munich where Mussolini is about to deliver his first speech since his liberation.

Leaping with a yell from the temporary bed, Claretta runs to the radio, which she hugs, almost wanting to snatch the voice from it. How it had been long since she'd heard that voice, and how she'd missed it! Now she knew that Ben was safe as she had the undeniable proof. That she didn't collapse because of emotion was only thanks to the cardiotonic opportunely given to her by her father.

The repairs to the car being completed, the group is able to get back on its travels towards Merano where they arrive at dawn.

But Marcello's castle, requisitioned by the Germans, was locked, and the keys couldn't be found, and because of this, it was necessary to go to the German Command. The Germans pledge to move out as soon as possible. In the meanwhile, the Petacci family settles in the Parco Hotel. "Miriam and I are overcome to see a bed with clean sheets and soft pillows," Claretta will write in her diary. "Casting off our dresses almost breathlessly, we get into it. Ah, Ben, I'll relive that moment for the rest of my life, when under my bruised and hurting back, I feel the soft, supple mattress; when my head, all painful and hurting, sinks into the feather pillows; when on my naked, dry skin, I feel the light and fresh caress of the linen and, turning my eyes, no bars, nor flaking walls, but a window with fluffy curtains and the sun streaming through the lace.

"Ben, my soul, you don't know, and I will never be able to tell you what pangs of emotion, what dreamlike sensations, after a few hours of physical and spiritual relaxation, hot water and a bath. My dry and dusty curls, my harsh gray skin, and the blessing of hot water that soothes my poor, thinned, small, tormented limbs. Oh, Ben of mine! And then ... breakfast in bed; warm eggs with ham! And fresh bread!

"Mimi and I were looking at each other like two shivering sparrows helped by a charitable person. We hugged each other while crying, and saying: 'Mimi, it's true, we're safe, the evil things are over, we are safe, are really safe, safe, we're not dreaming! The torture is over; we're still alive! Thank you, thank you God. For him, for us, thanks!'"

The Petaccis stay at Merano for a few weeks, weeks that were neither restful nor serene. Actually, besides the sad news emanating from Rome—Dr. Francesco Saverio's mother had died, and La Camilluccia had undergone an umpteenth break-in—the new German commander, the lanky General Wolff, augured nothing good. He was one of those laconic officers, suspicious and authoritarian, who only see their own way of doing things and who want to impose this on others, no matter what.

When he summons Claretta to the hotel lobby, she couldn't imagine, even distantly, what he was going to ask her to do: that was to try to convince Mussolini to have Ciano, his son-in-law, extradited to Italy.[40] Only in this way—according to Wolff—could the former Minister of Foreign Affairs be tried and condemned to the penalty that the furious Hitler deemed absolutely necessary and worthy for the "treason" of 25 July. Who better than she—asks the important officer at this point—the dictator's intimate friend, to be able to succeed in this very difficult task?

Claretta listens to him for a few minutes, then she interrupts him dryly: "I must remind you that my relations with Il Duce are of a personal and private nature. If the government of the Reich desires to inform him of something, why aren't the usual avenues used?"

Wolff objects that personal channels are much more useful, but the woman reiterates her personal unwillingness to do this, adding categorically: "I'm not in Germany's service, and even if I could influence Il Duce, I wouldn't do it." At which the angry general rises and leaves.

From that moment on everything becomes more complicated for her, even the secretive meetings with her lover whom she finally sees again soon afterwards at Lake Garda.

As always, with eyes only for each other, hand in hand as before, they spend "marvelous" hours together telling each other what had happened since the last phone call on the day after the Grand Council meeting.

But Ben was no longer himself. He'd lost his old self-confidence and in his appearance, it was possible to read only a deep sorrow and nostalgia for a time that would never return.

Seventeen

The Unwilling Mayor

H itler almost didn't recognize Mussolini when the latter went to Rastenburg, the Führer's General Headquarters, from Munich. The man before him was only a shadow, a pathetic spectre, of that Duce that he'd admired so much, and for so many years. He was now a pale man, thin, with a vacant look, devoid of ambition, and with only one desire: to retire from public life, to finally bring down the curtain on a glorious, but now buried past.

But it was too late. From the whirlwind that he'd created himself, he would never emerge. From that prison whose bars he had put up, he would never escape. And to keep him from actually doing so would be Hitler, his old friend.

Because of the Führer's headstrong wish, he would have to return to his former post, but not to recapture his previous power, now irrevocably lost. He would still be called Duce, but even better, at the official level, he would enjoy an absolute double, prestigious title: not merely Head of Government, but also Head of State. The part of Italy not yet in enemy hands would become a republic, in fact.

Before saying goodbye to him, Hitler tells him in a tone that would not permit any excuses, that the conspirators of 25 July were to pay for their betrayal with their lives. And, above all, Ciano was to suffer the consequences as well.

Mussolini had been on his guard against raising objections and, running into his son-in-law, he'd done his best to hide his personal quandary.

However, Rachele was violently against the former Foreign Affairs Minister. "If I see him, I'll spit in his face," she threatened. "Il Duce is not a piece of furniture that can be placed in the attic when someone gets tired of it."

All in all, from the beginning at Rastenburg, it was clear that the Head of Fascism, or rather what was left of Fascism, would no longer be giving any orders, but he would be receiving them. Hitler would now be the Chief, he the servant.

There was nothing to do but to make the best of things, and to draw up a semblance of a government, like an Italian Quisling, recruiting members from the remaining faithful of the now defunct Regime. This was a task that showed itself quickly to be almost hopeless since most declined any post, finding various reasons, either because of fear, or due to skepticism.

The task of choosing a Capital for the new "Republic," called rather controversially "social," because it was founded on socialistic ideas, was not less difficult. Amongst the various towns considered, Gargano on Lake Garda finally prevailed. On returning from Rocca delle Caminate, he moved quietly into one of the many requisitioned villas (the new State was called "di Salò", since that was the name of the main town on the Brescian side of the Lake).

His residence, which bore the name of Feltrinelli, its owners, even if it didn't compare with the grandeur of Villa Torlonia, was amongst Gargano's most renowned houses. Built in the late nineteenth century, decorated with stained glass windows and columns, possessing an olive grove, and facing the Lake, it also had a landing pier for small boats, and a jetty protected by an anti-aircraft battery unit. The marble floors and the wood paneled walls gave the inside a solemn appearance and, perhaps because of this, the Mussolini family never felt at ease there.

At the beginning, the building served as his office, as well as his private residence. Later the office was moved to the Villa of the Ursulines, also owned by the Feltrinellis.

As his office, Il Duce chooses the largest room, with a terrace overlooking the Lake, and as a desk, a walnut table previously standing by one of the walls, which he has moved to a corner, as at Palazzo Venezia.

Here, or more probably at Villa Feltrinelli, he receives Claretta a number of times before his wife and children join him in November of the same year. La Petacci requests to be close to him, but he tries to dissuade her: their relationship—he says—is on everybody's lips by now, and her move to Lake Garda would be bait for too much gossip.

Not only this. The Fascists who had followed him to the Lake, instigated by Rachele no less, wanted him to get rid of her, "the source of so many problems" (there were even those who talked of her connivance with the Germans, or worse, with the Anglo-Americans and the Partisans).

Claretta answers that these allegations were all lies, that she was the only one who loved him, and that he should rely solely on her. Then she'd burst into tears, begging him again to keep her with him. In the end he gives way, setting only one condition: that she not live in Gargano where she would be recognized too easily.

Radiant, she calls Buffarini Guidi, the Interior Minister, so that he might help her find a house (Miriam maintains that she approached Wolff instead).

At the beginning, the choice falls on a small residence on a hill on the other side of the Lake, in the town of Malcesine. But after a visit to the spot, the building is rejected because it is too secluded and too far from Gargano (eighty kilometres by road, more than one hour by car). She prefers Villa Fiordaliso, four kilometres from the Capital.

This is a three-story building, bordering on one side a villa that Vittorio, the Duce's second son will move into, and with the Lake on the other side. The house, which was surrounded by a vast garden, was owned by Polenghi, the industrialist, who had furnished it in the baroque style.

The Petacci family install themselves on the ground floor and first floor of the structure, the upper story being occupied by German workers. Naturally, Claretta takes the nicest room where she puts up some of the items she'd brought with her from Rome (amongst other things, the picture with Ben's dedication that she'd carry in her purse when she went out, fearing thieves).

Even if welcoming, the villa is not comparable to La Camilluccia, but of what importance is that now? The house was close to her man and, although she couldn't see him every day, talk to him every day, or every day declare her love to him, even if the secret of this house would be broken and become common knowledge, the dream had not vanished, even with so many nightmares and tears. Fate had decreed that to rebel against its occult laws would only make things worse. Better accept them and hope for a better future.

She also saw, actually she more than others, that her Ben was only a mere shade of his former self. Deprived of the power that he loved so much, and from which he'd enjoyed so much, what was left him now? No more wildly applauding crowds; no more flashy parades; no more pompous interviews; nothing more of anything. Only memories, sweet and overpowering ones, remembered in a Lilliputian lakeside town, within the walls of a gloomy, bare office, without even a direct telephone line.

Not having seen him since the spring of 1943, when Miriam meets him again, she feels a sudden sadness. "He seemed to have lost weight, he'd become old and tired, but what was most striking was his expression. Something had gone out of his eyes, and a type of dark resignation—so unlike him—mixed with despondency in his features. Only when he talked did he become the Mussolini of the past; gradually his self-confidence re-appearing in his eyes, and this was transmitted to the person with whom he was speaking. And then, inadvertently, the impression returned that, perhaps, everything was not over, that maybe there was still some hope.

"It is possible that Mussolini infused himself with courage while speaking, but, without doubt, he passed this on to others as well … He didn't hide his personal disappointments though his tone was very far from the optimistic stance of the official press … 'I've been reduced to the level of a podestà [mayor] of Gargano,' he'd say with bitter irony, referring to the Germans who were doing everything to isolate him and to hold him prisoner. He remained at his post only because this was one way to prevent northern Italy from sharing Poland's fate."

He was now an idol thrown off his pedestal, defrauded by his own myth, who for the first time had no more belief in himself, an involuntary victim of a fate now suffering its punishment.

But far from having a chilling effect, or merely cooling down Claretta's heart, this actually speeded it up. Until now, she had needed him. Now, even he needed her.

Ben no longer possessed that arrogant sureness that had fired her up so much, subjugating her to her adolescent fantasies. By now he was a spent hero, admitting his personal failures, feeding himself on regrets, having no more ambitions, and not sitting on any more hopes, either for himself or for anyone else.

In this wreck without goals or redemption, once again, though more than ever, Claretta sees her very own man. If the idol has fallen, being the upright and passionate Vestal that she was, she would maintain his cult, until death and beyond.

In any case, they see each other ever more infrequently, sometimes weeks going by without meeting, and every time they had to resort to the most unthinkable subterfuge.

At sunset, Mussolini would leave his office, and would re-enter the villa's bunker by a service entrance. Then, crossing a garden, he'd climb into his car, destination the Vittoriale, where d'Annunzio's tower was placed at his disposal. This was a round building with single rooms one above the other, linked by a winding staircase.

They were brief meetings, filled with bitter outbursts, faint remembrances, and long silences. She would go up to him joyously, throwing her arms around his neck, steering him towards the sofa near the window overlooking Lake Garda. In his threadbare, shabby suit, without stripes, he'd follow her like a robot.

He'd sit beside her and he'd tell her what he'd done, whom he'd seen, the voice feeble, eyes lost in space, his unmoving hands between her warm, pulsating ones which try, in vain, to instill a little hope in him.

Returning home, she'd recopy on her quality paper the words she'd confided the previous day to a piece of loose leaf at the wharf. "Dear Ben. I dream about us. I dream of white clouds above us, spotless clouds; the wind that touches them, also touches your somewhat tired eyelids, touches your delicate essence! I am reading these verses under a clear light-blue crystal sky, and all of d'Annunzio is reflected in this transparent Lake, which looks like silver, as in a delicate pastel painting. D'Annunzio announces, forecasts sunshine, and light perhaps for our great, tormented, incomparable Italy. I am lying down on the wooden walkway of the wharf, only as wide as my body. Above me is the sky and the Lake is under me, the Lake with its incessant rhythms, continuous, now easy, now strong, slow, even, reminding me of the sea, our divine sea. I look upward with the rays of the sun in my eyes. I see blue beyond the pine branches extending their limbs open to the sky; the tops perfect, shining in the sun, white, very pure, swaying like the promise of an evanescent dream. A high cloud passes slowly, swollen, and with a touch of color, cutting off the top. To be floating between heaven and Lake is sweet and good."

But how much was left of all this? How long would the fantastic vision last? The time to look up to the sky, to look deeply into the waters of the Lake, throw together these few lines, make a fair copy of them, stuff the sheet into an envelope, give it to a messenger? Then reality would carry her off once again, entrapping her in her treacherous noose.

The routine was daunting: hours that never passed in the leaden sitting room of Villa Fiordaliso, with its walls covered with crimson brocade; it's gold-colored, coffered ceiling; and outside, the trees, the Lake, a wearisome and monotonous silence. Her mother Giuseppina, always more sick; her father Francesco, quiet and far-away in his armchair; Miriam who traveled back and forth from Milan; and Marcello with his grandiose, chimerical projects: to save Mussolini, Fascism, and Italy. And over everything, the oppressive shadow, the frightened spectre of "Him."

To get away from these feelings and to improve her moods, Claretta would take long walks with SS officer Franz Spoegler, from the Alto Adige. He was a young man of twenty-eight, of severe appearance, but well-mannered, eager and affable, who was living in a small room on the upper floor, and who had been placed in her company by the German Command to spy on her.

They become friends quickly, going fishing together, she opening her heart to him day after day, making him her confidante. One of the few, along with mother Giuseppina, and Miriam.

Every so often she meets one of her old friends, is visited by Buffarini Guidi who continues to keep a foot in both camps, dividing his time between the mistress and the wife of the Capo.

A large part of the time she spends alone, however, under the illusion that the great wheel of life will turn again to become what it was. But then ruthless, bitter reality seizes the upper hand again: "I live as a hermit. Outside the doors of the house, I realize that no one would be able to understand me or would want to listen to me. To avoid the worst, I go out at night as bats do and hide in a cave until dawn breaks. Out of one hundred persons that I pass on the street, at least ninety would want me dead and everybody says that they would do it for him, so that in this way he could save himself."

She is not mistaken as Rachele assures us in her memoirs. "Exasperated by the situation, I had to take care to stop the impulses of many loyal persons who offered either to abduct the Petacci woman, or to eliminate Buffarini, or of some of the German notables ... Actions of this sort were devised by members of the *Decima Mas*, led by Prince Valerio Borghese, by the 'Young Republicans,' and by the officers and Militia of the Duce's bodyguard."

At the end of 1943, these threats induce Claretta to move temporarily to Merano where her sister and her parents were celebrating Christmas with Zita and Marcello. Before leaving, she invites Ben to join her, and he promises to do so. Then however, not only does he not come along, but he asks her not to return to the Lake before better times are re-established. At this she rebels: "No. I shall not remain far away. Don't you remember what I've been through for you? I was in jail, I was insulted, I am hated, and some people want to kill me."

Before too long she begins to suspect that there's another woman, that Ben doesn't love her anymore and that he is planning to replace her: her nightmare, her usual terror. With the holiday season over, against the wishes of the Capo, she is once again in Gardone, actually to ensure herself that he is not deceiving her.

One afternoon after sunset, Ben calls her and she unburdens herself at length. He was more dejected then ever, but he doesn't tell her the reason. Just at that time, the fate of his son-in-law, prisoner at Verona, in the eighteenth century convent-jail of the Carmelites, along with the five other "traitors" of 25 July who had not managed to escape, was being decided.

After some months in Germany, apparently free, but in reality under very close surveillance by the Führer's police, Ciano was sent back to Italy, precisely to Verona, and here he fell into the hands of the "Republicans." As we've seen, the one to demand the extradition was Hitler, livid against the nineteen Grand Council members who had booted out the Regime. The Führer demanded an exemplary punishment, something that only his Ally could inflict legally.

The German request was seconded vigorously by the Fascist Party and by Pavolini, its fanatical secretary. No leniency for those who'd knifed the Duce in the back: the perpetrators were to pay with their lives, and at the earliest possible moment, their action being more wicked since this move was against a man who had loaded them up with honours and benefits.

Mussolini found himself between the anvil of fatherly love (he adored Edda) and the hammer of State law. Then there was also Hitler's justice and that of the extreme "Republicans," hostile to any act of clemency.

Claretta helped accentuate his anxiety. In a state of fear, just at that time she writes to him. "Ben of mine. I've had a terrible night. Nightmares, fears, blood, ruin. Amongst the human and monstrous faces stood out Ciano's, in a red cloud. Ben, save the man. Show Italians that you are still master of your will. Probably destiny will be kinder to us then ... I await you soon and I hold you tightly to my heart." But in the light of what happens, he doesn't reply.

Instead, his son-in-law answers. "Signora, Frau Betz spoke to me, and your Christmas thought succeeds in moving me.[41] But this can't be all. The accusation, the arrest and worse will be nothing if I am not permitted to prove that I acted honourably, and performed my duty. You are the only person in the world who can affect the sentence. Let the trial come quickly; the verdict is already decided, but I shall let everyone know the truth, especially him. I am not defending my life, but the name of my father who honoured Italy, and that of my children, his grandchildren, so that the day will never come when they are pointed out as the children of a traitor."

Having read the message, Claretta sought to see Mussolini immediately, a meeting that she will recall later this way. "Ben was destroyed. His eyes rolled in their sockets, and often he covered his face with his hands. 'I can do nothing, nothing,' he kept repeating. 'A bloody orgy is being organized around me, and I cringe at the thought that someone awaits the dawn of execution as something festive.' He would shake his head and repeat: 'Think about it, just think about it. Galeazzo ... the father of my little grandchildren. ... Even in other cases they tried to force me to agree to capital punishment. I always refused, and when it happened, I swear before God, it happened without my knowledge.'"

Was he right? Was he lying? Up to what point could he oppose the Führer's will and that of his own powerful followers? What would have happened had he resisted a sentence not yet carried out, but about whose outcome no one had any doubts? There are those who contend that he would have saved his own life had he intervened, at least for his son-in-law. But there are also those who allege that the dice had been cast, by now—Hitler's, naturally—and that all he could do was to carry out the sentence.

The debate is still on as to whether the requests for clemency for the five condemned to death did or did not reach his desk. Assuming that he did not receive them, he could not but be aware of what was being carried out. He was still Il Duce, even if Hitler had weakened him, and the extremists of Salò were throwing monkey wrenches into his wheels.

If this matter had depended solely on him, such a sentence would not have been carried out after Edda's threatening letter. "Duce. I've waited until today for you to show me a minimum of human feeling and friendship. It is too much now. If Galeazzo is not in Switzerland within three days according to the conditions that I have worked out with the Germans, all that I know, with proof in hand, I shall use without pity.[42] In other words, if we are left in peace and safety (from tuberculosis to car accidents) you will no longer hear speak of us."

But the sentence on which he had to yield no longer depended on him, and this was a terrible blow, the worst after the death of his brother Arnaldo and of his son Bruno.

On the eve of the execution that took place on the morning of

11 January 1944, he didn't sleep a wink, and he didn't want to see anyone. He remained by himself in his bedroom seeking to read or to write, but he was able to do neither, his mind obsessively turning to the drama that was about to take place.

He gets the official announcement from Dolfin, his secretary, in the Villa of the Ursulines, a short time after the platoon had carried out the sentence. He does not flinch, makes no comment, and does not touch any food. At supper, he limits himself to a little fruit, and he goes to bed earlier than usual, without saying a word.

Claretta waits in vain for a telephone call from him, but perhaps for the first time she understands his silence and she forgives him. Even she is disturbed greatly by the killing of Galeazzo, because even she abhorred violence and she feared the devastating psychological effect that this would have on Ben, something that did happen, in fact.

When they see each other again, she finds him gloomier and more demoralized than ever. He tells her that he is a destroyed man, and he urges her to flee to Switzerland or to Spain with her family while there is still time. This raises in her large and fragile heart for the umpteenth time the suspicion that he has ceased to love her, or worse, that he loves someone else.

The visit to Villa Fiordaliso a few weeks later (it was the end of February 1944) of Eugenio Apollonio, the Chief of Staff and the head of the police, seemed more or less to be confirmation of this tremendous, but unfounded, fear.

According to the story related by the high public servant to Silvio Bertoldi, being embarrassed by the presence of the Petacci family at the Lake, Mussolini orders that they be arrested and moved to Merano. One night at about ten, Apollonio presents himself to Claretta and her family to carry out the order, but everyone beginning with the Duce's mistress refuses to comply with it. He threatens, then, to have them removed forcibly, and only after five hours of heated discussion is a compromise reached: Claretta and her family would leave Gardone, but "spontaneously," and without escort.

Whether this evidence is true or false, Sig.ra Giuseppina, her husband, and Miriam will soon say "ciao" to Lake Garda. The indomitable Claretta chooses to remain on that shore. And, on 29 July, while her man is meeting with Hitler, survivor of an attempt on his life by Colonel Stauffenberg, she will live through horrible hours, and only after he returns to Gargano and he calls her will she calm down. "At last! I'm so glad to hear your voice again, Ben. You don't know how much I've missed you."

"I would have wanted to call you from Germany as I'd promised you, but it was impossible for me to do that."

"I waited anxiously for your call, but instead of that I got the terrible news of the attempted assassination. I shuddered at the thought of the risk that you were exposed to. What a horrible, monstrous thing! Certainly Hitler was helped by surprising luck."

"I'd say miraculous. According to him, this was a sign of special protection on the part of Providence. He was very calm, and he extolled his luck and his destiny. But the fact that an attempt of that type took place in his Headquarters has surprised me very much."

"It was treachery."

"Now the Germans will no longer be able to talk only of the Italian betrayal. Perhaps because of this, Hitler agreed to all my requests."

"I'm happy about that. But you still have piles of things to tell me. About the trip..."

"Yes, but let me get to work now. I shall come to visit you tomorrow."

"Okay. I can't wait to see you again."

Eighteen

Miss, or What?

The autumn of 1944 was a sad one for Claretta. Things were going steadily worse, Il Duce seemed more discouraged then ever, and German pressures were becoming much heavier. The Fascist extremists continued to rail and to intrigue against the favourite with the aim of inducing Mussolini to release himself from her "nefarious" influence.

Even Rachele was getting excited (although without resorting to the unfair and hateful weapon of defamation) and when Nino Martini, one of her faithful supporters, a small industrialist from the Romagna who had moved to the banks of Lake Garda, mentions to her the existence of secret photostats made by La Petacci of some of her husband's letters, she decides to unmask her rival.

According to Martini, Claretta was being watched not only by the Germans through Spoegler and various gadgets of control and interception, but also by the Anglo-Americans through one of their own men, presumably working as a waiter in a trattoria in Torri del Benaco. The goal of the one and of the others was to learn Mussolini's disposition and his plans, which La Petacci knew, thanks to the letters that he wrote to her regularly.

Always according to Martini, Claretta would give a copy of these letters to the Germans, a second copy she'd mail outside the country, but she'd keep the original for herself.

One day, Rachele rushes into her husband's office with her own informer, and he comes out, or pretends to come out of his dream world. The scene was tempestuous and painful. Provoked by Rachele, Martini spills the beans: Rachele rails against Claretta and her man (actually the man of both); the very annoyed Duce, tries to calm down his wife, setting himself the task of shedding some light on the matter, and of teaching his mistress a lesson. In fact, as soon as his wife and her friend leave, he calls in Emilio Bigazzi Capanni, the chief constable, and orders him to search Villa Fiordaliso.

Accompanied by the same Martini, by a public security officer, and by the two guards, Musella and Mosca, the group leaves quickly for Gardone. Reaching the villa, they are admitted by the maid to the living room on the ground floor where they wait for Claretta who is on the floor above.

She is still in her dressing gown, her head wrapped in a rose-colored turban, and wearing men's slippers. After a quick and formal exchange of greetings, she asks Bigazzi the reason for this unexpected visit. The constable tells her that he'd been ordered there by the Duce personally, and with a very specific goal. When he is asked what that might be, Bigazzi replies, "To seize your correspondence with the Head of Government, along with the cards, the books and the photographs that you received from him."

"This is too much," replies a bewildered Claretta, "I can't imagine such a thing. What pictures are you talking about? There are no photographs of his letters … Word of honour, I never thought of having photographs taken of Mussolini's letters."

Since the public servant insists, she goes to the telephone and calls her lover. The switchboard operator answers that Mussolini is extremely busy and that he does not want to be disturbed. At this, first she bursts into tears, then she runs up the stairs, and locks herself in her bedroom. After a moment of perplexity, the head policeman and the three other men follow. But the door is bolted from the inside, and therefore the only way to breach it is with vigorous pushes.

Claretta is standing by a mirror, pointing a Beretta 7.65 at the intruders. Bigazzi jumps on her to disarm her. She presses the trigger, but fortunately no shot is fired because the safety catch is set. The two other policemen hurry to immobilize her, after which the chief officer begins rummaging through the wardrobes and the drawers, looking for incriminating letters and other items. He finds five of them on a piece of furniture, and eight in a leather bag that he puts in a larger bag, along with the Beretta, a second revolver with various cartridges for bullets, and a tommy-gun.

If this tale of Martini's is not taken with a grain of salt, it should be seen as highly embellished. Comparing this one with the version reported by Bigazzi, Claretta does use the pistol to threaten the visitors, and although the pistol is "loaded and without the safety catch," she does not press the trigger because perhaps there wasn't enough time.

She falls in a faint after being disarmed, and she is placed on the bed. Then, she drinks a small glass of brandy and swallows a few drops of a cardiotonic. As for the photographs, she herself gives them to the officer, pulling them out of a leather purse, along with two pictures of Ben with dedication, a few books, a tommy-gun, and another pistol, all gifts from her lover.

Before the five men leave, she asks if she might send the Duce a letter. At the "yes" from the constable, she goes to her desk and dashes off four dense pages in which, amongst other things, she tells him: "Something unchangeable has come between us, and it is the revelation that your love is finished. Now I see in you, and only now I understand with terror and affliction that I've loved uselessly, and even more than that, I have suffered in vain …This is the most atrocious delusion that I have had from you and from life. To have given so much without being allowed anything … Now that I've seen the inside of you, up to the deepest corners, after you have even thought of sending a policeman to my house because you don't want to let me keep a sign of your feeling for me, not even those lines that were my salvation and my sunlight in the pain which was tearing me apart, Ben, I can no longer remain near you. Everything is really over now; there is nothing more to do … I've loved you since the beginning of my life, to the threshold of the other one as well. The sun shone at dawn, but now it is night, night without a morrow and everything is already dark in me. Be happy, Ben, because never were truer words spoken."

Bigazzi repeats his apologies to the woman, says goodbye and returns to Mussolini on whose table he places the seized materials and the letter. The Head of Government glances rapidly at one, scans the letter quickly, then, turning to Martini purposely called in, blows up: "So you think you're right, and with this? Do you think that you've succeeded in halting Alexander's tanks?" Then he says goodbye to all, and gloomier than ever returns to work.

Forgetting what he'd said to the constable a few hours before ("If you bring me even only one photocopy, I'll have that woman arrested"), not only does he let her remain free, but he punishes the zealous performer of his orders instead, banishing him to Modena.

This, at least, is the version that Bigazzi relates to Silvio Bertholdi but contradicted by Miriam. Claretta's sister contends that the assistant head of the police, entering her sister's house forcibly, and after having thrown her to the floor and pinned her down, turned the villa upside down without finding anything that he was looking for (the senders, then, not being the Duce, but the extremist "Republicans").

In the same month of October, a few weeks after Bigazzi's raid, Claretta has another equally stormy and dramatic invasion, but from Rachele this time. How matters really unfolded, what the women actually said to each other with any degree of accuracy, we only know the Petacci version related by her sister Miriam, and differing in various details from the one provided by Mussolini's wife. We reproduce the two stories as faithfully as possible, despite some one-sided and biased aspects.

According to Miriam "Claretta knew that a belated attack of jealousy had struck Sig.ra Rachele, and she was aware of the arguments that the woman was having with her husband after so many years. As well, that day she had received a phone call from Gargano. 'She's coming to see you,' Mussolini told her. 'I tried to dissuade her, but it was not possible for me to do so. Don't have her come in. She's irate and I fear she may be armed.' Claretta summons Spoegler and has him lock the gate.

"When Sig.ra Rachele arrives at the villa, Buffarini Guidi and other unknown persons were with her. They stop in front of the gate, and they ring a couple of times. The sky is gray and a steady rain has been falling for several hours. Sig.ra Rachele continues to ring; then seeing that no one is answering, puts her finger on the bell and she keeps it there. The situation was annoying, and Claretta who had adhered to Mussolini's wishes to the letter, was beginning to regret having done so. She sends Spoegler to tell the visitors that she could see no one, and asks them to leave. This is almost like being baited. Suddenly, Sig.ra Rachele begins to scream. Then she seizes hold of the bars of the gate and tries to climb up so that she might jump over the barrier, while Buffarini, all wet due to the rain and sweat, tries to keep her from doing so by pulling at her skirt. This time Claretta doesn't waver. Spoegler returns to the gate, asks Sig.ra Rachele if she is armed, and when she replies that she is not, he allows her to enter. Buffarini also comes in while the others remain outside.

"The two women meet on the ground floor. Claretta descends the stairs slowly, and stops. Sig.ra Rachele remains quiet for a few moments, almost as if her anger has boiled over and she is trying to bring it up again. She must have succeeded because her greeting is extremely rude. 'What are you? Married or single?' 'I am married.' 'Then good evening, signora.'

"The intonation of the last word was obvious, but Claretta chooses to ignore it. 'You wanted to see me?' she asks, forcing herself to remain calm.

" 'Yes, I certainly did. I wanted to see you only to tell you one thing: that you must go, that this place doesn't need you, that no one wants you here. Go away and leave my husband alone.'

" 'I beg you to understand that if you think you are going to give me orders you are mistaken,' says Claretta, trying once again to keep the conversation at an endurable level. But by now this was useless. Rage had once again taken control of Sig.ra Rachele, and nothing could stop her. All at once Claretta warns her: 'Watch your language!'

" 'Oh, yes? A mistake. Why, who do you think you are? I will tell you myself who you think you are: you think that you've made my husband lose his head, but you make me laugh because he's had many, very many women, you know, and he's even betrayed you, not only me, and perhaps he's deceived you more than he has me. Because I knew about this affair, and I asked him about this right from the beginning: 'Who are these Pedaccis, or Pidaccis, or Petaccis? (since there were supposedly two, but where is the other one? I don't see her), and then he would reply: 'No Petacci exists,' and then I thought: 'This must be one of the many,' but then they said that this was love, and then I said: 'How stupid she must be if she thinks he loves her.' Because he really doesn't love you, you know? He told me yesterday that he doesn't love you, and that if you'd get out from underfoot you'd be doing him a favour, and now get out from underfoot and you'll be doing everybody a favour, understand? Because he doesn't love you, he loves only me, understand?'

"Claretta interrupts that outburst by leaving the room for a moment. She returns with some of Mussolini's letters. 'Signora,' she says, 'I know that I have no right, I know that I am to blame. I love the Duce, and for a long time too. I am ready to go, if necessary; I am ready for whatever sacrifice. But he must be the one to ask me. As for his feelings for me, here is the proof.'

"Sig.ra Rachele gets excited: 'I don't want to see the letters! They are of no interest to me! I don't want to take anything away. Keep them because, really, you will regret this, and even he will regret this, because a man who doesn't respect his wife ...'

" 'I must tell you that the Duce has always shown the greatest respect for you, as the mother of his children.'

" 'What mother? What children? What do children have to do with all this? When you get married you have children, no?' She stops for a moment before continuing. 'And then no one even says that you have to marry because many people have children without getting married, and perhaps you will also have them, even if you didn't marry him, but perhaps not because he'd have joked about it, as in other cases, and anyway with that shape you probably can't have any.'

"She'd hit a sore spot and Claretta's eyes well up with tears. Rachele's attack changes direction. 'Look, why are we arguing? Why don't we join forces? If you like, I'll take you with me, come to stay with me and we'll give him the lesson that he deserves.'

"'Can't we speak a little more calmly?'

"'What calm! Tell me rather that you wouldn't stay because if you come with me you will have to eat pasta and beans, not those dainty morsels that you eat. And you'll have to dress like me, not in silk stuff. Because I really want to see where you got that silk stuff and all the airs that you give yourself and ...' While still talking, Sig.ra Rachele approaches Claretta threateningly and grabs her arm. Then all of a sudden she begins to insult her.

"'Signora, watch your language and remember that you are in my house,' Claretta says loudly, but the other one doesn't pay attention. Buffarini and Spoegler who had remained on the side until then, overcome by the commotion, intervene now. Sig.ra Rachele calms down for an instant, but soon resumes her tirade. She says: 'If you really love him, you'll have to give him up.' Then she says: 'Woe to you if you don't go. You'll end up badly.' And she continues in that fashion, alternating between threats and offers of a common cause to return in the end to insults.

"At a certain point a worried Mussolini telephones. He speaks first to Claretta, and then he asks for his wife and he insists that she calm down and that she go back home. That was the coup de grace. Sig.ra Rachele loses all self-control, and the words that come out of her mouth from then on are absolutely unprintable. She herself admits, however, that she doesn't remember what she said. She was, I repeat, completely enraged. After the meeting (which lasts more than three hours) she has a collapse and—to use her own words once again—'was on the verge of committing a foolish act.'"

Here is Rachele's version: "At that time I'd learned that people without scruples, interested in fishing in muddy waters, seeking to create scandal, were trying to use her (Claretta) as a pawn in the terrible game that had as a goal the ruin of my husband. I thought that in her inexperience with political intrigue she could not possibly be aware of such things and I decided one day to talk to her myself. I also wanted to warn her that her very life was in peril. Before facing that very trying meeting, I phoned Benito to tell him that I would be going 'over there.' 'Do as you like,' he answers me. I have my driver take me there with two friends from the Romagna following in another car. I also wanted Buffarini to be present at the meeting because he was aware of everything ...

"It was pouring rain when we got out in front of the villa ... Buffarini demanded that my friends stay far away (they had arrived soon after us), but they didn't follow his orders, remaining off a short distance. I rang the bell twice: no one answered. A short time later, a German officer looks out the door, and while he is talking to Buffarini, he is trying to let me know through signs that it is not possible to go in, that to insist is useless. Therefore, I grab hold of the gate, and I try uselessly to climb over it ... At a certain point, my friends from Romagna approach Buffarini and they begin to threaten. This was a useful tactic of his. Very pale, wet like a big fish, he begins to tremble, to make signs towards the window to come to open up. Soon the German officer throws open the gate. 'Are you armed?' he asks me, noticing that I was upset. I reassure him. 'I don't make social calls carrying weapons,' I reply. He says nothing else and he comes beside me.

"An elderly woman (I don't know who she was) has us come into a small room that I can't describe because my anger was such that I didn't notice anything. Buffarini, the German, and another officer remain standing without saying a word. Finally, after about a quarter hour, a 'shadow' descends the stairs. She was clutching a gauze handkerchief between her fingers, like a French woman, and she seemed defenseless, similar to a fragile plant from our country districts.

"Perhaps I avoided looking at her during our painful talk. I was too upset due to irritation, by a desperate anxiety to find the words most suitable to convince her to get out of my husband's life forever. 'Are you married or single?' I ask her as soon as she is in front of me, I being the first to break the trying silence. 'Married,' she replies (she had a low raucous voice, a very strange contrast to the slenderness of her body). 'Signora,' I continue, 'I shall try to remain calm. I did not come to see you to insult you spurred by jealousy, neither to threaten you. Our country is living through dramatic times, and our personal feelings count for little now. I've come to ask you for a special favour. My husband needs peace and tranquillity so that he can work, but above all it is necessary to stifle the scandal created by your presence here, at this Lake, a few kilometres from my house. When you love someone you are able to make whatever sacrifice for him. I, who am his wife, to save Benito, would be inclined to go away, or to lock myself up in a castle, at the top of a mountain. And if you really love him, you must give up seeing him.

"Claretta Petacci listened to me silently, curled up in an armchair. She said nothing when I stopped talking, and I continue after a few seconds. 'Benito has always been a good father, he's always adored his youngsters. You know that he has five children. Now there are four, since the death of my Bruno. Even for them and for my little grandchildren I beg you to leave Lake Garda, not to disturb the peace of our family anymore.' I would have wanted her to rebel, that she'd try to defend herself in whatever way. Instead she was crying softly, her head thrown back onto the chair, as if she didn't even have the strength to listen to me. Then, exasperated, I told her that I couldn't stand women who tried to solve all their problems with tears and fainting spells, and I reproached her for many things: for having had photographs made of some very sensitive letters that my husband had written to her during their long relationship and of having these hidden in safe places in Switzerland and Germany (Benito himself had ordered his police constable, the consul Bigazzi, to seize those letters at the Petacci house); to have permitted the installation of a direct telephone cable between our villa and her house; and finally of having contact with some suspicious persons.

"I never heard her voice and to convince myself that I wasn't dealing with a shadow, that I wasn't merely talking to myself, I shook her by the arms until she said to me: 'Il Duce loves you very much, signora. I was never able to utter a word against you.' The instinctive pity that I felt for her quickly overcame my rage. I couldn't forget that she'd suffered after 25 July; that to defend Benito, she'd sent from the Novara jail where she'd been imprisoned, bitter but brave letters to Badoglio, our common enemy. This is why I begged her: 'If things are really the way you say they are, why don't we try to do something together for my husband? Why don't we help him in this most grave moment of his life?'

"She gets up slowly from the armchair and disappears up the stairs. When she returns she has in her hands some rolled up white sheets that she thrusts at me saying: 'Here are thirty-two letters that your husband sent me.' I only needed a quick glance: they weren't letters, they were typewritten copies. Then I shout: 'I don't want to take away anything of yours. This is not the reason for my coming here.' Now I realized that I had deluded myself into hoping to be understood by her, and I don't remember what I said to her, beginning with that moment. Naturally, forgetting my prudent intentions, I behave as all jealous women who decide to wage open war against a rival. From time to time Claretta keeps fainting (and the upset Buffarini would run over to her with a bottle of cognac); but between collapses, she finds the means to tell me that my husband couldn't live without her. 'That's not true,' I interrupt, hurt, 'my husband knows that I'm here, you can ask him if you don't believe me.' I myself push her towards the telephone while the trembling Buffarini rushes once again to help her; and Benito confirms to her that I hadn't lied.

"The talk continues at length, being both useless and distressing. I scream at her vainly that everybody hates her, whether Fascist or Partisan. I warn her in vain that her life was in danger (to protect Il Duce from scandal some adherents of the *X Mas* had sworn to kill her). I tell her everything: that the phone calls that she exchanged with Benito were recorded, and that five copies of the text of those conversations were sent to the German Command. That the English and American intelligence services were keeping tabs on her in order to watch Mussolini, and that she had to beware of everyone, even of a waiter who worked in a trattoria in Torri, a nearby town. He was called Edward Como and no one could have guessed from his simple and ordinary appearance that he was an American spy.

"Instead of answering me, Claretta Petacci continued to surrender to fainting fits on the chair, or to collapse in tears. I couldn't stand the nervous tension anymore, and finally I got up, my head very hot, and my heart beating furiously. Being extremely weary, I say to her before leaving 'You'll end up badly, signora.' Just a few days before I'd received an anonymous letter containing a poem whose cruel refrain repeated: 'We'll take them to Piazzale Loreto.' Obviously, that letter was sent to me by a Partisan, and it had created a violent feeling in me. Those were the only words I could think of at that moment and I repeated them mechanically to Claretta: 'They will take you to Piazzale Loreto."[43]

Finally, there exists a third, shorter version, by Spoegler, according to whom Rachele declares: "What elegance! The mistress dresses really well! So this is the way that the mistress of a Head of State dresses! And look at me who married him!" Then when the rival shows her the letters, Rachele tries to tear them up, but she doesn't succeed, being prevented from doing so by the

German officer who is rewarded with a scratch on the hand.

Who is more believable? Both Rachele and Claretta (this through her sister) in reporting their single meeting, or rather, confrontation, were thinking more about posterity than the truth, and worrying about not appearing hysterical and quarrelsome. Both force themselves to remain calm, imputing the provocation to the other person. There can be no doubt that the quarrel was turbulent. But which of the two, from the beginning, lit the fuse, transforming the scene into a commotion?

Neither Claretta nor Rachele were compliant women, above all in matters of the heart. Both were ready to fight and set down proprietary limits. Therefore, an agreement between them would have been virtually impossible, each claiming for herself the right to dominate the feelings of a man who had sought, and was seeking—this being a very great search—to reconcile the rights of his wife with the claims of his mistress. That is, the ho-hum happenings in the marriage bed, with the extramarital love nest.

In the end he was the real victim of that altercation since he neither had the courage to call Claretta that night, nor the bravery to return home (he spent the night on a cot in the little room near his office without, perhaps, even closing his eyes).

Nineteen

Following the Master

As soon as her rival leaves Villa Fiordaliso, Claretta succumbs to an hysterical fit of crying. She knew that Rachele was aware of the love intrigue, but she'd never imagined that her reaction would have been so violent.

She loved Ben at least as much as did his wife; she'd given up everything for him, lived only for him, and was ready to die for him. They'd known each other for twelve years, and for eight of those years, submissive but headstrong, she'd remained near him. How could she part company with him now, meekly exchanging goodbyes? Prisoner of a glorious past, hostage to a sombre present, subjected to a fearful, uncertain future, right at this moment he had need of her more than ever. Only in one particular case would she step aside, putting her illusions and dreams in storage, affixing the cruelest seal to the most exultant of loves: if he'd ask her to.

But he hadn't asked her to do this. Actually, he'd told her to remain nearby, asking her only to move from Villa Fiordaliso to more secure lodgings.

A short time later she moves into Villa Mirabella, inside the Vittoriale, in the residence willed by "The Prophet" to his widow, Maria Gallese di Montenevoso.[44]

She occupies the princess' room, whose walls were covered with costly damask, in whose centre was an enormous bed, also having access to a room in an upper level that becomes her usual sitting room.

She'll spend the remaining months of her life there, reading, listening to music, keeping company with the other two tenants, the married couple Carlo and Caterina Cervis, she the lady-in-waiting to La Gallese, and receiving irregular visits from friends and acquaintances while awaiting the ever rarer and hasty ones from her lover.

Although more protected in this house than at Villa Fiordaliso, even here she is assailed by threats from those Fascists who see her as the evil counselor of the Leader.

They were probably the ones to install bugs in the bedroom chandelier and in the telephone to record her conversations with Mussolini and her other habitual callers (Spoegler, Buffarini, her parents, Miriam, Marcello). A disgraceful plan that yields no results, however. Claretta never knew anything more than what her lover wanted her to know. She was never privy to important political, diplomatic, or military secrets, but also because he never revealed any to her. Something which doesn't prevent her from giving him advice, but this is merely because she is his woman.

Such as in December 1944 when everything really seemed to be lost, when under the heavy firepower of the Anglo-Americans the days of the Axis were beginning to appear numbered. Even she urges him to show himself to the people then. "They say that you are sick and that you are a German prisoner. It is necessary for you to be seen. The people want to know that you are alive and that you are the master of your own will. They want to hear your voice ... So speak, speak ..."

On the sixteenth of the same month, at eleven o'clock of a cold Saturday, the struggling dictator thus gives his last speech at the Lyric Theatre of Milan, relayed to the piazzas of the city by a network of loudspeakers. The theatre was jam-packed, the crowd being curious, excited and cheering.

As if re-invigorated, the old tribune delivers more of a winner's speech than that of a failure, almost as if he'd never doubted the outcome of the war, which seemed to be—and was—lost at that moment in time. "We'll defend the Po Valley tooth and nail," he thunders at one point, unleashing a flood of praises, worthy of the ones that had risen from Piazza Venezia in the past.

Claretta couldn't hide her own jubilation when she was listening to him: so, the Italians still loved him; so, the game was not up; so, there would be a recovery.

But this was only a nine day's wonder: the last and, perhaps, the most illusory and pitiful. The Mussolini who, at the podium, had read the speech with astounding vigor, written in huge letters, not wanting to use eyeglasses, had nothing left of the lictorial Caesar: neither the bold poses, nor the bombastic frown, or the arrogance of a visionary.

The return to the bleak and sleepy Gargano helps to chase away the excitement of the 16th of December, the town being his prison and his hell. Of the short-lived Milanese victory, all that will be left will be the memory, while the sadness will mount steadily.

As if this weren't enough, towards mid February, a violent quarrel breaks out between Claretta and Ben, as reported by Apollonio, which we reproduce scrupulously, but with reservations.

At about nine o'clock one night, Mussolini climbs into his car and, accompanied by another car carrying the above-named official, a brigadier and Leppo, a member of the medical corps, heads for Villa Mirabella.

Arriving here, Il Duce proceeds to the gate with Apollonio, but he crosses it alone, while the other man retraces his steps to the car. "All of a sudden," we read in the interview given by the police official to Silvio Bertholdi, "we heard female shouts and shrieks coming from the villa, but such loud ones that I thought it best to remain nearby to see what was going on. It was obvious that a violent quarrel was taking place inside Villa Mirabella, and that the incident was becoming a serious matter. Therefore, I stayed back, and I remember very well that after a half hour, the gate opens to allow through an enraged and fuming Mussolini.

"I went towards him. As if I knew what was going on between him and Claretta, and the reasons for that screaming, he tells me: 'Finally that damned woman has revealed her hand!' ... Those were his exact words; and so surprising, coming from his mouth, as to remain impressed in my memory to such an extent that I still seem to hear them. Then, almost as if continuing a discussion that we'd never actually had, Mussolini adds: 'The only thing missing is that we name her father Minister of Health!' He'd come to his car. Still upset, he gets in, and I linger behind, silently dismayed, without daring, naturally, to ask him to supply more details ..."

Il Duce returns to Gargano, and Apollonio enters the villa. And what does he see? Claretta in a fainting spell on the couch, and on his knees beside her, old Dr. Francesco Saverio, giving his daughter an injection after attending to a bruised hip.

The zealous officer also gets to work to try to revive the young woman, giving her a cardiotonic, while members of her family tell him what he later relates to Bertholdi. "Mussolini had arrived at Villa Mirabella with already taut nerves after a tough day. He'd received many reports of bad news. Perhaps he was looking for relaxation and sympathy, certainly a variance from his usual routine that was becoming ever more dismal. Instead, as soon as he enters the sitting room, Claretta confronts him literally with a series of incredible requests. This was enough to turn him into a raging beast. It is thought that the Petacci woman asked him to decide at once to nominate her brother Marcello to the post of Finance Minister, and Mancini, a lawyer and friend of the family, Public Instruction Minister. Those requests didn't seem to be completely mad. Marcello Petacci was always in need of money and the position chosen by him, undoubtedly was selected with imagination. As for Mancini, it was evident that he sought a political career that would give him some prestige.

"The overwhelmed Mussolini reacts violently. Therefore, taking a pistol from one of the pieces of furniture, a small weapon decorated with mother-of-pearl, Claretta points it at him. Mussolini jumps at her; and to be able to disarm her, he gives her a punch or a kick to her hip until she faints and falls limply at his feet. Meanwhile, her mother and father, the two old Petaccis, peer out from the second floor after hearing all the commotion and the sound of body against body, trying to find out what was going on. By this time, Mussolini had left the house."

It is possible that things really happened that way, but we rather doubt it. Everyone knew that Marcello was a megalomaniac, and that his dream of heading a Government Ministry could also possibly be true, but that after the gold scandal and the subsequent loosening of the love bond Claretta would pull strings to get him a post in the Salò Government is incredible. No less than the one of having Mancini the lawyer named to head the Ministry of Public Instruction because he was a friend of the family. The Petaccis had many other things to worry about at that time.

At Mussolini's request, they'd finally decided to move to a neutral country, safe from reprisals with the fatal results that the fall of the Regime would bring to them.

They would seek safety willingly in Switzerland or Spain. But the Swiss border seemed to be less accessible than the Iberian one that Miriam the actress had penetrated at various times in search of work.

According to the plans and the desire of the family, besides that of the lover, Claretta would also have had to go, but instead she was determined to remain behind. Under no circumstances would she pry herself away from Ben: in good or in ill luck, his destiny was her destiny. How often Spoegler had talked to her of a hiding place in the Dolomites, at a height of 2 300 metres, which could be reached by mule, and in winter by sleigh, after riding hours and hours!

One day she'd gone there on an excursion, met an old mountaineering couple that would have rented a wing of a hut to her for one thousand lire a month.

She'd discussed this with Ben, who consulted Spoegler about the main details.

The latter had shown him a series of pictures and, while Mussolini was looking at them, lingering on the more scenic ones, Spoegler had said to him: "Duce, this is the asshole of the world." The dictator replied that he'd think about it.

But time was short since the already dramatic situation rushed things: on April 11th, the Americans land on Elba, the 13th, they occupy Vienna, on the 16th, Nuremberg.

That same day, Mussolini announces to his Ministers the departure for Milan, where the bulk of the "Republican" forces were centered. There—he said—he would decide if they should head for Switzerland, or fall back on the Valtellina for a last ditch, desperate defense. "In any case, in whatever spot, Fascism must fall heroically."

But he also leaves the Lake because, or perhaps above all, in the hope that Cardinal Schuster, the Milanese Archbishop, would put him in contact with the main representatives of the Resistance.

He arrives in Lombardy's main town on 18 April, at about nine in the evening, with his closest associates, and a small escort of SS that he would willingly have done without.

Mario Bassi, the prefect, is there to receive him in the Government building in Corso Monforte. The latter puts three rooms on the ground floor at his disposal, and here he improvises a sort of General Headquarters. This soon becomes the goal of an agitated and picturesque pilgrimage of people, with the strangest suggestions, and the oddest proposals, (he'll listen to all of them, except for the Germans, whom he'll distance from the prefecture with very few exceptions).

Claretta telephones him the next day even though she'd promised not to leave the Lake in anticipation of his return. Instead, as soon as he departs from Gargano, she runs to Spoegler to beg him to take her to the Lombard city. The young officer tries to dissuade her, reminding her of the pledge made to Il Duce, but she won't listen to reason.

That day, when she announces to Ben that she is a few hundred metres from his office, in a building in the then Corso Littorio,* he has a fit of rage. At this, to calm him down, she explains that she'd come to Milan to say goodbye to her parents and to her sister who were about to leave the country. She wasn't

---

* Now Corso Matteotti.

lying though he was the real reason for her trip.

She asks to see him, even if only for a few moments, just long enough to hold him to her and to have a look at him. His face was not recognizable now because of so much misfortune. But his was the look that had charmed her since childhood, seduced her as a young woman, and that continued to race her heart and to make her suffer.

He replies that in dangerous times such as these it is much better to stay far away, but she begs him to phone her, at least. On hearing his voice, she'd feel him so much closer. But when again he urges her to flee to Spain with her family, she is the one who becomes riled. And with such heat that he changes subject.

Chaos was reaching its greatest extent in an indescribable jumble of fears, hopes, betrayals, misunderstandings and deceit. Everyone was giving orders, but no one was obeying them. Pavolini wanted to retreat to the Valtellina, to set up a final redoubt and put up a fierce struggle, while Graziani described the idea in the same words as Il Duce, "bullshit," crazily unreal.

On the 21st, the elderly Marshal of Italy announces to Mussolini that the Americans had established a bridgehead at Mantua, on the east bank of the Po River, and that the next day they could enter Milan, if they so chose. Graziani, therefore, asks Mussolini what he intended to do now. "As always happens in such situations, at certain points events take the upper hand and dictate the consequences," replied the dictator rather cryptically.

In fact, even he didn't know, victim to the most changeable swings of mood, at the mercy of frightened advisors, incapable of action (he even conceives the notion of transferring power to the Partisans of the north, without the Communists, but then he abandons this idea).

On 25 April, in this very irresolute atmosphere, takes place the historic meeting at the Archbishop's palace, in attendance being General Raffaele Cadorna, representing the *Corpo Volontari della Libertà*, the lawyer Achille Marazza and the engineer Riccardo Lombardi, delegates of the *Comitato di Liberazione Nazionale Alta Italia*.

Mussolini, with Graziani, Zerbino, the Minister of Internal Affairs, Undersecretary Barracu and Prefect Bassi, arrive at about five in the evening, and are received by the Cardinal and his secretaries. They are escorted to the Hall of Audiences with its walls covered in crimson damask, containing a large red sofa and, facing this, eight armchairs placed in a semi-circle.

With the pleasantries over, Schuster offers his guests a drink of a cordial and some biscuits. Then the Cardinal gives Il Duce a book on Saint Benedict's life, for which he supplies a dedication. During the meeting, he couldn't keep himself from condemning bitterly the Regime fallen—he said—because of the faults of the Capo, above all, but also because of ill service by his entourage.

Representatives of the Resistance join them at about six o'clock and, with some embarrassment, the Archbishop proceeds to make the introductions, sealed by formal and quick handshakes. Then, everyone sits down: Mussolini and Schuster on the couch, the others on the armchairs.

Marazza breaks the ice. In order to avoid a misunderstanding, he says quickly, the *Comitato* would accept exclusively, and only, an unconditional surrender. "That was not why I came here," replies an offended Duce. Lombardi answers rudely that, in the light of the accords with the Allies, the *Comitato* would offer to the remaining forces of the Social Republic, including the voluntary corps such as the *Decima Mas*, the guarantees as provided for in the international conventions, of course, as long as the enemy would lay down their arms immediately. As for the families of Fascists, they would not be harmed in any way, while the diplomats would have all their rights respected.

On the basis of these conditions—comments Mussolini—it is also possible to bargain and, perhaps, negotiations would have ensued had it not been for Graziani who mentions that he'd learned in the outer rooms a short time before of a parlay going on between the Germans and the Anglo-Americans. All the more reason, Graziani adds, to postpone an agreement that the Germans would interpret as an act of treachery.

Il Duce is dumbfounded and, turning to the Partisan delegates asks what they make of all this. "The reports of an agreement with Germany are of no interest to us; we are still at war with Germany," Lombardi answers dryly. Marazza in turn observes: "The Germans have been discussing a surrender for some days and, it would seem, haven't bothered informing the Government of the Social Republic."

Now Schuster begins to speak affirming the truth of the previous statements, and turning to Mgr. Bicchierai (intermediary between the Cardinal and the Chiefs of the Resistance), the latter states that only the signature remains to be added to the surrender. At this point, perhaps aware or not of the negotiations (and if he were, his own being just a bluff), the Duce blurts out: "For once it will be possible to say that Germany stabbed Italy in the back. They have always treated us like servants ... and at the end they have betrayed me." The prelate seeks to calm him down, but without success.

A short time afterwards, in fact, he gets up brusquely: "I've decided. I'm going to the Germans to settle accounts." Taken by surprise, the opposing conferees ask him when he would return. In an hour, he replies, making for the door with the Cardinal.

Waiting for him at the prefecture is an unseemly, stunned and vociferous crowd, unaware of what has been going on in the Archbishop's palace. Crammed with cars loaded with bags, suitcases and trunks, the courtyard of the building seems to be the bivouac of gypsies. There are families of the *gerarchi*: complaining women, crying babies, all amidst Black Shirts and gray-green uniforms. An anxious coming and going that Mussolini's arrival renders even more clamorous.

Some people keep asking themselves what the Duce has in mind, the latter continuing to curse the Germans. He reaches his office quickly along with about ten advisors. After a half hour of discussion, he announces: "On to Como."

No Valtellina, then, and no resistance in the prefecture until the arrival of the Anglo-Americans as his son Vittorio had suggested, and to whom he'd replied: "If they think they will put me in the pillory in the Tower of London like a ferocious beast, or in a cage at Madison Square Gardens, they are deluding themselves."

Why Como, exactly? According to Bianchi and Mezzetti because from the small Lake Como town, a removal to the Ticino Canton would be much easier: "... refuge in Switzerland would seem to provide the ultimate secure exit, perhaps to re-enter Italy across the Alto Adige border. Mussolini knew after discussions with his son Vittorio and the Head of Cabinet at External Affairs, Mellini Ponce de Leon, that the Swiss Confederation would not welcome him officially: from which stems the idea of crossing the frontier secretly, and creating a fait accompli." Had he not ordered Rachele, along with Romano and Anna Maria a few days earlier, to leave Gargano, go to Monza and then, with a few helpers to get to Como ?

And Claretta?

On the 21st, in the Corso Littorio lodging, she'd just said goodbye to her parents and sister about to depart Italy. They had begged her to leave as well, threatening absolutely to remain in Milan themselves in case of refusal. Miriam to whom we owe this remembrance, is taken aside by her sister: "I can't give you orders, but I am your older sister and I implore you to do what I tell you. Take away our parents. Have them leave immediately. Don't think of me: I must remain alone." "Why?" questions Miriam. "Because I will be calmer this way. I will have more freedom to move about, I'll be able to safeguard myself more easily. And I will save myself, you'll see. Now if you want to help me, you'll have to do as I tell you."

The plane obtained for them by Il Duce was to have taken off that night but, at the last minute, the fuel tanks are found to contain water, instead of fuel, and therefore the departure is postponed to the next day.

Returning to the house unexpectedly after midnight, Miriam and her parents find that Claretta is still awake, in bed, the image of St. Rita in her hands and lying on her heart. Seeing her family, she jumps out of bed beaming: "My God, I thank you ... What happened?" Miriam relates the incident, repeating once again the request that she join them: "There is nothing else to save, and you know it. He himself, on the other hand, must have many things going through his head. If you come with us, you'll relieve him of a worry. Then, when everything is over, you can return."

Losing her patience now, Claretta replies imperiously: "And you think that I could come back? That I'd be able to look him in the face after having abandoned him while in danger? No, it's impossible. Too many people are turning their backs on him for me to do him this wrong as well. Please don't make things more difficult for me." All that Miriam could do was to wish her sister a good night and leave the room. The choice was really final.

The second departure the next day was even more trying.

Accompanying her parents and her sister to the elevator, Claretta stoically tells them again that she would soon be safe herself. Then, she throws her arms around their necks, this becoming the most horrible moment because so many chaotic and dramatic moments come back to life in their memories and in their hearts, superimposing now, then mixing themselves up, only to evaporate or to mutate into unmentionable premonitions.

A hint of a goodbye, whispered almost for luck, seals the last farewell. While the emptiness is swallowing the elevator, Claretta brings her soft, sad face, now ruthlessly creased by the first wrinkles, to the small window allowing her to follow her loved ones until they are gone from view. Only then do her large eyes moisten, and two heavy tears roll down her cheeks. The hourglass had run out of sand, and a terrible fate was preparing itself: nothing was left except her love for Ben.

After a very harrowing flight, as soon as they arrive in Barcelona, with trembling hands, Miriam extracts from her purse a letter that her sister had given her before leaving, urging her not to open it before landing: "Don't worry about us … I am following my destiny which is also his. I will never abandon him, no matter what happens. I will not destroy with a vile gesture the total love-liness of my offering, and I won't give up helping him or being with him as long as I am able to … You know where all my papers are. Keep them and look after them. Keep them yourself: I bequeath them to you, and you in turn, entrust them to your son if God gives you one, or to Benghino.[45] You will know which of the two will be able to understand them. You know everything, you who have lived all through my life of love, you who saw things since you were a little girl, you who were the 'peacemaker,' the 'food suppli-er,' our own 'little idiot' of happy times. No one better than you can be the custodian of my writings, of all my soul given to him. You'll find his letters; perhaps in time you'll be able to come across the other ones. Obtain them from the thief in whatever way. They are part of me, a sacred record and an indivisible property … I beg of you, whatever happens, make sure that the truth about me, about him, about our sublime, beautiful, divine love, beyond time, beyond life will finally be known. You know.

"I am giving you this very delicate task with a loving heart, and sure that you will do what I would have done. Don't cry because of what I am telling you. This is neither pessimism, nor gloom. It is the desire for me to feel sure of what is most dear to me. Only you can understand me. This is not to say that I will not survive, no, darling little one, my destiny will not be so cruel, but there is the possibility that I shall not return and …"

A short time later she leaves Milan, against the wishes of everyone, heading for her Duce's column. She has a fur coat on her shoulders and, as her only luggage, a small suitcase with a few garments, her cosmetics, and the ever-present medicines. But she is happy. She had just said to a friend: "A dog goes where the mas-ter goes."

Twenty

Go, Duce, Go!

The mixed-up caravan reaches Como a little before nine in the evening, and heads directly for the prefecture.

Even here a great disorder reigns in a frenetic overlapping of orders and counterorders. Everyone fears the worst, but what this could be no one has the faintest idea. Not even Il Duce, by now in thrall to unforeseeable and uncontrollable events. Some envision a flight to Switzerland, others a retreat to the Valtellina, or a final last ditch defense within the walls of Como, the provincial Capital.

In the main Government building, the fallen leader eats a simple meal, prepared by Prefect Celio's wife who gets her chance to dust off the ceremonial china and silverware. Rather than this being a banquet, it is the funeral vigil over a corpse, that of Fascism, waiting only to be placed in a coffin and lowered into a tomb.

With the meal over, Mussolini retreats to Celio's office from which he telephones Rachele, the latter having arrived at six o'clock the previous evening at Villa Mantero, along with Romano and Anna Maria. What they said to each other we do not know but, more than a "See you soon," no doubt. Perhaps, it was a last good-bye. Before hanging up, he tells her that some very loyal visitors will come to see her to whom she should hand "the stuff" (personal effects and documents, perhaps).

It seems just under such conditions that Mussolini sends her his famous letter that his wife will destroy "in a moment of distress" a few years later after having memorized its contents: "Dear Rachele. Here I am at the last step of my life, at the last page of my book. Perhaps we will never see each other again. This is why I am writing you this letter, to ask your forgiveness for all the hurt I have inadvertently caused you. But you know that you have been the only woman that I have truly loved in my life. I swear it to you before God and our Bruno, in this last hour. I am trying to reach La Valtellina, but you should try to cross the frontier with the children. You'll be able to make a new life for yourselves there. I don't think that the Swiss will refuse you entry because I've always helped them in all circumstances and also because you and the children have had nothing to do with politics. If this is impossible, present yourselves to the Allies: perhaps they will be more generous than the Italians. I entrust Anna and Romano to you, especially Anna who is so young and who needs so much care and affection. You know how much I love them. I embrace you and the children. Your Benito."

According to Rachele, the letter was written with a blue pencil and signed in red, just as those that he had sent her from Ponza and La Maddalena.

More than one historian has cast doubt on the authenticity of the letter. Not that his wife didn't receive it, or that she'd invented it, but that she could have changed its contents, here and there, for understandable human concerns. This might have been to prove the fundamental devotion of the husband to his wife, the lover of so many women, the frequenter of so many love nests, but the unshakable defender of the marriage tie.

We do not reject that Mussolini really did write those words, and in absolute good faith. He'd had relations with at least two other women, and one had been his paramour. But neither for La Sarfatti, nor for La Petacci would he have left Rachele, the fighting companion of his entire life.

Down deep, he only felt a tender gratitude for Claretta now. If she had not been so attached to him, he probably would have loosened himself from her some time before. The dream was over for him, and all that was left was a submissive routine. Fire for her, ashes for him: embers ever weaker and cooler, as his reaction when he is told that his mistress had reached Como with Marcello, Zita, and her nephews, and that she was at the prefecture: "In these emergencies, it is best that women stay home!"

Not only doesn't he want to see her: he orders her categorically to leave Como. But once again she disobeys him, having decided to share his fate with him until the end, whether good or bad.

While awaiting new developments, Claretta heads for the Firenze Hotel where the other members of her family were already staying. She lies down on one of the two beds with one of her two nephews, while Zita installs herself in the other one with her younger son, Marcello having to do with a cot.

Colonel Casalinuovo of the Militia appears at midnight to inform her of what is going on in the prefecture. She asks him how the Duce is, if she might see him, and when. The Colonel answers that he'd inquire from the involved persons, but not before the arrival of the Black Brigades from the Lombard main city.[46] Then he says goodbye, promising to return as soon as possible.

He shows up four hours later with fresh, but bad news: "The Duce left suddenly and we don't know where he went." At this Claretta jumps out of bed screaming: "That's the usual dirty trick. They've taken him to die." She dresses again in a fury, her family doing the same, while Casalinuovo goes out to try to find out something more on the unexpected departure of the Capo.

He returns quickly stating that the Duce had taken the road towards Menaggio, and Claretta turns to her brother: "Get the car ready, I want to go there as well. I'll join him anywhere, even at the ends of the earth."

Arriving at their destination, they park the cars in a vast open space adjacent to a large villa where there are already dozens of other vehicles. Marcello and Casalinuovo begin to look for the Duce immediately, while Claretta, Zita, and the children remain in the car. After an hour, the two come back stating that Mussolini is in the Town Hall. "I want to see him. I want to see him immediately," exclaims Claretta all excited. "I am certain that at this moment he has need only of us ..."

No, he didn't need anyone now: only a miracle could save him.

His exodus from Como had been particularly difficult. As suggested by Party Secretary Porta, very familiar with the passes for Switzerland, he'd had to deal with the opposition of the Germans and of Birzer, their commander, personally placed on his heels by Hitler: the dictator's car was blocked at the pass, and he was finally forced to acquiesce to their desires. They would leave for Menaggio together.

Here they accommodate themselves in the villa of Enrico Castelli, the Assistant Party Secretary for Como, where Il Duce requests to be able to rest, being very tired from all the wandering. He would discuss later the eventual departure from Italy, with greater calm and with a clearer mind (a few hours before, Rachele and the children had tried to cross into Switzerland, but the Swiss authorities had turned them back).

According to Porta, the best road to cross the border was at Grandola, a handful of houses above Menaggio. However, it was best to go there quickly, before the Partisans scattered in the region and armed to the teeth would set their traps. Thus they get back to traveling along a dusty, steep road full of curves, Mussolini at the head, the others following.

The caravan heads for Hotel Miravalle, transformed into a command post by the 53rd Company of the Border Militia (taking advantage of a fork in the road during the short trip, the Duce's car tries to lose Birzer, but the trick fails). The procession stops here and Mussolini gets out of the car, while the others gather in front of the hotel.

Happening to note Claretta's car, Ben goes to her, helps her get out of the vehicle, then turning, to the *gerarchi* who were in a semi-circle around him, says: "This woman who has already suffered jail, and who has lost everything because of me, has wanted to follow me even now ..."

Flattered and moved, she thanks him with a smile, which quickly vanishes when she catches sight of Elena Curti Cucciati, a young woman of whom she was extremely jealous and said by some to be the dictator's illegitimate daughter.

But she doesn't say anything, or bat an eyelash, and she proceeds angrily towards the hotel where a short time later Ben joins her to give her an explanation.

At one in the afternoon all of them eat a frugal meal prepared and served by the soldiers of the Company, while the radio announces the success of the revolt in Milan.

With the vice tightening and thus diminishing the possibilities of escape more and more, Buffarini Guidi proposes crossing the Swiss frontier at Porlezza, but he finds only Tarchi and Fabiani, two *gerarchi*, ready to follow him. The three leave Grandola together by car (Buffarini Guidi will be executed by the Partisans into whose hands he will fall).

At four o'clock Ben goes to see Claretta who, after the morning's incident, has locked herself up in her room. "What is that woman doing here?" she assails him. "She must go, I want her to go away." He tries to appease her but she is incensed. "Enough, enough!" he replies, losing his patience, and heads towards the window from which comes an annoying draft. However, while trying to close it, he trips over the couch near the same window, striking his forehead on a corner of the frame. Alarmed and forgetting her "rival," Claretta rushes to help him and to dress the wound, while Zita who'd arrived in the meanwhile, prepares some tea for him.

Having recovered, but ever gloomier, he begins a tirade against the English: "You don't know them well enough and Italians will learn to know what they are like finally only when it is too late. They are only waiting to get their hands on me to turn me into a sideshow. Their hatred is pitiless because they only know how to hate ... It is my turn now, tomorrow it will be the turn of the others. They will knock down all of us, one by one.."

La Ritossa, who tells this story, interrupts him: "In any case the Partisans control all the roads by now and they are shooting at us from everywhere." "And so? What is to be done?" he asks her. "Everyone should go off on his own business," answers Zita. "That would certainly be much easier," agrees the dictator, getting up and arranging to meet the Petaccis in the safer Menaggio.

In Menaggio, La Ritossa, Marcello and their children will stay in the rooms of a villa, while Claretta will be lodged in a building a few metres from the barracks of the Black Brigades where Mussolini is housed, kept under guard by adolescents in gray-green uniforms.

It was about eight in the evening and no one knew yet what to do. Whether it was better to move towards the Valtellina, to try the road to Switzerland again, or to stay there, and await Pavolini who finally shows up at two in the morning with Elena Curti Cucciati who'd gone to look for him by bike, and six Militiamen (instead of the more than one thousand promised).

The arrival during the night of a motorized brigade of Germans in flight, a division of the *Flak*, the anti-aircraft battery commanded by Lieutenant Fallmeyer and heading for the Alto Adige, gets the group going.

Mussolini quickly gathers together his *gerarchi* and after a feverish secret meeting, decides to join the German forces because they were many and well armed, but above all, also because they had a clear plan of retreat.

First, however, he sends Claretta a message in which his tone is worried and imploring, urging her once again to find safety. But she disobeys him once more, and not for the last time either. In fact, a short time later, she climbs into a car, followed by Marcello with Zita and the small children.

She is wearing a brown suit and a cashmere blouse, and on her arm, she carries her fur (the small handbag containing her personal effects and her make-up kit she'd entrusted to a reliable assistant). She is destroyed: her face is pale, she has circles under her eyes, her spirit being in confusion: after so much happiness, so much suffering; after so much good luck, so much misfortune; after so many illusions, so much sadness. But what could one do?

Rebel? Oh no, that would be useless because the Fates already seemed to have issued their irreversible judgment. There was nothing else to do except submit to the inevitable, entrusting oneself to their mysterious mercy.

The sky was gray, and a thin, overbearing rain was drumming on the shiny roofs of the cars and on the rough canvas of the trucks, ready to leave. At the head was Pavolini's armoured tank; then, on a truck, Birzer's SS; then, the cars carrying Mussolini, Barracu, Bombacci and the *gerarchi* with their families, their secretaries and their maids; at the end, the German trucks (totaling forty German vehicles and twelve Italian cars, in a line stretching about a kilometre).

The column heads immediately for Dongo.

There are frequent pauses along the way and, at a stop longer then the previous ones, Mussolini leaves his personal Alfa Romeo with Barracu to move into Pavolini's tank. He carries with him two pouches filled with documents and money, this vehicle guaranteeing him a greater degree of protection.

But, at less than a kilometre from Musso, at the height of a curve, the caravan finds the road blocked by a walnut tree trunk and large stones which force them to draw back and halt. Without even enough time to remove the blockage, a volley of gunfire is discharged on the column, but without hitting any victims in that group (although a worker at a nearby quarry does lose his life). A short time later—it was about seven-thirty—appear some Partisans of the "Luigi Clerici" 52nd Garibaldini Brigade, Puecher detachment, commanded by the twenty-five year old Tuscan nobleman Pier Bellini delle Stelle, but better known as Pedro.

The small group comes towards the military vehicles and the head Partisan asks to talk to the commanding officer. Finding out where the caravan is headed, Pedro objects that without his superior's authority, at that moment in Chiavenna, he cannot let them through.

The two have a long discussion, then decide to proceed together to that town. They return after several hours with the reply: the Germans are free to continue up to Ponte del Passo where they would have to stop to await further orders. As for the Fascists, they would all be handed over to the Partisans.

While the bargaining is going on, a great uneasiness spreads over the people in the caravan and some, smelling what is in the wind, seek refuge in the nearby houses of Musso and of Dongo, bartering their jewels and money for safety. Then, at twelve-thirty, after the rumour spreads that only the Germans would be allowed through, the agitation transforms itself into alarm and deserters become ever more numerous. Taking advantage of the growing chaos, other *gerarchi* including Bombacci, slip away and ask asylum from Padre Mainetti, Musso's parish priest.

Claretta is particularly jittery, especially about the fate of her Ben that she is able to see again during the long stop. She asks him if she could occupy a seat in the tank beside him, and he finally yields to her pleading (before getting in, she pulls on blue mechanic's overalls, and places an aviator's cap on her head).

They are not together long, in any case, since at a predetermined signal as in the agreement, the German column moves away from the Italian one. It is at this point that Kisnatt and Birzer approach the tank and invite Mussolini to join them.

The dictator refuses at first. He didn't want to save only himself. To abandon the *gerarchi* to their fate seemed, and was, too vile an act: either all or no one. Some of his most loyal followers, supported by Claretta, intervene to get him to change his mind. She implores him in tears: "Go, Duce, go!" (she is so upset that Casalinuovo has to scold her: "Signora, stop it! Shut up!")

Finally, the Capo climbs into one of the trucks, after having put on, against his will, the great coat of a Wehrmacht corporal, and a helmet, so as not to be recognized (the understanding with the Partisans stipulated, in fact, an inspection in the main piazza in the nearby town of Dongo).

Perhaps at the moment of leaving he really utters the historic sentence: "I am leaving with the Germans as I cannot trust the Italians." Many writers have commented on this statement, but to us it seems to be an unlikely sentiment. Mussolini had been harbouring bitterness towards Hitler for some time, the latter being guilty of having reduced him to the rank of a puppet proconsul. Most probably he says nothing, being in a state of inertia just then.

With the lifelessness of a robot, he climbs aboard truck no. 34, crouching in a corner, at the back. He'd have wanted to take Claretta as well but, precise as a good Teuton to the order received, Birzer answers that this was impossible.

As soon as the truck begins to move, freeing herself from Casalinuovo's grip, the latter holding her by the arm, the mistress begins to run, fooling herself into thinking that with that touching and impassioned gesture, the German officer would be affected enough to allow her to climb aboard the vehicle which had not yet attained its full speed.

Reaching it, she grasps the tailboard with both hands, but a mallet-like blow on the fingers from the butt-end of the soldier's gun forces her to let go. She continues to run, however, moving in a zigzag, almost as if she'd been struck by a sudden perdition.

She stops only when the truck disappears from view, swallowed up by a curve. Defeated then, her head in her hands deadened by the blow, she falls to her knees, breaking out into uncontrollable weeping.

Getting up, her look somewhat dazed, her steps erratic, she retraces her path to her family who, along with the *gerarchi* are waiting for her. Zita advises her to remove the overalls and to get back into her suit. She does that quickly, and then taking shelter in her brother's car, they proceed to Dongo with the rest of the column.

The drama was reaching its epilogue, but the curtain hadn't descended yet.

Twenty-One

The End Is Near

The Partisans are ready to search the German convoy at Dongo, as previously agreed.

Up to and including the fourth truck, everything goes according to plan; at the fifth, the dramatic turn of events. Giuseppe Negri, a shoemaker, one of the improvised inspectors, notes a sleepy man, shoulders turned towards the left side of the vehicle, with the collar of his great coat raised up, helmet riding low over his forehead.

Coming closer to check his identity, his path is blocked by the Germans who tell him that this is a drunken comrade: better just let him sleep. But Negri becomes suspicious, and elbowing his way through, moves forward anyway. As soon as he is in front of the man, he pulls down his coat collar. A quick glance at the unmistakable profile is enough. Other than a drunken soldier, that is Il Duce!

Although he is very excited, without showing any emotion, he rushes to Bill, the political vice-commissar of the 52nd Garibaldi Brigade, also known as Lazzaro Urbano, who later, with Pedro, will write the most detailed report on the capture of the Duce, of Claretta, and of the *gerarchi*. "The big cheese is here," he whispers in the other's ear, using his dialect.

Lazzaro asks him if he is certain, or if under the exceptional confusion and tension he is just seeing things. "I recognized him," he answers promptly, "I recognized him! He's the one!"

Bill warns him not to mention this to anyone because if the Germans are apprised of this fact, they can even begin shooting. He goes to the truck himself, to the side where Mussolini is seated, the collar of his coat now being raised up again.

"Comrade," the latter addresses him, but the other man doesn't move. He tries again with the title "Excellency," without better results. Only when he calls him "Cavaliere Benito Mussolini" does the startled dictator open his eyes. Now Bill jumps into the truck, and placing himself squarely before the dictator, takes the helmet and the glasses from him, and then the tommy-gun that the latter holds between his legs. He asks the Duce then if he has other weapons, and, unbuttoning his overcoat, the fallen leader pulls out a Glisenti nine-calibre pistol, missing one of its two facings.

"His face is waxen, and in that steady but faraway look, I read an extreme weariness, not fear," notes Lazzaro. "Mussolini seems no longer to have any willpower, being spiritually dead."

In the meantime a crowd surrounds the truck: the people want to see, to know, many not yet having understood what is going on. The Germans are mystified, fearing that they won't be able to continue on their retreat, and that they will have to surrender to the Partisans.

Bill declares the Duce under arrest "in the name of the Italian people." "I won't do anything," replies the dictator, looking at Lazzaro who reassures him with unintentional irony: "Not a single hair of your head will be touched." "Thanks," answers the bald prisoner, moving towards the back of the truck, hands up and eyes lowered, where Bill and another Partisan help him to descend. Hindered and jostled by the loud mob, in an indescribable crush, they head in the direction of the town hall, about sixty metres from the fateful truck.

Crossing the threshold, the Duce and his captors now including Rubini, Dongo's Mayor, enter a corridor leading to a plain, large room on the ground floor, lighted by two windows that look out onto the piazza. Along the wall are a pair of tables, as many benches on one of which the prisoner sits, his expression more dumbfounded than pained, his movements slow and mechanical. He takes off his coat and places it on the table after folding it carefully. He wears his Black Shirt, military officers' pants, and boots. According to Bill and Pedro, he has a leather bag with him (other witnesses say two), which he puts on a wooden box to his right.

At a certain point, the door is thrown open and the *gerarchi* Barracu, Casalinuovo, Utimpergher and Porta enter, escorted by Partisans of the 52nd Brigade. On seeing Mussolini, his associates spring to attention and exclaim differentially and in unison: "Hail, Duce," receiving in acknowledgment an absentminded, hardly noticeable nod of the head.

Bill now comes forward, positioning himself to Mussolini's right, behind one of the two tables on which the new arrivals have piled up their wallets and briefcases. The chief Partisan examines these items carefully, one by one, then he grasps the dictator's bag. But when he is about to open it, the latter takes his arm and softly, politely, suggests to him: "The documents in there are secret. I must advise you that they have a very great historical significance." At this point the Partisan hesitates for a moment, then proceeds to examine the contents.

There are many papers, all confidential: some refer to the situation in Trieste, others to an eventual flight to Switzerland; still others deal with the Verona trial.[47] There is also a bundle of letters in German exchanged with Hitler, with the relevant Italian translations, and a dossier titled "Umberto di Savoia." At the bottom of the roomy bag are one hundred sixty British pounds, three drafts of a half million lire, one of fifty thousand and four of twenty-five thousand lire issued by Italian banks. Finally, a pair of black leather gloves, a handkerchief, and a pencil that Bill returns to the prisoner, keeping however the documents and the money.

The news of Mussolini's arrest spreads throughout the region. Excited and incredulous hordes of the curious descend on Dongo from the nearby towns. Shouts are heard of "Death to the tyrant." There are those who want to try him immediately, and then execute him, while others, more expeditiously, demand a shooting at once.

Having decided to protect the prisoner from such frenzy, but also from the possibility of attempts by other Partisan groups or of fanatical "Republicans" from trying to seize Il Duce, Pedro talks with Pietro, also known as Michele Moretti, political commissar of the 52nd Brigade, and with Neri, aka Luigi Canali, inspector of the military regional command of Lombardy.[48] Together they decide to bring Mussolini and Porta to Germasino, to the barracks of the Customs Officials.

And Claretta?

Her brother's car in which she is also riding, along with Zita and her young nephews, is stopped by the Partisans after reaching Dongo. Coming close to Marcello, Bill, one of the leaders, demands to see identity papers. "I am a Spanish citizen and I am going to Switzerland," replies the inventive Petacci, lying. "This is my wife and these are my children." "Now you're not going to tell me that this is your sister?" the Partisan retorts with suspicious irony. "No, no, she is a woman who asked me for a ride."

Now Bill confiscates the passports, promising that he would return in a few minutes.

He reappears fifteen minutes later with orders to take them all to the municipal building. Together they make their way to the town hall. After crossing the corridor, the Petaccis enter a large

squalid room, lighted by a window overlooking the teeming piazza, swarming with men and women sporting red neckerchiefs.

After looking about her (there is only a pilot with them,
almost certainly Calistri, having joined the fleeing column acci-
dentally), Il Duce's lover loosens her blouse and pulls out a letter
that Ben had written to her that very morning, hoping that at
least she would be able to save herself. This was the last message
from her man and she would not have parted with it, but the fear
that someone would find it induces her to tear it up and discard it
in the refuse pile heaped up in the corner of the room. A knot was
tightening up her throat and her heart was becoming leaden.

In the meantime, Bill had examined Marcello and Zita's passports: one was made out to Don Juan Munez y Castillo, the other
one for his wife, the third one for the two together. In the two single ones, the date of birth of Marcello and Zita was entered as
1914, while in the combined one, La Ritossa's date was 1912 (but
besides this, rather than being embossed, the stamp was an oil
one). There was enough here to place them under arrest.

Feigning anger, Marcello protests with a threat: "You will pay
dearly for this. I have an appointment with Sir Northon in
Switzerland at seven this evening. I am expected then. Is it possible to imagine such nonsense?" But he isn't believed, and before
too long, Pedro conducts another interrogation, asking him who is
the brunette woman. "We don't know her," retorts the false envoy.
"She asked us for a ride and we had her get in." "I am an ordinary
citizen," affirms Claretta. "I found myself in Como during these
disorders by chance, and to avoid the danger of finding myself in
the midst of some battles, I asked these people for passage to try
to reach a safe spot. I really turned up at the right moment! What
will you do with me?"

She was seeking reassurance, but Pedro answers her with a
mysterious "We'll see," which makes her more nervous.

If she is worried about her fate, that of Ben positively alarms
her. What would happen to him? Would they hand him to the
Liberation Committee, or the Allies? Would they save his life or
would they take it from him? And, if he'd be condemned, would she
be able to see him again, to declare her love for him for the last
time, to give him a final farewell? Oh, if she were only allowed to
join him again, to die for him and with him, just as she'd lived for
him!

This is all she desires; this is the only wish she wants granted. If this drama is to end, let it be done cleanly, but with the shar-

ing of their destinies, not separating them, but sealing them as in the old mutual vow "Clara, I am yours, you are mine, Ben."

Meanwhile the Duce arrives in Germasino—it is not yet seven in the evening.

He is offered a mousse in the office of the head of customs. It is cold and he warms up by pacing to and fro in the room, while Porta throws on his shoulders, shawl-like, a military blanket obtained from the guards.

Brigadier Buffelli, one of the guards who will later provide the detailed narrative on Mussolini's brief stay in Germasino, is entrusted with the prisoner by Pedro, the latter having to return to Dongo.

However, before leaving, the Duce takes Pedro aside and asks him softly to greet "that person who is already at Dongo and who is under arrest as well." To Pier Bellini's question, "Who is that?" surprised and almost annoyed, he doesn't answer. "In any case, we're going to find out any way," the Partisan says curtly, at which the dictator stammers: "La ...la ... Petacci." The head Garibaldino promises to do so, and leaves.

Left alone with Buffelli (Porta is outside smoking a cigarette), Mussolini questions him. "Why have you arrested me?" "We haven't arrested you, but we've stopped you," states more precisely the customs guard. "Why?" "Because you are an Italian and we don't intend that more Italians go to Germany to be slaughtered by Germans." "What can you blame on me?" "Nothing except of having brought us to this state of affairs. Do you have any idea of the marvels that the war has wrought to our country?" "The people wanted war, the King signed the decree." "And you were the innocent broker." "If you remember well, in June 1940 all Italians wanted war." Buffelli reminds him then of the Alliance with the Führer, at which the prisoner cites the German proverb "No plant goes to heaven," observing philosophically that "all human endurance has its limits," and that Hitler shouldn't forget this.

With badly hidden apprehension, he asks the sergeant at this point what would happen to the Fascists, but the latter replies that he doesn't know. Porta then returns with his guard and Buffelli goes out, re-entering about ten minutes later.

The bickering resumes. The war is brought up again, and America, and the Soviet Union, and Roosevelt, and Stalin, then on to 25 July, to 8 September, to the speech at the Lyric Theatre. Being confronted with his real responsibilities, the prisoner defends himself energetically, deflecting many of the accusations towards his German ally: "All that is missing is that a member of the SS got into bed with me."

The talking continues until about eight-thirty when a meal is served consisting of a light pasta, vegetables with kid, Parmesan, mousse and tea. Mussolini eats heartily, but slowly, his left hand in his coat pressing against his stomach.

At nine-fifteen he gets up from the table and he begins to walk about the room, to digest better. He returns to sit down when Buffelli asks him to prepare a written declaration about his arrest.

The demand makes him suspicious and he refuses to do this. Then the brigadier explains the reason behind the request and in the end he consents: "But only as a type of historic relic." "Fine," answers Buffelli. "What must I write?" he asks. "The 52nd Garibaldini Brigade arrested me today, 27 April, in Dongo's piazza," the customs' officer prompts him with embarrassment, choosing the words carefully. "The treatment accorded me, during and after the capture was correct." The prisoner writes this, signs the declaration, and hands the paper to his guard.

They talk about Germany again, of its imminent surrender, of the missed refuge in Switzerland, of the *gerarchi* detained at Dongo, of the right of the people to freedom, but also of a certain man who got fifty thousand lire from the Duce in exchange for the formula for the fusion of two metals, of nickel and copper.

The time is now eleven, and the exhausted prisoner would like to lie down. But before going to the little room that the command has prepared for him, Mussolini asks to use the washroom, and Buffelli accompanies him personally. Assuring himself that the bed is satisfactory, the blankets sufficient, the sergeant wishes the guest a good night, which the latter reciprocates with cordiality.

In the meantime, once again at Dongo, Pedro inquires on the fate of the "Spaniards," and he is told that they have been moved to a hotel, but that the woman who is traveling with them is still in the town hall. In line with the task that he undertook, he goes to her and finds her sitting down, more frightened and nervous than when he'd left her.

Seeing him again, Claretta's face exhibits a touch of alarmed curiosity. Why does the head Garibaldino return to her? To question her again? To free her? To imprison her as at Novara?

Pedro who relates the following dialogue, senses her anxiety and, without beating around the bush, tells her: "Signora, I have been asked to relay greetings." "Greetings? From whom?" she inquires, coming out of her confusion. "From a person that I've just left; from one of my prisoners ..." "But you're joking. It's not possible ... I don't know anyone here ... Perhaps the Spanish gentleman who was so kind to offer me a lift? ..." "No, signora; from another person that you know very well. From Mussolini ..." "Mussolini said something?" exclaims Claretta, pretending dismay that amazes even her questioner. "But I don't know him! How is it possible for me to receive greetings from someone that I don't know?" "Signora," replies the annoyed Partisan commander, "it is useless for you to try to deceive me. I know who you are: Mussolini told me himself." "But look," insists the woman, "there must be some mistake ... I don't understand." "I assure you," he pursues, "I know perfectly well who you are, and therefore your efforts to hide your identity are useless. But, if you insist on not believing that you are the person for whom the greetings are meant, there is no use for me to repeat what he begged me to tell you."

And still in Pedro's narrative of the long emotional talk that he has with the Duce's mistress, he pretends to leave the room at this point, but she detains him, seeking to have him amplify what she's just heard. Finally, realizing that she can't extricate herself from the situation in which she finds herself, she discloses her identity: "Yes, it's true, I am Clara Petacci. I'm relying on you; I hope that you aren't trying to trick me. Tell me, tell me ... what did he tell you to tell me? Where is he now? Is he in danger? How is he? Who is holding him? Who commands here? ..." In her changed attitude, and in her agitated questions was the pain of one who first denies to protect her personal relations (rather than herself), then confesses so as not to betray her actual love.

"Stay calm, signora," Pier Bellini reassures her. "Mussolini is in no danger, and he won't be as long as I have him in my charge. I am not linked to my superior command and, therefore, I don't know when I might receive orders ... For the moment, therefore, no evil will befall him, be assured of that ... barring that no attempts are made to free him. Under those circumstances, I really don't know what might happen."

Throwing her hands into the air, he hardly has time to finish before Claretta, selecting her words with care, interrupts him scornfully: "Free him? But who do you think is going to free him? If you only knew what I've seen in the last few days! My God, what miserable things! Absolute ruin! Everyone is running, everyone is thinking only of saving his own wretched life, but no one is thinking of protecting the life of the man that for so many years they had proclaimed to love and had sworn to save with their lives. Everyone is treacherous. Everyone has abandoned him in these dangerous hours ... My God, who knows what pain, what grief for him alone, abandoned, defeated, to see that his followers were faithful only when they needed him, and now that he is the one who needs help, everyone turns his back on him and repudiates him."

Pedro cuts off the outburst with the observation that this is the fate of the powerful, victims of ambitious and treacherous advisors, besides their own personal folly. Claretta retorts bitterly that in misfortune a person is always alone, after which she asks anxiously: "Then you can assure me that he is well? What did he ask you to tell me?" "Oh, nothing important," minimizes Pedro. "He only asked me to give you his greetings, and to tell you not to worry about him since he needs nothing and he is treated well."

But she insists. She wants to know what will become of Ben, but Pedro doesn't know, limiting himself to asserting: "I've already taken steps to communicate to the high command in Milan that Mussolini was captured with almost all his governmental associates and I await the decisions that will be taken." "You, however, should hand him over to the Allies," naively suggests the woman. "He'll be safer with them."

But the chief Garibaldino doesn't agree: "The Allies have nothing to do with all this," he says. "They must not get involved in any of these matters. Only Italians have the right to judge one who governed them for twenty years, dragging them into a suicidal war."

The conversation is interrupted when a Partisan enters to tell Pedro that he is wanted outside. The chief Garibaldino gets up, but an extremely rapid, unexpected question causes him to retrace his steps: "Tell me, what will happen to me?" "I don't know," he answers. "... The authorities will decide." The prisoner asks him what these people could possibly want from her, and he reminds her that she was Mussolini's advisor for a long time. "Even you believe all the things that have been said about me," she bristles resentfully. "But what should I do to have you understand that there is nothing true about all of this? How can I have you understand that I was with him for such a long time only because I loved him? I loved him so much that I made his life my life, that I did not exist except in those few instances when I could be with him. You must believe me." And, sobbing painfully, she withdraws into herself, covering her face with her hands.

"Please calm down, signora, I beg you," Pedro urges her. "I believe everything you've told me ... Don't look at me as an enemy, even if unfortunate circumstances have placed us in conditions to consider ourselves such ... I've changed my mind about you and now I see you more as an unlucky person than an adventuress. But you must calm down."

Claretta looks up again, daubs her eyes and her cheeks with a linen handkerchief, and thanks him with a faltering voice: "I never thought of finding so much goodness and understanding in an enemy ... Your words have given me the strength to request a favour, a great favour, that I wouldn't have the courage now to ask of anyone else but you. Will you grant it to me?"

The man asks her what the favour was concerning, and she hesitates for an instance, as if to make her wish more dramatic, then impulsively: "My love for Mussolini has been, and remains, very great. Perhaps you are too young to be able to understand me, but life's circumstances may lead you to recall my words one day ... To become Il Duce's mistress, of the man who at that time was at the apex of power, had become the secret or open ambition of many women. This position represented almost one of pride and conceit ... that was not really what I wanted, not what I was looking for. I'd never ask for anything; I'd only wanted him to consider me a sweet and dear friend, one to whom he could run when the need arose to escape for a while from the storms of life, to find refuge in a tranquil spot, in a serene and peaceful atmosphere ...

"Irrevocably, little by little, the simplicity of my tenderness and the sincerity of my love modify his closed and exclusive character even regarding his thoughts, so much so that little by little we finally attain an intimate, spiritual coalescence. Only then am I rewarded ... If, at times, I used the sway that I had on him, it was merely to sponsor someone who'd come to me to beg me to plead a case with Il Duce ... I endured all his philandering stoically ... When the hour of the Regime was up, it never occurred to me, even fleetingly, to abandon him. I followed him to Milan, to Como, to Menaggio, and I would have followed him anywhere in all his sad wandering as a fugitive, exposing myself to all the dangers. How easy it would have been had I not loved him to go on alone, unobserved, and flee outside the country with my family. Don't you think that this is the best proof that my love was true love, and not base reckoning or self-interest? Don't you also believe that?"

"Yes, I believe that," Pedro answers laconically but compassionately, while Claretta seems a little heartened: the unburdening was good for her, and now her questioner is looking at her through different eyes. If he could, he would grant her wish. "Put me with him, put me with him. Why is that bad? Don't tell me that you can't. Don't tell me that you don't want to."

"No, signora," replies Pier Bellini, pulling back gently the hand that she had taken hold of. "You are asking me for something that I wasn't expecting and which involves a certain responsibility. I wouldn't want anything to happen ..."

"What do you expect to happen? You don't think that I could help him escape?"

"That's not it, but look ... the situation is still so fluid ... it is possible that Fascists would try to free him ... and once together, if something happened to him, even you would be in danger, and I wouldn't want to have such a responsibility ..."

At this moment Claretta has a fit of pique. Her cheeks get red, her eyes cloud over, her voice, at first mournful, rages in a spiteful denial: "That's not true, that's not true. Now I understand. You want to shoot him. That's it, that's it. I know, I know. Oh my God! You want to shoot him!"

"But signora, I want to tell you ..." Pedro tries to explain.

"No, don't say anything, I wouldn't believe you anyway," Claretta continues imperiously. "You want to shoot him, I know it, I feel it. Perhaps you've received orders to do so ... But I will ask you this now, and this you can't refuse me. I have no crimes or faults to answer for. I can't be accused of anything and therefore they can do nothing to me and I will certainly be allowed to go free. But now you must promise me that if Mussolini is shot, I will be able to be near him until the last moment, and that I shall be shot with him. I'm not asking too much, am I?"

"But, signora, I repeat ..." the chief Garibaldino tries once again to interrupt her.

"Don't talk," she retorts combatively. "You've got to promise only this, understand? I want to die with him. My life would have absolutely no purpose after his death. I would die as well, only slowly and very painfully. This is the only thing that I ask of you: to die with him. You can't deny me this request."

Pedro asks her to calm down once again, telling her that he has no intention of shooting her man: "While I have the power to look after him, nothing bad will happen to him."

"Really?"

"I give you my word."

"I believe it. But, why then don't you want to put me with him?"

"I didn't say that I didn't want to put you with him. I was only wondering if I could do that ... In any case, I'll consult my friends." Then he leaves.

He returns a short time later to inform her that he spoke with Canali and Moretti and that they agree with him. Then, in a rush of gratitude, she takes his hand to kiss it, but he is embarrassed and he fends her off.

"Are we leaving soon?" she asks him. "No," he replies ... "we have to move Mussolini to a safer place, and we will take you also."

"Then we will make the trip together," exclaims Claretta.

"We'll see," replies Pedro. "Stay here now for a little while and remain calm. Try to rest because we won't leave for two or three hours."

In fact, the head Garibaldino must go to the hotel to Marcello who has asked to see him: he wants Pedro to telephone Milan to ascertain his identity and his position as legate. Pier Bellini promises him that he will do this, and says goodbye. Then he returns to the town hall where Pietro and Neri are waiting for him to decide together the plan for the removal of the Duce from Germasino to San Maurizio, to a house on the other side of the Lake.

Pedro himself goes to fetch Mussolini from the barracks of the customs officials where he arrives at about thirty minutes after midnight. He is received by a Partisan who rushes to Buffelli, the latter then going to awaken Mussolini: "Orders have arrived to leave. You need to get up." "Very well, I imagined that," complies the Duce who dresses hurriedly, exchanging the loathsome German overcoat for a similar garment of the customs officials.

He is then brought to Pedro who has a large bandage in his hand. "Will you allow me to blindfold you?" he asks the prisoner. "We have to go through various barricades and it is better that you are not recognized." The dictator raises no objections, muttering a baffled "Yes, yes." After this he inclines his head docilely to Buffelli who carries out the procedure, leaving his eyes and nose uncovered.

At one thirty-five, one hour later, the head Garibaldino and that of the dying Fascism, climb into a car with one of Pedro's Partisans. Goal: the bridge that leads to a forge, prearranged spot for the meeting with another car in which are Neri, his Partisan girlfriend Giuseppina Tuissi (Gianna), Pietro, a Garibaldino and La Petacci. While heading towards Dongo from Germasino, the Duce asks the Partisan commander if he's spoken to "la signora"

and how she is. "Very well," he replies, expecting the Duce's surprised reaction. "She wanted to join you. She begged and implored
so much that we decided to accommodate her."

Mussolini gives a stupified start: never could he have imagined that he'd be sharing with Claretta even this last dramatic
adventure.

At the bridge, under a heavy pelting rain, La Petacci followed
by Neri, and the Duce, escorted by Pedro get out of their respective cars to greet each other. A few exchanges, rapid and without
sadness, almost a meeting of strangers who have nothing to say to
one another. "Why did you want to follow me?" asks the dictator.
"I prefer it that way," answers his mistress. "But what's happened
to you. You are bandaged." "Nothing, nothing, it's only a precaution." No handshake, no embrace, no gesture that could even
remotely betray their lengthy intimacy of so many years.

Before getting back into the car, Claretta reminds Pedro of
the promise he'd made. "Why don't you put us together. You promised that to me ..." But the Garibaldino commander says that this
is not the time: until Como it is best to travel in separate cars (in
the meantime, taking advantage of the stop, Gianna moves into
Mussolini's car).

The cars are forced to stop at various barricades where
Canali is always recognized. To the inevitable question "Who is
the man wrapped in the large piece of gauze?" he answers that it
is someone who is wounded requiring urgent care.

A little before Menaggio, some Partisans, more suspicious
than others, fire a round of machine-gun bullets at the cars, fortunately without hitting anything. Pedro gets out of his vehicle and,
hiding behind a rock yells that this is not the way to carry out an
inspection. Neri arrives, the misunderstanding is cleared up, and
the cars continue on their journey.

Something more serious happens at Moltrasio. Alarmed at
the echo of gun fire, Neri stops the car in the deserted piazza and
gets out, heading for one of the nearby buildings. A few minutes
later he reappears, worried and hesitant. The Allies, he says, have
reached Como during the night. To continue towards the main
town of that region is to risk falling into their hands, provided that
they do not fall first into the hands of the "Republican" Brigades
still active in the region.

He suggests that perhaps it would be best to turn back. About
forty minutes from Moltrasio, at about mid Lake, is the little town
of Azzano, and a little further up, in the hamlet of Bonzanigo, is a

farmstead of some friends where he'd often found shelter. The dictator and his mistress can be accommodated there temporarily for the night. Then it would be necessary to see. Nobody objects and the cars turn back.

Claretta and Mussolini follow the goings-on with indifference: she doesn't open her mouth for the entire trip, deep in her own unhappy thoughts. From time to time, in a monotone, he asks how much further before reaching their destination.

At Azzano, they get out of their cars, with their respective escorts, two by two, to negotiate the steep trail that leads to the farmhouse (Canali and Moretti in front; then the prisoners; then Gianna and Pedro; last, the Partisans Lino and Sandrino, the latter better known as "Menefrego").

According to Pier Bellini, the only source at our disposal, Claretta is pale and exhausted: tested by so much suffering, humiliation, and disillusion, her face reveals an immense sadness and an infinite bewilderment. She'd never felt so unhappy, but never, as now, was she forced to hide this. Not for herself, but for him. To encourage him, even with so many doubts and fears that, if the settling of accounts is near, the decision may not be unchangeable. She pretends to be strong, to give him some strength as well, suffocating the tears that flood her heart and macerate her soul because this finale will be so costly for them.

She climbs up the path with difficulty since her heels bother her on the wet pebbles of the mule trail. Pedro and Mussolini offer her their arm and, after a few minutes, they reach the yard of the farmhouse. Neri, who is a few metres ahead, loudly calls De Maria, his friend, who peers out sleepily from the open gallery and invites them all to come in.

Using a small stone stairway, they reach the first floor where the kitchen is located and welcomed by Lia, the lady of the house, who has already taken care to make a fire in the fireplace.

In the large, simple room, the main piece of furniture is the wooden table, surrounded by six chairs, on which Claretta and her lover almost collapse.

Not recognizing them, Lia says that the two newcomers can sleep in their children's room, the latter will move into the hayloft. Then she prepares an ersatz coffee that the Duce refuses. After this, she goes to make the bed.

When she returns, Pedro, Neri, and Pietro each choose to have a look at the room that is on the same floor as the kitchen. The centre of the room is occupied by an enormous double bed, above whose headboard is a reproduction of the Madonna of Pompeii, two heavy bedside tables, a couple of chairs, a chest, a clothes tree, a lamp with a moveable lampshade, and a tripod with a basin and a jug for water. In the wall is set a small window, with wooden shutters, which looks out onto the courtyard cluttered with farm equipment (the drop is at least five metres: too high to try to flee through there).

Coming back into the kitchen, Pier Bellini summons Lino and Sandrino and he puts the prisoners in their charge: the Partisans are to leave the lovers alone in the room, but with the door left ajar and, at the first sound, weapons in hand, they are to take immediate action. As soon as he can, he will send other men for a change of guard.

After this, he approaches Mussolini and La Petacci, the latter asking him to fetch her overnight bag left in Dongo. Then, he wishes them a good night.

While going out, he casts a last glance at the prisoners, motionless before the fireplace: he with his hands on his knees, his face as if swallowed by the flames that were gradually fading into ashes, an ominous metaphor of a fate inescapable by now; she, bending forward, her hands supporting her chin, her eyes mesmerized by the dying tongues of the flame.

At a certain point, Claretta gets up and asks to use the toilet. The woman of the house replies that a toilet as such does not exist there, but only an outhouse in the yard, to which she accompanies her personally, lighting the way with an old oil lamp, both escorted by Sandrino who releases the safety latch on his tommy-gun. Carrying a towel and a piece of soap, La Petacci crosses the threshold of the outhouse, banking the door without closing it, however. But she notices that there is no water, and she mentions this to Lia who goes to fill a bucket after having handed the lantern to Sandrino.

With the brief wash completed, Claretta moves into her assigned room where she finds Giacomo De Maria with Ben, standing at the window. She approaches the bed and with the tips of her fingers feels the softness of the mattress. Satisfied and smiling, she invites her lover to lie down.

Seeing then that a pillow is missing—Mussolini uses two— she tells Lia who quickly brings another one, with a mended pillowcase. Claretta positions the two already on the bed at Ben's spot, reserving the threadbare one for her own use. After a short time, the De Maria couple take their leave, while Lino and

Sandrino station themselves on the gallery to keep an eye on the inside of the room whose entrance is not completely shut.

Left alone with her man, Claretta helps him to get rid of the bothersome bandages, and to undress. Then she also removes her clothes, keeping on her underwear. He gets into bed heavily, she lies down beside him, taking one of his hands and bringing it maternally up to her lips. After this, she turns towards him and throws her arms around his neck. Ben takes her in his arms, exchanging a lethargic smile because of her emotional gesture. Outside the rain continues to fall, and it will soon be dawn.

At a certain point, a small noise rouses the suspicion of the guards and they barge into the room. At their appearance, she pulls the sheet to her eyes, while the Duce sits up and scolds them: "Away, children, don't be bad boys now." The two return to the gallery. The time is not yet five.

At about ten, the prisoners rise. Although very tired, neither he nor she have slept a wink, perhaps. Claretta had wept, and her mascara, mixed with the tears, had left a stain on the torn pillowcase. This is the first, and last, night that she spends entirely with her man.

As if in a crazed kaleidoscope, her mind is filled with the magic afternoons within the austere walls of Palazzo Venezia, the endless waiting, the fleeting meetings in the Room of the Zodiac, and the very lovely verses of Elizabeth Barrett Browning:

_____ I love thee with the breath,
Smiles, tears, of all my life! _____ and, if God choose,
I shall love thee better after death.

Years of superb happiness, marvelously carefree, which seemed meant to last an eternity. But, instead, all is finished, overwhelmed by a horrendous shipwreck: without even a raft to pull oneself onto, no safe harbour to drop anchor, and no guiding star in the heavens. Only one thing has escaped the dreadful disaster: her love for Ben, that love that only her sublime dedication and her intensity immortalizes. He will be forever her Duce, in whom she will blindly believe, and whom she, absurdly, would like to see rise again. A childlike, deceptive, desperate illusion!

In the meanwhile, the De Marias have awakened also, and Giacomo goes to visit the couple.

At the sight of the prisoner without his bandages, he is dumbfounded and he staggers: never would he have imagined that, one day, he would be host to Il Duce of Fascism!

Regaining his composure, he asks the two what they would like to have for breakfast; then, he goes to his wife and tells her what he's just seen. The woman thinks that's all a prank, but when she enters the room bearing a rough tray with a pitcher of milk, polenta, and salami, she doesn't believe her own eyes. With trembling hands, she places the platter on a wooden box covered with an old napkin, and she goes out.

Claretta eats the polenta and milk heartily, while Ben listlessly tastes a slice of salami and drinks a glass of water.

The rain is no longer falling, but the sky is still sulky. The clock in the nearby belfry strikes eleven.

Twenty-Two

A Lame Horse for a ...

The news of the arrest of Mussolini and of his *gerarchi* reaches Milan in the late afternoon of the 27th.

The first to hear about this event is Colonel Alfredo Malgeri, the commander of the Customs Service who is in the Government building conferring with Riccardo Lombardi, the new prefect.

Immediately he informs the Headquarters of the *Corpo Volontari della Libertà*, a member of which is Colonel Valerio, also known as Walter Audisio, a thirty-six year old accountant from Alessandria, an ironclad Communist, under Longo's direct orders, and assistant to Cadorna, head of this same Corps.

Audisio would like to know more, but the chaos is enormous and the information contradictory. At eleven-twenty in the evening, Malgeri who has in the meantime received a second message, reveals to Valerio that the hiding place is at Germasino. "The Command," says Audisio to him, "has charged me with the task of capturing Mussolini and transporting him to Milan. Under no circumstances is he to fall alive into the hands of any other persons."

Actually, the Allies are carrying out an indefatigable hunt for him as is shown by the message radioed from Siena earlier at six by the Special Commands Unit of the American Office of Strategic Services, seeking from the highest officials of the Milan Partisans "Mussolini's exact location" and his "delivery." But the heads of the Resistance who just that morning had had a lengthy and heated discussion on the fate of the Duce and of his associates, don't intend—at least not in the majority—to give up carrying out their own form of justice.

The most resolute are Pertini the Socialist,[49] Valiani of the Action Party, and the Communists Sereni and Longo, in favour of immediate shooting of the dictator. Even Cadorna seems in agreement and, perhaps because of this, he signs the laissez-passers immediately for Audisio and for Aldo Lampredi, a forty-six year old Tuscan, Longo's right-hand man known as Guido, who will accompany Valerio on the dangerous mission.

Since the Allies persist, at three in the morning of the 28th, the Command of the *Corpo Volontari della Libertà* radios them this message: "Sorry not to be able to hand over Mussolini who's been tried by the People's Court and was executed at the same spot where previously the Nazi-Fascists had executed fifteen patriots."[50] Three hours later, Valerio, Lampredi, and a select platoon of twelve men, headed by Riccardo the Partisan, also known as Alfredo Mordini, set out for the trip to Como.

At about eight, Valerio and Guido reach the prefecture of the main town of the Como region, where they meet the heads of the local "Liberation Committee," the latter wanting to imprison the Duce and his *gerarchi* in the jail of the small town. The Colonel replies that the persons arrested must be taken to Milan as soon as possible on board a "large covered truck." But such a vehicle cannot be found. At eleven, seeing that time is passing, he calls Luigi Longo in Milan for instructions. The future Secretary and President of the Communist Party of Italy has only one, final and irrevocable: "Either you get rid of him or we get rid of you."

A half hour later, the anxiously awaited truck arrives, an ancient charcoal-powered vehicle that Valerio rejects, however. One will be provided later, he says. He is, in fact, in a great hurry as he is to reach Dongo quickly, and in the town hall he has a violent encounter with Pedro, the latter not wishing to hand over the prisoners, and also opposed to summary execution. "You are only a subordinate, and I am one of your superiors. Your only duty is to obey," rams in Audisio, asking for the names of the persons arrested.

Pier Bellini gives the list to him reluctantly, and the other begins to check it, putting a cross beside many names: "Benito Mussolini, death. Clara Petacci, death ..."

"Death for La Petacci?" rebels Pedro. "You want to shoot a woman? She has absolutely no responsibility." "She was Mussolini's adviser," rages Valerio. "She abetted his policies for all these years. She is as blameworthy as he is." The head Garibaldino doesn't concede defeat: "What advisor! She was only his mistress!" "I am not the one condemning her," replies Audisio tersely. "She's already been condemned."

The list of the persons to be executed now settled, learning that one of the detainees is passing himself off as a Spanish legate, Valerio sends Bill to get him. As soon as the "Spaniard" is before him, he questions the latter in his "own" tongue that he knows having fought alongside Longo in the Iberian peninsula during the Civil War there. But, not being able to make heads or tails of even one word, the dumbfounded Marcello remains silent.

Convinced that this is Vittorio, Mussolini's son, Audisio then hands him back to Bill with orders to shoot him. Then he rises and, with Lampredi and Moretti (who knows where Mussolini can be found), leaves for Bonzanigo in a black FIAT 1100, with a Rome license plate, requisitioned along with its driver. The time is now three-ten in the afternoon of 28 April.

But here is Valerio's 1973 version, the last one, time-wise, in a disconcerting and suspect series.

"After Mezzegra, leaving the route along the Lake, the next narrow and deserted road on which the car chugged up labouriously, led us to Bonzanigo. Along this street I chose the site for the execution: a curve, the closed gate of an orchard, a house at the end clearly deserted.

"The spot, about a kilometre from Bonzanigo, was called Giulino di Mezzegra. But this detail I learn from Pietro after the sentence is carried out, because at that moment I had made the choice mentally, without mentioning it either to Guido or to the other two. A suitable site was thus chosen. A little further along I have the car stopped. I get out, remove the safety catch from the tommy-gun, and fire a shot to try out the weapon. It was in working order.

"We continue on foot: Pietro first, followed by me and by Guido; I give orders to the car driver not to move from there until our return. During the brief walk, I turn and say to Guido: 'You know what I've just thought of? I'll tell him we've come to free him.'

" 'He's not an imbecile,' observes Guido, 'how do you think he's going to swallow that?'

"Wait and see. He'll lap it up," I insist.

"In any case, I thought that even if he were incredulous, it would be much easier to take him away under that pretext.

"The small house of the De Maria farmers was half way up the slope, set on the mountain. The two Partisan guards were standing on the landing near the door, at the top of a stairway cut into the natural stone. Pietro the commissar speaks briefly to the two Partisans and then, turning to me calls out: 'Come along.'

"One of the two men on guard pulls the bolt, the door opens and I enter the room alone, stopping just inside the threshold. Everyone else is silent and motionless on the landing.

"Mussolini was standing to the right of the bed, observing, in uniform, wearing a hazel-colored overcoat. La Petacci was in bed, under the covers, all dressed. He looks at me frightened and whispers: 'What is it?'

"I was looking at him straight in the face. His lower lip was trembling. This was, perhaps, the first time in his life that he found himself completely without cover before danger. Between him and his enemies there had always been a wall of tyranny: first the *squadristi*, then the police. Now, instead, we were face to face.

"I thought that for him, perhaps, this might be a perfect occasion to show an enemy that he was a man. If not for honour, at least to be remembered in history, as they say. But no, that man was trembling with fear; that man didn't even have the power of conceit. Before my tommy-gun he was even giving up the idea of history.

"Standing by the door, I exclaim: 'I've come to free you,' and I continue to look at him. At my words, the expression on his face changes: 'Really,' he grunts quickly; and he says nothing else to me: neither seeking information, or details of that 'liberation.'

" 'Quickly, you must move quickly. There's no time to lose,' I add. Meanwhile, he regains his self-confidence; the fear of a moment before gives way to the old cockiness of Il Duce, to his familiar imperialistic stance. 'Where are we going?' he asks, already sure of his business.

"Instead of answering him, I ask him: 'Are you armed?' My question was in the tone of one who is concerned about supplying him with a weapon.

" 'No, I'm not armed,' he replies. And now, suddenly, there was no longer any terror, nor cockiness in him, but he was in a hurry. He moves, in fact towards me, towards the door.

" 'Let's go,' he says. He'd entirely forgotten the woman in bed and I remind him of her.

" 'Before you, the woman,' I say. And turning to La Petacci, I press her with a glance. She hadn't caught on to what was happening yet since she certainly had not understood the meaning of the words spoken. Nevertheless, to my coaxing looks, she hurries up anxiously to collect her personal things.

"At this point Mussolini tries once again the motion of going out and I let him pass me before La Petacci. At that instant, his face transfixed, turning his head towards me he says in the re-acquired tone of a First Marshal: 'I offer you an empire!'...

"We were still at the doorstep of the house. Instead of answering him, I urge along La Petacci. 'Let's go, let's go,' I mutter.

"Thus La Petacci catches up to Mussolini. The two are followed by me and by Guido; Pietro precedes all of us. We set out for the mule trail that descended from half way up the slope to the place where our black FIAT was stopped. La Pettaci was teetering about hesitantly along the steep path, bothered by the high heels of her small, black suede shoes.

"More than ever Duce, he was walking at a brisk pace, sure of himself, with the air somewhere between that of a soldier on the march and a man in a hurry. If I hadn't led him to believe that I was there to save his life, we'd probably have been forced to take him away in the state of collapse in which we found him. Instead, he was once again himself: the Man of Destiny.

"While we were going down, I almost felt tranquil: I was certain that my mission would be reaching its goal. This is what I was thinking of. I was thinking that 'he' was there before me, and that in a few minutes the justice of the people would be carried out.

"Along the way Mussolini turns around only once, and I whisper to him: 'I've also freed your son Vittorio' (thus trying to squeeze out of him some indirect indication on the unknown diplomat arrested at Dongo).

" 'Thanks from the bottom of my heart,' he says and then he asks: 'Where are Zerbino and Mezzasoma?'

"I reply: 'They are also being freed.'

" 'Ah,' he utters, and he doesn't turn around again.

"It was obvious that he knew nothing about his son Vittorio. He wasn't even bothering to find out about Pavolini and the others.

"Reaching the car, Mussolini seems convinced that he is a free man. He makes the gesture of giving precedence to La Petacci, but I say to him: 'You climb in first; you'll be better protected there. But that Fascist cap is a bit thick. Take it off.'

"And he actually removes it, but then he passes his hand on his big bald head. 'And this?' he asks.

" Then put the cap back on and lower the visor down to your eyes.

"By now, for me, matters would have gone well no matter which way. We leave. On the back seat are Mussolini and La Petacci; in front, the driver and Guido. Pietro is standing on the footboard on the woman's side. I sit on the back fender on the right, with my back to the road, and my face turned towards Mussolini. That way I have him constantly in view.

"Slowly the car begins the descent. Only I know the site chosen, and as soon as we arrive before the gate, I order a halt, signaling to Mussolini not to talk. In a soft voice, drawing close to the car window, I whisper to him: 'I heard some suspicious sounds. I'm going to see.'

"I move to reconnoiter the road to make sure that no one is coming towards us. After I retrace my steps, I notice that Mussolini's face has changed: it is now showing signs of fear. Guido tells me then that he'd said to him already that 'the party's over.'

"It was obvious anyway that by looking at him carefully, I could see that Mussolini was only slightly suspicious. I send Pietro the commissar and the driver in opposite directions to be lookouts about fifty to sixty metres from each other.

"Then I have Mussolini get out and I tell him to go between the wall and the post of the gate. He obeys as tractable as a lamb. He doesn't believe yet that he is going to die, he isn't yet aware of the real world … He walks heavily, dragging his right leg a little. The open seam of his boot is clearly visible.

"Then La Petacci gets out of the car as well and quickly, on her own initiative, she goes to him, he having reached the spot indicated obediently, with his back to the wall. It all took a moment. Suddenly I begin to read the text of the death sentence of Benito Mussolini, the war criminal:

'By order of the General Command of the *Corpo Volontari della Libertà* I am charged with the task of rendering justice to the Italian People.'

"I think that Mussolini didn't even understand those words. He was looking at the tommy-gun pointing at him with eyes wide open, horrified. La Petacci throws her arms around his shoulders.

"I say, 'Get away from there if you don't want to die as well.'

"The woman understands immediately the sense of the 'as well' and she moves away from the condemned man. As for him, he doesn't utter a single human sound: not the name of one of his children, not of his mother, of his wife; not a scream, nothing. He was trembling, overcome with terror, and he was stammering convulsively with those huge lips of his: 'But, but, but … my colonel … but, but, but … my colonel.'

"Not even a word to that woman who was hopping about near him, who was moving here and there, displaying a look of absolute confusion, not a single word to her. No, he was begging, in the most vile way, for his fat trembling body. That's the only thing he was thinking of, of that fat body that he had leaned against the small wall.

"I've said that as a precaution, I had tried out the tommy-gun a few minutes before entering the De Maria house; so, I pressed the trigger, but no shots fire. The weapon is clogged. I work the breech-block, try to fire again, but the weapon wouldn't discharge. Guido seizes his pistol, fires the gun but—it seems a stroke of fate—the pistol is blocked. Mussolini appears not to be aware of this. By now he is aware of nothing.

"I pick up the tommy-gun, grabbing it by the barrel, ready to use it as a bludgeon, expecting—despite everything—some reaction. Any normal man would have tried to defend himself, but Mussolini was way beneath what a normal man should be, and he continues muttering, trembling, without moving away, his mouth still slightly open and his arms dangling by his side.

"I call the commissar of the 52nd Brigade loudly who comes running to bring me his weapon. Pietro exchanges his weapon for mine, ten paces from Mussolini, and then he runs back to his guard post.

"In all, only a few minutes have passed, time that anyone condemned to death could have used to make a desperate escape or, at least, an attempt to struggle. Instead, he who was supposed to live like a 'lion,' was a poor, trembling defeated rag, unable to move.

"In the brief period that it took Pietro to bring me his tommy-gun, I had the feeling that I was really alone with Mussolini.

"The watchful and involved Guido is there.

"La Petacci is also there, beside 'him,' almost touching him with her elbow, but she doesn't count.

"'He' and I are the only ones there.

"In the damp air, the silence is heavy. The short panting of the condemned one is clearly visible. On the other side of the gate, between the green mass of the orchard, appears a part of the white façade of a house. Beyond this, the mountain.

"The blocking of the automatic weapon certainly had not provided Mussolini with even a shred of a hope, knowing by now that he had to die. And with this feeling, he is enclosed, as if by a cloud of unconsciousness that is protecting him from sorrow. He isn't even aware of the presence of she who'd been his woman.

"Even I have no more hatred for him; there is only the inflexible need for justice for the thousands upon thousands of dead, for the millions of starving and betrayed. I even don't have the feeling that I am going to kill a man.

"When I am once more squarely before him, I fire five bullets from the submachine gun into his trembling body. The war criminal collapses onto his knees, leaning against the wall, with his head inclining towards his chest.

"Stunned and frantic, La Petacci moves confusedly, is hit, and falls to the ground beside him.

"The time was 16:10 of 28 April 1945.

"The weapon carried the following markings: '7.65 cal. L. MAS model 1938 – F 20830' and it bore a small red ribbon at the extreme end of the barrel."

This is the official version, the last in order of time, penned by Valerio and confirmed by the Headquarters of the Communist Party of Italy.

Of the others, also bearing the official stamp of the Communists, two are dated 1945, and one 1947; discrepancies abound, as also does a particular slant.

In the first one published by *Unità* in the Rome edition of the 1st of May, the anonymous author (Valerio, it seems) fires five shots, doesn't refer to the blocking of the weapon and, where Claretta is concerned, writes: "Then it was La Petacci's turn" (she also, then, condemned to death).

In the 2nd version, of 13 December of the same year, always in *Unità*, signed by a certain Valerio, the bullets become ten and Claretta is hit by accident.

In the third, of 28 March 1947, once again in *Unità*, the declared author is Walter Audisio, the shots remain ten, and La Petacci is hit because of destiny.

In the fourth, as we have seen, the shots go back to being five and Claretta falls because she "moves in a confused manner."

Now for a few questions:

1) Why is Valerio accompanied in the second version (1945) by Guido (Lampredi) and by Bill (Lazzaro), the assistant political commissar for the 52nd Garibaldi Brigade, while in the third (1947) and in the fourth (1973) Bill's place is taken by Pietro (Moretti), political commissar for the 52nd Garibaldi Brigade?

2) Why is the Autopsy Report Number 7241, prepared by Professor Caio Mario Cattabeni of the Institute of Forensic Medicine of the University of Milan, silent on the number of bullets recovered? (there were so many of them);

3) If Valerio fires from a MAS 7.65, why were two 9 caliber bullets found during the identification of Claretta's body asked for by her family?

4) Did Walter Audisio, the Communist senator, really state to a parliamentary colleague in 1971: "But do you really think I was an assassin?"

5) What was Valerio hiding when he confided to journalist Silvio Bertholdi in July 1959: "If I wanted to, I myself could create a great journalistic scoop, a positively sensational one. I would only need to write five short chapters for a glossy magazine on the history of which I have been a protagonist ... and I assure you that there would be a run on the publication ... Never mind *Grand Hotel!* "

6) Did Lia De Maria really say: "We all knew that things happened differently" in an interview with a writer for *Il Giorno* in February 1973?

In what way "differently?"

Franco Bandini, the scholar who has studied most closely the last "95 hours" of Mussolini's life has no doubts: the Duce and his mistress were shot twice: at about noon the first time, and at about four the second time. "Valerio," he writes, "whoever he might be, was in charge of the second shooting, which was also a false shooting or, as in fact he says, a 'tidying up' ... That of Villa Belmonte was a performance which was to mask an alternative reality, of which Walter Audisio probably hadn't the faintest notion, except on the sly ... Mussolini and Claretta's end will forever more remain a mystery."

Twenty-Three
The End Is Here: Part 1

D espite its inconsistencies and gaps, many scholars have accepted the version of Mussolini and Claretta's death offered to History by Valerio. But other accounts exist that it might be worthwhile to examine as, for example, the following unpublished one.

Because of the Partisan past of the person who has provided the narrative to us is, by and large trustworthy, we present it to the reader as a complement to the story.

Although the motives and details raise some questions, the statements, which follow, may help to reach a conclusion in an event that is still fraught with obscurity.

Mussolini and La Petacci were not executed either by Walter Audisio (Valerio), or by Michele Moretti (Pietro), or Aldo Lampredi (Guido), but by Bruno Lonati, using the nom de guerre of Giacomo, who is the one supplying this "true" version, and another man known as John.[51]

Although he was already the political commissar for the 101st Garibaldi Brigade, Giacomo, a young man from Legnano, strong, of medium height, having a frank, open face and with a decisive manner, holding the rank of Head of Division and Liaison Officer, was given the task of reorganizing the 111th, 112th, and 113th Garibaldi Brigades, operating at least on paper, in the Sempione, Magenta, and Vigentina zones (besides disarming isolated "Republican" Militia, these commandos attacked Fascist bases and road blocks in metropolitan regions).

In February 1945, Giacomo moves into a small boarding house in Via Vallazze so as to be free to go about and not attract attention.

In mid March, during a Partisan gathering, Lampredi introduces him to John, Marshal Alexander's Chief of the British Information Service, an Englishman of regular features, with black crew-cut hair and brown eyes. He was the son of a Sicilian man from Enna who had moved to the British Capital at the beginning of the century and who became a manufacturer of men's

218

suits, after having started out as a simple tailor. Although of Latin blood, John exhibited prudent Anglo-Saxon coolness.

After completing his studies at Oxford, he took up a military career. He spoke excellent Italian, having lived in Florence for two years before the outbreak of hostilities.

Having fought in Normandy, at the end of November 1944, he'd been parachuted into northern Italy to establish contact with the Committee of National Liberation. He'd then gone to Switzerland, returning subsequently to Milan where he put together a network of agents and informers, spread in almost all of Lombardy, especially in the Como and Varese regions.

Varese was his centre of operation, and this allowed him access to nearby Switzerland. Thanks to him, the Partisan Brigades in the Sesia, Ossola and Olona valleys received generous and frequent help in the form of arms, food, medicine, money and munitions.

More than once John mentions to Giacomo whose group efficiency he quickly tests, the fears of his Government for the post war period. Differently from the Americans, he explains, who know how to make war very well, but who weren't quite as capable at making peace work, for the British this time was fraught with risks and heavy with uncertainty.

Meanwhile, having established a headquarters for his command in a school on Viale Lombardia, on returning to the boarding house on the evening of 24 April, Giacomo finds the Englishman waiting for him.

"The Duce," says John to him, "is in Milan with his *gerarchi*. It will be necessary to nab him."

"Someone will do that," replies the Partisan commander.

"We should be the ones to do so," says John.

"You bet!" exclaims Giacomo skeptically.

An enormous confusion reigned in the Lombard Capital, and even if the war was officially over, Partisan commands continued to grab as many Fascists as they could, real or presumed ones, which irregular tribunals of the people subjected to rushed and often arbitrary judgments.

Giacomo sought by every means possible to prevent summary executions, based, it seems, more on the settling of personal hatreds and private revenge than seeking legitimate punishment (in this just task, he was aided by two like minds: a lively and sensible farmer using the name of Bruno, and a fantastic driver known as Gino).

In the early afternoon of 27 April, this time in the Viale Lombardia school, the Partisan commander sees the Englishman again, the latter wearing semi-military garb: high boots, gray-green cloth trousers, and a heavy, light-colored sweater of the British Navy. Hanging from his belt is a Beretta nine calibre pistol, and from his shoulder, a Sten gun. He also carries a knap-sack containing, amongst other things, an identical uniform to the one that he wears. He is very tense, and this worries Giacomo.

"You must help me," he says to the latter, pushing him towards the window.

"To do what?"

"To pursue and catch Mussolini."

"Why us in particular?" asks the Italian.

"If not us, who else?"

"The others know?"

"No. Neither must they know."

"But where is the Duce?"

"In Como. With a group of Fascists, it seems, wanting to head for the Valtellina. As you can see, there's no time to lose."

"Why are you so interested in him?" presses Giacomo.

"What's the use of winning a war without capturing the enemy chief?"

"He won't be able to run away or to hide," observes the Italian. "The area is crawling with Partisans. Perhaps he's been caught already."

"Follow me and let's go," replies the Englishman crisply.

"Who's coming with us?"

"Two or three of the most trustworthy associates. But we'll also need a car."

"We have one in the street. A FIAT 1100, requisitioned from a Milanese doctor," Giacomo assures him, he having already summoned Bruno and Gino in the meantime.

"Dress like me," John says at this point, pulling out a sweater and pants like his from the knapsack.

Heading for the exit, the Garibaldino commander notes that perhaps four men are not enough.

"Who else could join us?" asks the Englishman.

Just at that moment, Lino, a young Partisan that Giacomo knew well, returns from Val Sessia.

"Are you coming with us?" the Garibaldino captain asks him. Lino nods okay and joins the others.

They all climb into the car: Gino in the driver's seat, Giacomo sits beside him, with the others occupying the back seat, and they leave.

"What road are we taking?" asks John.

"The surest one, even if it is the longest one," answers Giacomo, consulting his watch that shows the time to be four in the afternoon.

They drive along the road going to Rho, and leading to Legnano, stopping at many roadblocks for an examination of their identity papers.

From Legnano, they head for Saronno, then on to Cantù and Como.

There was a great coming and going of Partisan vehicles, from whom they receive warm greetings, Bruno having raised on the fender the small scarlet pennant of the Garibaldi Brigade (during the trip Lino and Bruno are informed of the journey's purpose, and they are told about John's identity. Even if they were accustomed to obeying without asking too many questions, they could not hide their anxiety and their emotional state).

From Como they take the Brunate route, turning again at the entrance to the town, onto a dead-end road, at the end of which, lingering in the humid shadows of the night stood out a small house with an open gate, looked after by a man.

Introducing himself as Franco, this person invites the five to enter. Since there is no electricity, he lights a couple of candles after which, turning to John, he asks: "All's well?"

"All's well," the Englishman reassures him, pulling him aside.

They chat for a few minutes, then Franco, about forty years of age, strong, bald, and smart, goes out, but not before having offered bread, salami, and cold cutlets to his guests.

John explains that Franco is a high-level Partisan, in the service of the Como Liberation Committee. He'd learned from him that the Duce had left Como at dawn with his *gerarchi*.

"What are we going to do now?" questions Bruno.

"Nothing. We're tired. Let's try to rest. Tomorrow morning we'll see," answers Giacomo.

"Franco has not gone to sleep, but to try to learn further news," states John. "When he returns we'll decide to continue or to go back to Milan. Agreed?"

"Okay," answer the four in unison.

Therefore, all of them, wrapped up in coarse blankets get to sleep either on the bed, on the sofa, or on old armchairs.

They wake at seven the next morning and, lacking anything else to eat, they polish off the leftovers from the previous night.

At about eight o'clock, Franco shows up, tired but smiling: "We're at the right spot, but you must hurry. We finally know Mussolini's hiding place. It is about a dozen kilometres from here, between Bonzanigo and Giulino di Mezzegra, in a house on a mountain."

"How are we going to find it?" asks Bruno.

"Don't worry," answers Franco. "After Tremezzo, on the right, you will meet a man smoking a pipe and wearing an Alpine hat. He will show you the place, or he will give you directions instead. The catchphrase is 'We are taking a lovely trip;' the answer is 'I know a lovely spot." Then continuing: "It seems that the Duce was arrested by a rather strange Garibaldi Brigade that was waging war as it saw fit. As far as I know the Public Command wants to transfer the dictator to Como and the Milan General Command has dispatched a detachment to grab him and to bring him to the Lombard Capital. But the residents of Como don't agree with this. Since the arrest came in their territory, they claim that the prisoner should be kept by them."

"Too many stories! Let them sort it out," bursts out John. "Tell us instead how he was caught."

"Something unforeseen must have happened because there was no military action. Now, therefore, it's up to you."

The five get into the car (occupying the same places they'd sat in the previous day), and follow the Lake road.

The time was slightly after eight-thirty and very few people were about.

Reaching the environs of Argegno, a Partisan patrol orders them to stop.

Giacomo gets out of the car, identity papers in hand, and he approaches the group who were handling their weapons rather threateningly. He doesn't even have the time to show his permits before the cry is raised: "They are Fascists: to the wall, to the wall!"

"No, we are Partisans," insists Giacomo, "and I am a Garibaldino commander. We've come from Milan. Look at this."

At this point, a youth levels his gun, ordering: "Have them come out."

Lino and John get out of the car, while the other lunatics shout: "Death, death!"

"Bloody pigs, get out of here," the Englishman begins to swear in English, rousing the suspicions of the brutes even more, now believing them to be Germans.

"Hands up! We've caught you! Everyone out!" shouts one of the Partisans triumphantly. At this Lino comes toward one of them who seems to be the leader: "Don't be an ass," he assails him in Milanese dialect, "don't you see that we're Partisans?"

This only takes a moment. From the group comes a blast of machine gun fire that grazes their shoes. Lino's response is swift. He fires at the group at leg level, but he, in turn, is struck in the chest and in the forehead.

Realizing that they are in a trap, and deciding to put up a fierce struggle, Giacomo and John throw some hand grenades, while Gino and Bruno who have jumped out of the car, spray the attackers with their automatic weapons fire.

The bloody skirmish doesn't last long because the attackers turn around suddenly and run away, leaving behind some of their wounded. They were unused to handling weapons and fighting.

Bruno and Gino lift the broken body of their dead friend and lay him on the right side of the road. Then they return to their bullet-riddled car with its shattered rear windscreen.

After Tremezzo, they meet the informer with the pipe and the Alpine hat: a somewhat short man with a wily look, made more prominent by his mustache.

After exchanging the passwords, Giacomo asks about the situation in the area.

"What happened to you?" asks the man in turn, looking at the car which now resembled a sieve.

"Near Argegno we were stopped and there was shooting," exclaims Giacomo. "They wanted to do us in, and one of our men was killed."

"Until two hours ago," continues the Alpinist, "the Duce was in a house on the mountain at Bonzanigo. He should still be there. But be careful! The region is under Partisan surveillance. I don't know what their intentions are, just as I don't know your plans. I'd willingly come with you, but I can't move from here."

John asks him further information about the location of the house, but receives only a very vague reply.

"Where are you going to wait for us?" asks the Englishman, quickly closing the conversation.

"In that little road on the right," points out the man with the pipe.

Gino who knows the area very well chimes in, asking for other directions

"After Azzano," continues the Alpinist, "is a sign that indicates Giulino di Mezzegra, to the left of the Lake. Continue on that road until Bonzanigo. Here, get out and walk along a trail. The house should be at the end of the path. I don't know which one it is, however. In any case, don't ask anyone anything, and keep your eyes wide open. If you see some Partisans, that is where Mussolini is being held." Then, he says goodbye and Bruno starts up the car.

Reaching the road sign, split in two and partially covered by bushes, they go by it and head towards Bonzanigo until they arrive at a pebbly mule path, facing a green space. They stop here and everyone gets out. It is cool and rainy and John pulls some raincoats out of his bag, but no one wants to put one on.

"What are we going to do now?" asks Gino.

"We'll go along the mule trail," answers Giacomo while walking with the Englishman. Following about twenty metres behind are the two other soldiers, so much more nervous than their leaders who seem to be almost at ease.

It was close to ten-thirty when, to their right, they note a small house on whose balcony are stationed three men wearing showy red neckerchiefs. They must be the Partisans described by the Alpinist.

Seeing the small group coming forward, one of the three informs the others. At this point, Giacomo hastens his pace, digging the documents quickly out of his pocket, and waving them yells, "I am a Partisan captain."

The three, arms in hand, rush down the stone steps, stopping a short distance from Giacomo, who comes close to them. "May I explain why I'm here?"

When they reply "Yes," he advances a few metres, the weapon at his shoulder with its barrel pointing downwards.

The three had a growth of beard. They looked exhausted because of the vigil and the tension, and were wearing brown uniforms. They did not seem to be more than twenty-five years old. One wore a helmet and had a submachine gun, and the others had short "91" rifles.

"What do you want? What are you doing here?" they ask suspiciously.

"We know that Mussolini is in there and we must see him. We have orders from General Command in Milan which concerns him," answers Giacomo.

"Nothing doing," rebuts one of the three imperiously. "No one can see him. Besides, what makes you think that he's here anyway?"

"We know everything," replies Giacomo. "But where is your

chief? I want to talk to him."

"He's in Dongo."

"What's his name?"

"Pedro, but there are others."

"This is a very good spot," says Giacomo ramblingly. "But you three are too few, don't you think?"

"Few, but on the ball!" they reply together. "In any case, soon others will join us."

"Is your chief coming?" continues Giacomo, "or should we go to him?"

"He's coming this morning. At least that's what he promised us last night before going off. He could arrive any minute now. He must be involved with the captured *gerarchi*."

"Where are they?"

"In Dongo."

" Fine. We'll wait for him together. I've absolutely no wish to have to come back here again," says Giacomo, offering them some cigarettes that only one of them refuses.

At the point of lighting up, pretending that he has no matches, he turns to John, who'd stayed a bit further back: "Do you have fire?"

"Yes," answers the other one, coming closer. While the Englishman fishes in his pocket, Giacomo rapidly turns the machine gun, pointing it towards the three: "Freeze! If you move I'll plug you full of lead."

No one moves and John disarms them without a hitch.

"Where is he?" inquires Giacomo.

"Upstairs," reply the three.

"Let's go," says the Garibaldino commander.

Reaching the landing, one of the guards points: "He's in there. But do you know what you are doing? You're not Fascists, are you?" Neither Giacomo nor John answer.

The Englishman pulls out some packthread from his knapsack and he and his friends tie up the ankles and the wrists of the three. Then, using their red neckerchiefs, they gag them and put them down on their stomachs.

Bruno remains to guard them while Gino goes down to the road to make sure that no one is coming along unexpectedly.

In the meantime, attracted by the confusion, a woman peeps out of a door. "If you value your life, stay inside until tonight," warns Giacomo.

The poor trembling woman does what she's told, and the

Garibaldino chief is able to reach the prisoner's room. He knocks but no one opens the door. Therefore, he enters resolutely.

With some surprise he discovers that the dictator is not alone, but is with a young woman that he recognizes as La Petacci.

"Hello," he greets them, but the two remain silent.

Claretta is seated on the right side of the bed. Tired and prematurely aged, Il Duce is standing. His face does not display any fear, but only dismay. But she seems tranquil.

"We've come to take you away. There's no time to lose," says Giacomo.

"Who are you?" asks the Duce, noting Giacomo's and John's uniforms, the latter also having entered the room.

"He's English," replies the Partisan captain.

"The papers, where are the papers?" asks John quickly.

"What papers?" asks Mussolini then.

"Don't try to be sly with me. Your papers!"

"But I only have this bag," stammers the Duce, lifting up a brown, faded leather one.

John grabs it quickly and empties the contents on the bed.

"They are papers of mine," the prisoner adds defensively, "nothing of importance, nothing that could interest you."

"That's for us to see," replies the Englishman dryly.

Her face pale, circles under her eyes, her hands very well manicured, Claretta watches everything from a corner. She wears a lightweight, long-sleeved wool suit and a blouse, sports a necklace, and on her finger a wedding band.

"Where do you come from?" she asks Giacomo with a weak smile.

"From Milan."

"What's going on there?"

"Nothing. Now that we're here."

"I thought so," she adds with another sad smile, while looking at her man who is silently helping John in his fruitless search.

While going through the papers one by one, John exclaims disappointedly: "Nothing, nothing" (there were only the Duce's writings from 1922 on, all previously published).

"You have other papers?" asks John.

"Yes, and very important ones, but they were taken from me last night," answers Mussolini.

"By whom?"

"By the others."

"Such as?"

"I don't remember their names. I heard so many. Pedro, Pietro, even a woman. I told them that they were historic documents, that I intended to hand them to the Allies, but despite this, they wanted the bag telling me that in their hands the papers were safer."

"We've been fucked," bursts out John in a rage, "and who knows where the papers are now!"

He rummages even through the night stands, in the chest, under the bed, in the woman's purse, irritating the prisoner that Claretta tries to calm down: "Don't you see that they aren't the same ones as yesterday?"

"Yes, yes," he murmurs, while John goes out onto the balcony, leaving the couple with Giacomo. ("I didn't know what to say," the Garibaldino chief will recall years later. "Despite my sense of security, I felt some uneasiness. She understood that, but she was the only one to do so.")

"You think I'm to blame, you think I'm a criminal," guesses Mussolini at a certain point looking at Giacomo, who doesn't have time to reply before La Petacci, going to her man, exclaims sadly: "They are all against you. Everyone has abandoned you. Fortunately we've been brought together, and this is a good sign."

"And where are you taking us now?" he asks.

"You'll see," replies Giacomo mysteriously.

Even though disturbed by the succession of dramatic events, the dictator does not seem to fear for his life, thanks to the feigned optimism of the woman who, according to Giacomo, "had already understood everything, and quickly at that. He was what really mattered exclusively to her."

A short time later John re-enters, still angry by the negative results of his search. After giving another glance around the room, he decides: "We can go, but you will have to walk a bit. Get ready."

Claretta gathers together some handkerchiefs, a sweater, gloves, a comb and other personal items that she stuffs into her purse.

Giacomo and John use up the time to go out of the room for a moment.

"What are we going to do now?" asks the Garibaldino chief, sensing already the Englishman's answer.

"We've got to kill them," replies John.

"Even La Petacci?"

"Even La Petacci."

"What did she have to do with all this?"

"She knows Mussolini's secrets and the contents of his papers. Besides, if we don't do that, others will."

Bruno and Gino are also present at the fast-paced conversation, but neither one says a word.

"Il Duce must be shot by an Italian, by one of you three," says John.

"I'll do it," says Giacomo. "Let's leave Bruno and Gino out of this. But where the woman is concerned, I disagree. Think about it."

"I already have," replies the Englishman. "If they catch her, they'll tear her to pieces. And if she could, she would do the same to us, along with all the others." Then they return to the prisoners.

While they are slowly going out the door, from the threshold where he already is, Mussolini could see the three gagged and bound men. This encourages him: if his jailers have been subjected to that treatment, that means that the newcomers do not intend to do any harm to him or to his companion.

He whispers this to Claretta who, looking at John and Giacomo, answers him: "I told you that they are different, that they want to find a safe place for us."

"Yes, yes, you're right," he mumbles, heading for the landing where Bruno and Gino can finally meet him.

John also goes out and Giacomo is thus left with La Petacci. "We exchanged a sad smile," he will recall later, "but perhaps the saddest was mine. When a person is young, he can't lie, at least with the eyes, especially to a woman like her."

"You didn't come to move us, true?" asks Claretta.

"Yes."

"Then it's over for us?"

"For him, not for you," answers Giacomo who, perhaps, was not expecting that question.

"Why?"

"Because if we don't do it, others will sooner or later. This time there's no escape."

"Yes, I understand that you have no alternative. Perhaps we were fools, perhaps we could have saved ourselves." She halts for an instant, then, softly, she implores: "I want to ask a favour of you."

"Like what?"

"Do it so that he's not aware of what is happening. I don't want him to suffer. He is certain that he's going to escape this fate, at least for now. I was the one to convince him of this. Promise me that?"

"I give you my word."

"Because look," she continues, "you have an honest face. I prefer that you do it, but I beg of you, not to the head."

Even though her hands are trembling, her look is firm, her spirit resigned to the inevitable.

At that moment John enters: "Shall we go? You are ready?"

"Absolutely ready," answers Claretta, grabbing her purse and throwing her fur coat on her shoulders. The small group—Gino and Bruno are already in the yard—passes by the three gagged men that Giacomo warns with a threat: "Forget our faces; you know that we're not joking. Wherever you might go, we'll come to get you."

The small group heads for the mule path: Bruno and Gino in front; the two prisoners in between, and fifteen to twenty metres behind, Giacomo and John.

"Where to?" Giacomo asks John at a certain point, the latter calling Gino over. "At the first alley, you and Bruno will stop, pretend that someone is approaching, and drag Mussolini and La Petacci into the alley. We can't take them elsewhere."

Claretta is holding tightly to the sleeve of her lover's coat, and with the other hand she hangs on to her purse. Every so often she'd turn around to look at Giacomo, perhaps to remind him of his promise.

Having covered about three hundred metres, Bruno and Gino halt, signaling to the others to slow down. When the prisoners are at the alley selected, the two Partisans push them along to a sheltered spot near a metal fence, commanding them to remain quiet.

Mussolini seems not to have understood, thinking perhaps that this is just a diversionary tactic, while La Petacci, still holding on to the sleeve of his coat, is trying desperately to hide her anguish. Giacomo and John overtake them while Bruno and Gino scrutinize the road beyond to ascertain that all is still.

In a flash, the Garibaldino commander turns to face the couple: "It was all very fast. The machine gun was ready to fire. At about a metre away from the man, I pull the breechblock and fire a shot at the heart. He remains standing, his eyes glued to mine, as if stunned, almost as if asking me 'Why?' I fire other shots—three or four—always at the left side of the chest. La Petacci places herself in front of him and, while Mussolini slides slowly to the ground, I move. Then John rushes from my right while the dejected woman is sinking down along with her lover. John fires at her chest: a discharge much longer than mine. No screams, no moans, only a strange grin, a forced smile."

"Are they dead?" ask Bruno and Gino coming close to Giacomo and John.

"I think so," replies the Partisan commander.

The Englishman places his hand first on the Duce's chest and then on Claretta's, exclaiming, "They seem to be."

"The shots hit the bull's eye," confirms Giacomo.

Mussolini was sitting, a little bandy-legged, his head bending forward. Pulled by the legs, he is stretched out on his back, beside La Petacci's body. The remains of the two are then covered with his coat. The time was a little after eleven, 28 April.

The job which took eighteen hours and which was almost an off-hand action (at least by the three Italians), was over.

As arranged earlier, Giacomo and his friends meet the Alpinist at Tremezzo and the latter takes them to a cottage in whose barn they park their car.

"We've not found the papers," laments John. "It is absolutely essential to know what's happened to them."

"Okay," replies the man with the pipe. "Stay here while I go to pick up other information." Then, serving his guests a simple meal of bread, salami, and cheese, he goes out, climbs onto a bicycle, and rides away.

The four eat hungrily, then John solemnly announces: "No one must know anything, at least for now. Whatever happens, we were not the ones who did that." Then, pausing briefly: "It's just fantastic that those American simpletons wanted to have him alive. Anyhow, the important thing is that a chapter is closed, even if it didn't end the way we wanted it to."

Meanwhile, the time was passing and the Alpinist hadn't returned. At about four that afternoon, the men are roused by the roar of an engine. Fearing an enemy raid, they take up their weapons quickly. But it is only the man with the pipe, returning by car: a black one like the car they'd used, except for the colour, to accomplish their mission), his bike having been left behind.

He relates that a column of Partisans had arrived in Como that morning and that they had continued to Dongo at noon where the arrested *gerarchi* were detained.

"And the papers?" asks John.

"Nothing," answers the Alpinist throwing up his arms. "Perhaps the 52nd Garibaldi Brigade has them and they might give them over to their associates who came from Milan, or perhaps they might make them vanish."

"However, you keep your eyes open," urges the Englishman,

"and if you learn anything, let me know about it immediately. We are going back to Milan. You know where to find me."

The man with the pipe salutes John and the others militarily, then they leave for Argegno, heading next for Como, already invaded by Allied troops. They decide to spend the night at Legnano to establish an alibi. Early in the morning of the next day, they proceed to Milan.

Reaching Corso Buenos Aires at about nine, near Piazzale Loreto, their progress is blocked by a huge, disorderly, yelling crowd. They ask what is going on. They are told that the Partisans had captured and executed Mussolini, La Petacci, and the *gerarchi,* now strung up at the same spot where fifteen hostages had been killed in August of the previous year.

They don't stay there, preferring to go on to the Command Post on Viale Lombardia. Here Giacomo, Bruno, and Gino get out while John continues, not before having urged them to keep everything utterly secret. He says that they shouldn't look for him, that he'll show up again soon.

"A few days later," the Garibaldino chief remembers, "in Via Moscova, in the office of one of the British Commands, I again see John in a British officer's uniform. I say to him – but he already knows this – that the responsibility for the killing of Mussolini and of La Petacci was already claimed by Partisans who'd come from Milan. We all knew the names of those involved, but we didn't talk about them. I ask him about the papers and the documents and he tells me that he had high hopes of recovering them. He adds that his mission in Italy was coming to an end and that he would return to London at the end of May. Before leaving, however, he wanted to see us and he asked me to telephone him before the 20th.

"In the following days, at a dance on Lake Maggiore, I meet Lampredi and his wife. By now the official story of the event was common knowledge. I ask him, in any case, how things had gone for him, and he answers that although he'd risked a great deal, all in all, things had worked out for him.

"I see John again one night at supper with Bruno and Gino. I ask him for news about the famous papers. He replies that many had been found, and that the others were being hunted down. For the umpteenth and final time he repeats that what had occurred was to remain secret, no matter what others might say. He adds that according to an old British honour code, we were to remain silent for at least thirty-five years, after which we would be free to divulge the truth. He said further that at the end of half a century, that is, in 1995, anyone would be able to know the truth through the English archives where a detailed account of the events would be on deposit.

"At the end of February 1946, after a brief and disillusioning political and trade union interlude, I realized that the ideals for which I had fought and risked my life had evaporated, and therefore, I decided to return to Legnano and dedicate myself to my family and to work.

"After so many years from such tragic events, I want only one thing: not to be judged. What I did I wouldn't do again. Don't ask me why.

"As for La Petacci, for me she existed for little more than a half hour."

Twenty-Four

The End Is Here: Variation: Part 2

Leaving Lino and Sandrino to guard the bodies of the Duce and of Claretta, Valerio returns to Dongo with Pietro and Guido to carry out the other sentences.

In the meanwhile, Pedro who had brought the accused together in the Gold Room in the town hall, was particularly astounded to see Colonel Audisio enter without the dictator and his mistress. When he hears from Valerio personally that the two prisoners had already been shot, and that the weapon used to do them in was Moretti's, he could not hide his absolute annoyance. He reminds Valerio that the plans as previously agreed to were different, but without supplying any explanations the Colonel states that time was tight, and that a great deal of it had already been wasted.

The only thing the Garibaldino commander could do was to grin and bear it: Valerio was his superior. He could not disobey him even if he found the other man's way of proceeding repugnant, brutal, and without any legal precedent. Equally vain was the protest of Rubini, the Mayor, who resigns from his post as soon as he is appointed to it.

The *gerarchi* are gathered together in the town hall's court-yard for the reading of the death sentences. After this, in double file—each one with a Partisan at his side—they march out into the piazza. Audisio wanted half of the execution platoon to consist of Garibaldini of the 52nd Brigade, but Pedro vetoes this. Further, he indicates that he would not participate in the executions. Valerio replies that this was an order, and Pier Bellini had to give in.

In the meantime, having lined up the prisoners at the wall overlooking the Lake, the Garibaldini, less four included forcibly in the platoon, yield their places to the executioners, commanded by Mordini.

At that moment, a friar from the Dongo convent comes forward seeking permission from Valerio to bestow general absolution on the doomed.

The friar was getting ready to fulfill the charitable act when Audisio realizes that Marcello Petacci is missing (being assigned the task of shooting him, after finding out his true identity—this was not Vittorio Mussolini after all—Bill had taken him back to the town hall). "Let's go! Bring him along with the others! Let's get this over with now!" he shouts angrily, but when the *gerarchi* see Marcello come forward as well, they rebel: "Away, take him away! We don't want him with us! He's a traitor!"

Not expecting such a reaction, Claretta's brother's face goes white and he moves back like a robot. Impatiently, Valerio repeats the order, at which the fifteen condemned men, more insultingly than previously shout out: "No, not him!" Pedro is forced to intervene with considerable effort to convince Valerio to respect the wishes of those about to die. Marcello is moved away and the *gerarchi* settle down.

Mordini approaches Audisio to receive the final instructions, which the latter gives to him with the fussiness of an accountant, but ever faithful to the ghoulish order of procedure.

"Prisoners! Attention! About face!" shouts the captain of the platoon. Some of the condemned raise their arms in the Roman salute, others exclaim "Long live Italy!" their faces turned towards the Lake. Barracu is the only one who doesn't do so, claiming the right as the holder of a gold medal for bravery, to be shot in the chest. Despite a further intercession by Pedro, Valerio denies him this provision, ordering: "In the back, like everyone else!"

Barracu's request throws the *gerarchi's* line into disorder, requiring Mordini to repeat the orders: "Prisoners! Attention! About face!"

"Firing squad, attention!"

"Firing squad, get set!"

"Aim!"

"Fire!"

A diabolical blast of gunfire strikes the victims, amidst acrid spirals of bluish smoke. The unearthly silence that had preceeded the shootings is broken by the brutal howls of a crowd thirsting more for revenge than for justice. At the foot of the parapet, in a pool of blood, lie the victims: some motionless, others wheezing in horrendous death spasms.

Now, a voice thunders: "Bring Petacci!" Dragged by two Garibaldini, in the throes of terror, Marcello is brought forward: "You can't shoot me, you mustn't! ... After all I've done for Italy!" he shouts, tossing about furiously.

Unexpectedly, at a few steps from the fateful balustrade, he succeeds in freeing himself from the two Partisans with a Herculean shake and, crossing the piazza, runs into an alley.

Covering only about a hundred metres, however, he is caught by four men who bodily carry him back to the execution site. But here, with an even more violent jerk than previously, he succeeds in freeing himself again, and dives into the Lake. Even now he doesn't get too far because, after swimming a few vigorous strokes, he is hit by a volley of gunfire. For a few moments his massive body, arms and legs spread out, floats. Then he disappears, leaving behind a lurid purple stain on the glassy surface of the Lake.

After this, pandemonium breaks out: all the persons bearing arms begin to fire in the air, perhaps as a release of tension, repressed for so long, or possibly to celebrate the end of an absurd and suicidal war with that impromptu slaughter.

A half hour after the execution of the *gerarchi*, at six-thirty that evening, the bodies, including that of Marcello, are hurled onto a truck which then heads for Como, along with two other vehicles: the larger one bearing Guido, Valerio, and Mordini; the smaller one carrying some Partisans.

At Azzano, the vehicles turn towards Giulino di Mezzegra where Lino and Sandrino are watching over the corpses of the Duce and of La Petacci. Lino had already removed her fur coat. The bodies are loaded into the car and the vehicle catches up to the truck onto which are transferred the two bodies, winding up on top of the heap.

The little procession now heads for Milan, destination Piazzale Loreto that is reached at three in the morning because of a hitch.

The site is deserted at that hour, and the bodies are piled under the roof of the gasoline stall.

The rumour of the macabre exposition spreads throughout the city in a flash, giving rise to an impressive, uninterrupted pilgrimage of the curious, the incredulous, the dumbfounded, and the excited: the tyrant, his mistress, and his lackeys, no longer able to do harm, now exposed to public scorn.

Most people pass in front of the bodies in silence, the remains now being rewarded by the punishment meted out to them "In the name of the Italian people." But others give way to the most vicious derision, attacking the wretched corpses without pity. Into the hands of the dictator whose head is lying against the breast of his lover, is forced a broken fragment of a pennant with the lictorial insignia, as if to symbolize the fall of the Regime, and the collapse of a myth.

But the height of shame is reached when, between insults, curses, jokes and grimaces, the most fanatical ones begin to kick at, and cover with spit (some even urinate on their faces) Claretta and the man for whom she had sacrificed herself.

At a certain point, either to remove the bodies from the havoc being inflicted on them, or to show them better to the maddened mob, Mussolini, La Petacci, and five *gerarchi*, are strung up by their feet from a metal trellis.

Claretta's skirt slips down, uncovering her body to the waist, and only the intervention of a merciful priest who pins together the poor woman's garment removes her from further gawking by the mob.

Unexpectedly, Achille Starace, the former Secretary of the Fascist Party, in sweat suit, comes along, escorted by some Partisans. Placed before an improvised firing squad, he faces the platoon's fusillade with pride, invoking "his" Duce: that same Duce who, after having dismissed him, no longer wanted to see him, neither did he respond to his heartfelt entreaties. Having died better than he had lived, even he is given the honour of being hoisted up onto the trellis, head down, at Barracu's place, who also cedes his rope to the other.

When Cardinal Schuster is informed of what is going on in the piazza, he telephones General Cadorna and Prefect Lombardi in order to have the madness stopped. "Enough of this obscenity!" shouts the commander of the Committee of National Liberation. "This is Mexican butchery!" rages an indignant Ferruccio Parri. "The Insurrection is dishonoured!" thunders Emilio Sereni. But only the will of Charles Poletti, the American Governor of Lombardy, succeeds in putting a stop to the repugnant, contemptible depredations.

The tortured and violated bodies are brought to a paupers' morgue, and some of them undergo a brief examination and autopsy.

The hardships continue for the cadavers of Mussolini and La Petacci. They are buried in the Musocco Cemetery in Milan but, after a year, on 23 April 1946, the Duce's remains are stolen mysteriously by agents of the Democratic Fascist Party, to be returned subsequently to Milan's police commissioner by two brothers. Today he lies in a tomb in the small San Cassiano Cemetery in Romagna, next to Rosa and Alessandro, the dictator's parents, to children Bruno and Anna Maria, and to that of Rachele, his wife.

Claretta's body, interred with her brother in Cemetery One Hundred Eleven, then in Cemetery Thirty-three, tomb 751 under the false name of Rita Colfosco, was given back to her family after eleven years of unbelievable vicissitudes and official rebuffs.

Since March 1956, she lies in the shade of the cypress trees in the Verano, Rome's cemetery, in a pink marble sarcophagus, above which rises a white marble, life size statue, showing her with her body and head bending slightly towards the front, her arms behind her back, as if defying an atrocious and inevitable destiny. On the headstone is her name and her birth and death dates: nothing more.

Sacrificing herself with him and for him, almost shielding him with her body, at last Claretta feels Ben to be finally hers, completely hers, only hers.

The tommy-gun of the executioner, whoever he might be, became for her, a woman like all other women, but a woman in love as no one else, the unexpected, selfless, munificent donor of all that she had hoped to have, but which had eluded her in vain until then.

In an instant, the circle of passion closes in tightly, and her heart pierced by that fatal firearms discharge, achieves in the most horrible of destinies the heroic dream of an absolute and everlasting coalescence.

End Notes

1. Tazio Nuvolari (1892-1953) Italian car racer of the era. [Please note that all unidentified explanatory remarks are by the editor. Author's notes are followed by the letters RG.]

2. Italo Balbo and crew flew several times across the Atlantic Ocean. The first trip was to Rio de Janeiro in 1931, and the next one to Chicago, via Montreal, in 1933. Federici was apparently preparing for the second flight, but there is no evidence that he landed in North America in one of the several dozen flying boats of that expedition.

3. A shoe size equivalent to today's size two.

4. The Italian manufacturer was an important producer of electrical equipment of the era.

5. The order to which belonged French Saint Bernadette.

6. Giacomo Leopardi (1798-1837), Guido Gozzano (1883-1916), and Francesco Petrarca (1304-1374), are important poets in the Italian literary pantheon.

7. Beniamino Gigli (1890-1957) and Ferruccio Tagliavini (1913-95) were celebrated tenors of the operatic stage.

8. On 4 November 1925, a few months before, Tito Zaniboni had carried out an unsuccessful assassination attempt. RG.

9. This sentence was underlined by Mussolini with his usual red pencil. RG.

10. Achille Starace (1889-1945), a Secretary of the Fascist Party of Italy.

11. (Jewish) Margherita Sarfatti (1880-1961), art critic and writer.

12. This may have been of a sexual nature.

13. Amongst many other admirers were New York Mayor Jimmy Walker, and Winston Churchill.

14. Poet Giosuè Carducci (1835-1907).

15. Leonida Bissolati (1857-1920) was a Socialist politician, a member of Giolitti's government, and a previous editor of *Avanti!* In 1912, he was expelled from the Socialist Party when he supported his Government's seizure of Libya from Turkey. The resulting disorder apparently resulted in a splintering of the Socialists into various factions and this split was reflected in the 1913 election votes. Socialists, it seems, could not adhere to their political ideology and be imperialists as well.

16. Futurist writer Tommaso Marinetti (1876-1944), Vittorio Podrecca (1883-1959), and conductor Arturo Toscanini (1867-1957).

17. In the Italian text, the author writes: "Diversamente da Maometto, papa Formoso e Casanova, non provò mai quell' *anelitus puellarum*, comune a tanti comuni mortali, che priviligia il fiore acerbo rispetto al frutto maturo."

18. The poem is "Sonnet 43" from Barrett Browning's *Sonnets from the Portuguese.*

19. Telephone surveillance began in Italy in 1903 in Giolitti's government. Mussolini and his successors made use of this system. Many conversations are reproduced in U. Guspini, *L'Orecchio del Regime.*

20. Francesca's story is found in Dante's *Inferno,* canto V.

21. Ministry of Popular Culture.

22. The French ambassador. RG.

23. Italo-German alliance. RG [Signed by Ciano in May 1939.]

24. The British ambassador. RG.

25. Attilio Teruzzi (1882-1950) occupied a number of posts in Fascist Italy including that of Governor of the portion of Libya called Cyrenaica.

26. In 1915, neutral Italy left the Triple Alliance that included Germany and Austria, and joined the Triple Entente. An action of this sort, with a country actually "changing sides," was not unprecedented. All the Great Powers had done so at one time or another. But political morality had changed by 1940. At least, this is what some writers would have us believe.

27. The relationship was to be a sexual one, rather than a purely consultative one.

28. *Istituto Nazionale per l'Assicurazione contro le Malattie* (a governmental agency for health insurance).

29. The Secretary of the Party. RG.

30. Mussolini's personal secretary. RG.

31. We'll see in what circumstances below. RG.

32. The first time was for his daughter Anna Maria, stricken with polio. RG.

33. Dr. Francesco Petacci wrote a medical column for that paper. RG.

34. *Ente Italiano Audizioni Radiofoniche*, the broadcasting service of the era, later replaced by RAI.

35. Raffaello Riccardi was the Minister of Exchange and Currency. RG. [He was dismissed in February 1943.]

36. The German ciphering code, generally called "Enigma," had been cracked in Britain so that the British knew quickly what their enemies were up to. This allowed them to dispatch ships or airplanes from Malta or elsewhere to send the Axis convoys to the bottom of the sea soon after they set out from port. Of course, only very privileged members of the military and government in the countries constituting the Allies knew about this development. Thus Britain in particular was able to maintain the fiction that the Allies were "more sinned against than sinning." The truth, as is often the case, was very different, however. The callous Allied Command was willing to sacrifice its own fighting men so as not to indicate to the Axis powers that the German code could now be read at will.

37. Carlo Scorza was the Secretary of the Fascist Party of Italy. RG.

38. In this particular letter, full of such emotion and passion, Claretta lets the words carry her forward. As such, this translation aims to keep the feeling of the original, rather than make changes to the basic structure.

39. Claretta's sister Miriam.

40. For some inexplicable reason, Ciano fled Italy for Germany, hardly the safest place, under the circumstances.

41. Dutchwoman Alice von Wendel, recruited by the German police to keep tabs on the former Foreign Minister. RG.

42. It would seem that the Germans were ready, at a certain point, to free her husband in exchange for the diary. RG.

43. Where in reprisals, fifteen hostages had been shot the previous August. RG.

44. Gabriele d'Annunzio's wife.

45. Marcello's son.

46. The Black Brigades (*Brigate Nere*) were formed for anti-Partisan warfare.

47. The trial of the conspirators who had brought down Mussolini's government.

48. The Partisans and Communists made extensive use of false identities. This was to allow them some protection in case they fell into enemy hands, no one being able to reveal the identity of fellow Partisans

49. Sandro Pertini became president of Italy eventually.

50. At Piazzale Loreto. RG.

51. John has been identified tentatively as Captain Malcolm Smith in an article by John Phillips and Richard Woods. See "British Agent 'ordered death of Il Duce,'" *Sunday Times,* 14 July 1996, p. 10.

Bibliography. 1. Books

Alessi, Rino. *Il Giovane Mussolini*. Milano: Il Borghese, 1969.

Amicucci, Ermanni. *I Seicento Giorni di Mussolini*. Roma: Faro, 1948.

Anfuso, Filippo. *Da Palazzo Venezia al Lago di Garda*. Bologna: Capelli, 1957.

Bandini, Franco. *Le Ultime 95 Ore di Mussolini*. Milano: Sugar, 1959.

_____. *Claretta*. Milano: Sugar, 1960.

_____. *Vita e Morte di Mussolini*. Milano: Mondadori, 1978.

Bertholdi, Silvio. *Mussolini Tale e Quale*. Milano: Longanesi, 1965.

_____. *Salò*. Milano: Rizzoli, 1976.

Buffarini Guidi, Glauco. *La Vera Verità*. Milano: Sugar, 1970.

Ciano, Edda. *La Mia Testimonianza*. Milano: Rusconi, 1975.

Ciano, Galeazzo. *Diario 1939 – 1943*. Milano: Rizzoli, 1980.

Collier, Richard. *Duce! Duce!* Milano: Mursia, 1971.

D'Aroma, Nino. *Churchill e Mussolini*. Roma: Centro Editoriale Nazionale, 1962.

Deakin, Frederick. *Storia della Repubblica di Salò*. Torino: Einaudi, 1963.

De Vincentis, Luigi. *Io Son Te ...* Milano: Cebes, 1946.

Dolfin, Giovanni. *Con Mussolini nella Tragedia*. Milano: Garzanti, 1949.

Dollmann, Eugen. *Roma Nazista*. Milano: Longanesi, 1951.

_____. *L'Eroe della Paura*. Milano: Longanesi, 1965.

Dulles, Allen. *La Resa Segreta*. Milano: Garzanti, 1967.

Fappiani, Antonio and Franco Molinari. *Chiesa e Repubblica di Salò*. Torino: Marietti, 1981.

Fortuna, Alberto Maria. *Incontro all'Archivescovado*. Firenze: Sansoni, 1971.

Gallo, Max. *Vita di Mussolini*. Bari: Laterza, 1967.

Gunther, John. *Faccia a Faccia*. Milano: Garzanti, 1967.

Guspini, Ugo. *L'Orecchio del Regime*. Milano: Mursia, 1973.

Hibbert, Christopher. *Mussolini*. Milano: Garzanti, 1962.

Kirkpatrick, Ivone. *Storia di Mussolini*. Milano: Longanesi, 1964.

Lanfranchi, Ferruccio. *La Resa degli Ottocentomila*. Milano: Rizzoli, 1948.

Leto, Guido. *Polizia Segreta* in Italia. Roma: Vito Bianco, 1957.

Ludwig, Emil. *Colloqui con Mussolini*. Verona: Mondadori, 1950.

Martinelli, Franco. *Mussolini ai Raggi X*. Milano: De Vecchi, 1964.

Mazzucchelli, Mario. *I Segreti del Processo di Verona*. Milano: Cino del Duca, 1963.

Mira, Giorgio and Luigi Salvatorelli. *Storia del Fascismo*. Roma: Edizioni di Novissima, 1952.

Molinari, Franco. *I Peccati di Papa Giovanni*. Torino: Marietti, 1975.

Monelli, Paolo. *Mussolini Piccolo Borghese*. Milano: Garzanti, 1954.

Montagna, Renzo. *Mussolini e il Processo di Verona*. Milano: Omnia, 1949.

Mussolini, Benito. *Opera Omnia*. 35 v. Firenze: La Fenice, 1951 - 1960.

Mussolini, Edvige. *Mio Fratello Benito*. Firenze: La Fenice, 1957.

Mussolini, Rachele. *Benito il Mio Uomo*. Milano: Rizzoli, 1958.

_____. *Mussolini Privato*. Milano: Rusconi, 1980.

Mussolini, Vittorio. *Due Donne nella Tempesta*. Milano: Mondadori, 1958.

Navarra, Quinto. *Memorie del Cameriere di Mussolini*. Milano: Longanesi, 1972.

Petacco, Arrigo. *Riservato per il Duce*. Milano: Rizzoli, 1980.

Petacco, Arrigo and Sergio Zavoli. *Dal Gran Consiglio al Gran Sasso*. Milano: Rizzoli, 1973.

Pini, Giorgio and Diulio Susmel. *Mussolini, l'Uomo e l'Opera*. Firenze: La Fenice, 1955.

Pisanò, Giorgio. *Storia della Guerra Civile in Italia*, vol. 3. Milano: FPE, 1974.

Rafanelli, Leda. *Una Donna e Mussolini*. Milano: Rizzoli, 1975.

Rossi, Cesare. *Mussolini Com'era*. Roma: Ruffolo, 1947.

Roux, Georges. *Benito Mussolini*. Roma: Lessona, 1967.

Sarfatti, Margherita. *Dux*. Milano: Mondadori, 1926.

Schuster, Ildefonso. *Gli Ultimi Tempi di un Regime*. Milano: La Via, 1960.

Settimelli, Emilio. *Edda Contro Benito*. Roma: Corso, 1962.

Susmel, Diulio. *Vita Sbagliata di Galeazzo Ciano*. Milano: A. Palazzi, 1962.

Whittle, Peter. *One Afternoon at Mezzegra*. London: W. H. Allen, 1969.

Zachariae, Georg. *Mussolini Si Confessa*. Milano: Garzanti, 1971.

Bibliography. 2. Periodical and Newspaper Articles

The number of periodical and newspaper articles published on Mussolini and La Petacci both in Italy and in other countries since 26 July 1943 is vast. To cite them all is beyond the capacity of this book. Included below are records of memories of some protagonists:

1. Walter Audisio. "Memoriale Postumo." *Corriere della Sera*, 11 and 18 May 1975.

2. Pier Luigi Bellini delle Stelle and Urbano Lazzaro. "Parlano I Protagonisti di Dongo." *Epoca*, numbers 4, 11, 18, 25 December 1960.

3. Pasquale Donadio. *Tempo Illustrato*, 22 September – 24 November 1962.

4. Myriam Petacci. (With the assistance of Giovanni Cavalotti.) *Oggi*, 2 March – 18 May 1961 (the most honest, complete and moving of the documentary material).

5. Zita Ritossa. *Tempo Illustrato*, numbers 6 – 19 of 1957.

Other articles:

6. Silvio Bertholdi. *Oggi*, numbers 17, 18, 19, 20 of 1963.

7. Ferruccio Lanfranchi, *Oggi*, 19 December 1948 – 24 March 1949.

8. Paolo Pavolini, *Il Giorno*, 24 February – 8 March 1968.

9. Ezio Saini, *Settimo Giorno*, number 13 of 1961.

10. Duilio Susmel, *Gente*, numbers 12 – 20 of 1958 and 41 – 48 of 1968.

Fundamental also are Claretta's *Diario* from the Novara prison, *Giornale del Mattino*, 27 January – 13 February 1946;

Lawyer Gino Sotis' *Diario* on the annulment of the Petacci-Federici marriage reported more or less widely in various newspapers of the era;

National Archives and Records Service, Washington, D.C. *Personal Papers of Benito Mussolini*. Mussolini-Petacci Correspondence. RG 242, reel 53, frames 026456–026491.

Bibliography. 3. Additional Titles.

Browning, Elizabeth Barrett. *Sonnets from the Portuguese*. New York: Harper, 1936.

Cannistraro, Philip V., and Brian R. Sullivan. *Il Duce's Other Woman*. New York: William Morrow, 1993.

Canosa, Romano. *I Servizi Segreti del Duce*. Milano: Arnaldo Mondadori Editore, 2000.

Bibliography

De Felice, Renzo, ed. *Bibliografia Orientativa del Fascismo*. Roma: Bonacci Editore, 1991.

_____. *Mussolini*. 4v. in 8. Torino: Einaudi, 1965 - 1997.

_____. *Rosso e Nero*. Milano: Baldini e Castoldi, 1995.

Fraser, George MacDonald. *The Hollywood History of the World*. London: Michael Joseph, 1989.

Luzzatto, Sergio. *Il Corpo del Duce*. Torino: Einaudi, 1998.

Moseley, Ray. *Mussolini's Shadow: the double life of Count Galeazzo Ciano*. New Haven: Yale University Press, 1999.

Meader, Edward, ed. *Hollywood and History*. New York: Thames and Hudson, 1987.

Petacci, Myriam. *Chi Ama e Perduto*. Gardolo di Trento: Luigi Reverdito Editore, 1988.

Phillips, John and Richard Woods. "British Agent 'ordered death of Il Duce,'" *Sunday Times*, 14 July 1996, p. 10.

Pisanò, Giorgio. *Gli Ultimi Cinque Secondi di Mussolini*. Milano: Il Saggiatore, 1999.

Ridley, Jasper. *Mussolini*. New York: St. Martin's Press, 1998.

Files of the Mondadori periodical *Storia Illustrata* and of *History Today*, amongst others, might be consulted for additional current material, especially on the controversy that has arisen in Italy lately on who actually pulled the trigger destroying the Duce and his mistress on 28 April 1945, and the related one of who ordered the killings in order to keep tales accumulating about "dead men," and others. Since the executioners have probably died as well, unless incontrovertible documents are found to help finger the doers of the deed, and of their masters, this question will remain the subject of speculation, joining the lengthening list of "who might have done what to whom." And why!

Index

Alexander, Harold 167 218
Amico delle Donne, L' 108
Antichi, Osvaldo 137
Antonetti, Luciano 60-1
Apollonio, Eugenio 163 177
Audisio, Walter (Valerio) 209-17
   233-5
Ausili, Maria 32
Avanti! 41 55 57
Avvenire del Lavoratore, L' 39

Badoglio, Pietro 79-81 89 134-7
   139-44 146 150 152 172
Balabanoff, Angelica 39 55
Balbo, Italo 33 49 78-9 84
Bandini, Franco 217
Barracu Francesco Maria 180
   190 194 234 236
Bassi, Mario 179-80
Bastianini, Giuseppe 121
Battisti, Cesare 40
Bedell Smith, Walter 142
Bellini delle Stelle, Pier (Pedro)
   190 193-206 210 225 227 233-4
Bertholdi, Silvio 163 167 177
   217
Bianchi, Michele 182
Bicchierai, Monsignor 181
Bigazzi Capanni, Emilio 165-7
   172
Bini, Giuseppina and Luigi 33

Birzer, Fritz 187-8 190-1
Boggiano, Armando 108-9 144
   151
Bombacci, Nicola 190-1
Borghese, Valerio 160
Bottai, Giuseppe 78 81
Briganti, Air Force Colonel 32
Brivonesi, Bruno 141
Bruno 219-25 228-9 231
Buffarini Guidi, Guido 83 88-9
   97 112 117 120-1 133 157 160
   168 170-1 173 176 188
Buffelli, Giorgio 197-8 203

Cadorna, Raffaele 180 209 236
Calamai, Clara 106
Calistri, Pietro 196
Canali, Luigi (Neri) 195 203-5
Cantoni, Guglielmo (Sandrino)
   205-7 233 235
Carducci, Valfredo 38
Casalinuovo, Vito 186-7 191 194
Castellani, Aldo 118
Castellano, Giuseppe 142
Castelli, Enrico 187
Cattabeni, Caio Mario 216
Cause ed Effetti 108
Cavallero, Ugo 89
Celia, Novara's Carabinieri
   Captain 149
Cervis, Carlo and Caterina 175

Index

Ciano, Galeazzo 78-80 84 87-9
  109 112-3 119-21 154-5 161-3
Ciminata, Dr. 91
Cinema 108
*Claudia Particella, l'Amante del
  Cardinale (Claudia Particella,
  the Cardinal's Mistress)* 40
Collier, Richard 139
Como, Edward 173
Coppola, Saverio 13-4 62
Cupini, Samuele 32
Curti Cucciati, Angela 118
Curti Cucciati, Elena 188-9

Dal Monte, Toti 107
Dalser, Ida 56-7
d'Annunzio, Gabriele 42 62 159
  175
De Bono, Emilio 84 89 129
De Cesare, Nicolò 88-9 133-5
Decima Mas (X Mas) 160 173
  181
De Maria, Giacomo 205-8
De Maria, Lia 205-8 217
De Sica, Vittorio 107
De Vecchi, Cesare Maria 129
de Vincentis, Luigi 31-2
Dolfin, Giovanni 163
Dollmann, Eugen 81 97 99
Donadio, Pasquale 59-60 73 88
  136
Dumini, Amerigo 47
Duse, Eleanora 106

Eisenhower, Dwight David 142
Europe Nouvelle 66
Fabiani, (*Gerarca*) 188

Facta, Luigi 43
Faiola, A 142
Falconi, Dino 108
Fallmeyer, Lt. 189
Farinacci, Roberto 78 130 133
Federici, Riccardo 13-5 23-5 30-5
  59-60 100-1
Federzoni, Luigi 82
Felës, Marco 100-2 104
Ferrari, Paolo 108
Franco 221-2
Frangi, Giuseppe (Lino) 205-7
  220-3 233 235
Frassati, Luciana 63
Frattoni, Raffaele 139
Frugoni, Cesare 118
Galbiati, Enzo 89 130 136
Gallese di Montenevoso, Maria
  175
Gasparri, Cardinal Pietro 32
Gasperini, Gino 32
Gasperini, Silvio 62 136-7
Gerlach, Heinrich 143
Gibson, Violet 20 47
Gino 219-20 223-5 228-9 231
Giorno, Il 217
Grandi, Dino 82 126 128-31 134
Graziani, Rodolfo 114 180-1
Gueli, Giuseppe 141-2
Guidi, Anna 40

Hitler, Adolf 49 75 77-8 80-2 94
  114 132 141-3 151-2 154-5
  161-4 187 191 195 197

John 218-32

Index

Kisnatt, Otto 191

Lampredi, Aldo (Guido) 209-16
  218 233 235
Lanfranchi, Ferruccio 60
Lazzaro, Urbano (Bill) 193-6
  210-1 216 234
Leppo, Edmondo 177
Linfozzi,Santo 135
Locanda Portoghese, La 107
Lombardi, Riccardo 180-1 209
  236
Lonati, Bruno (Giacomo) 218-32
Longo, Luigi 209-10
Lorraine, Sir Percy 78
Lotta di Classe, La 40
Luccichenti, Amedeo 85
Ludwig, Emil 49

Mafalda di Savoia 140
Mainetti, Father 191
Malgeri, Alfredo 209
Maltoni, Rosa 30 36 48 76 236
Mancini, Enrico 178
Marazza, Achille 180-1
Marie José di Savoia 107
Marinelli, Giovanni 47 136
Marinetti, Filippo Tommaso 42
Martini, Nino 165-7
Mastrocinque, Camillo 108
Mastrofini, Carlo 90
Matteotti, Giacomo 46-7
Mellini Ponce de Leon, Alberto
  182
Messagero, Il 101 109
Mezzasoma, Fernando 213
Mezzetti, (Gerarca) 182

Monaco, Vincenzo 85
Monelli, Paolo 53 59 108
Montagna, Ugo 146
Mordini, Alfredo (Riccardo)
  210 233-5
Moretti, Michele (Pietro) 195
  203 205 211-6 218 227 233
Mori, Cesare 48
Mosca, (Guard) 166
Moscardi, Lisetta 142
Musella, (Guard) 166
Mussolini, Alessandro 36-7 40
  236
Mussolini, Anna Maria 92 140
  143 182 185 237
Mussolini, Arnaldo 36-7 57 162
Mussolini, Benito Albino 56-7
Mussolini, Bruno 89 95-6 135
  140 162 172 185 237
Mussolini, Edda 41 79 83 123
  161-2
Mussolini, Rachele 29 40-1 44
  48 53-7 74 83-4 89 96 115 133
  136 139-40 155-6 160 165
  168-75 182 185-7 237
Mussolini, Romano 140 143 182
  185
Mussolini, Vittorio 83-4 108 139
  182 211 213 234
Mustafà, Omari 97-9

Navarra, Quinto 26-7 45 49 53
  57 62-3 97 117 119-20 123 127
  136
Negri, Giuseppe 193
Nenni, Pietro 140
Noccioli, Dr. 91-2

Index

Pareto, Vilfredo 39
Parri, Ferruccio 236
Pasinetti, Francesco 108
Pavolini, Alessandro 121 161 180 189-90 213
Persichetti, Giuseppina 13-7 22-4 31-5 59 66-7 85-7 93 106-11 123-4 136-7 144 146-9 159-60 163 178 182-4
Pertini, Sandro 209
Petacci, Benvenuto 111
Petacci, Edoardo 22
Petacci, Ferdinando 111
Petacci, Francesco Saverio 15-6 22-3 32 85-6 91-2 95 120 123 137 146 149 154 159 177-8 182-4
Petacci, Giorgio 89
Petacci, Giuseppe 22
Petacci, Marcello 16 34 61 69 85-6 97 107-13 118-20 123 136-7 144 151-3 159-60 176 178 186-7 195-6 203 210-1 234-5 237
Petacci, Miriam 13-6 23-9 34-5 65 67-70 73 77 81 83 86-8 92 99 101 106-12 123 127 137-8 144 146-9 153 157-60 163 167-70 176 178 182-4
Petacci, Stefano 87 89
Pius XI (Achille Ratti) 48
Pius XII (Eugenio Pacelli) 80
Podrecca, Vittorio 42
Poletti, Charles 236
Polito, Saverio 140
Poncet, French Ambassador 78
Popolo d'Italia, Il 41-3 56-7 108
Porta, Paolo 187 194-5 197
Pozetto, Father 149

Rafanelli, Leda 55-6 .
Ribbentrop, Joachim von 121
Riccardi, Raffaello 112-3 120
Ricciotti, Giuseppe 140
Ritossa, Zita 73 86 107-11 123 136 160 186-9 192 195-6
Rivera, Cesare 32
Roatta, Mario 89
Rommel, Erwin 114-6
Roosevelt, Franklin Delano 80 197
Rubbiani, Dr. 91
Rubini, Giuseppe 194 233

Santillo, Dr. (Major) 135
Sarfatti, Margherita 29 53 55-8 84 186
Schuster, Cardinal Ildefonso 179-82 236
Sciaretta, Police Officer 44 116
Scivicco, Giuseppe 135
Scorza, Carlo 126 129-31
Sebastiani, Osvaldo 89
Serena, Adelchi 88
Sereni, Emilio 209 236
Skorzeny, Otto 142-3
Sogno d'Amore 108
Sorel, Cécile 54
Sotis, Gino 100-4
Spoegler, Franz 160 165 170-1 173 176 178-9
Stalin, Joseph 197
Starace, Achille 21 78 83 236
Stauffenberg, Claus Shenk von 163
Storia di un Anno 141
Student, Kurt 142
Susmel, Duilio 97

Index

Tarchi, Angelo 188
Teruzzi, Atillio 79
Thaon di Revel, Paolo 120
Torlonia, Prince Giovanni di 49
Toscanni, Arturo 42
Tuissi, Giuseppina (Gianna)
  203-4

Umberto di Savoia 107 195
Unità, l' 216
Utimpergher, Idreno 194

Valliani, Leo 209
Valli, Alida 106
Venturi *(Gerarca)* 120-1
Vidussoni, Aldo 119
Vie del Cuore, Le 108

Vigneri, Paolo 134-5
Visconti Prasca, Sebastiano 89
Vita di Gesù Cristo
  (Life of Jesus Christ) 140
Vittorio Emanuele III 43 67 80
  129-34 132-4 136 140 142 150
Volta Matteucci Cattaneo, Alma
  della 101

Wendel, Alice von (Frau Betz)
  161
Wolff, Karl 154 157

Zamboni, Anteo 47
Zaniboni, Tito 20 47 140
Zerbino, Paolo 180 213